THE ENGLISH
COUNTRY
HOUSE
PARTY

THE ENGLISH COUNTRY HOUSE PARTY

Phyllida Barstow

SUTTON PUBLISHING

First published in 1989 by Thorsons Publishing Group Limited

This edition published in 1998 by Sutton Publishing Limited

A catalogue record for this book is available from the British Library

ISBN 0 7509 1849 7

Cover illustration: Evening (The Ball), c. *1878 by J.J. Tissot (Musée d'Orsay, Paris/photograph Bridgeman Art Library, London/Giraudon*

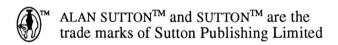 ALAN SUTTON™ and SUTTON™ are the trade marks of Sutton Publishing Limited

Printed in Great Britain by
WBC Limited, Bridgend, Mid-Glamorgan.

Contents

Introduction

The English landowner's attitude to country life has always been markedly different from that of his Continental counterparts. As far as a French, Russian, Prussian, Italian, or Spanish nobleman was concerned, banishment to his country estates was a punishment only slightly less feared than death itself. The country was dull, dirty, poor, backward, lacking in all excitement or amenity; its inhabitants were at best docile serfs and at worst dangerous malcontents bent on the destruction of their masters. Isolated, uncomfortable, and horribly bored, the banished nobleman would spend his years in the country intriguing tirelessly to be restored to favour, so he might plunge once more into the glorious hurlyburly of city life.

For the Englishman, the threat of rustication never carried a comparable menace. He actually preferred living in the country, finding in his own broad acres opportunities for a wide range of sporting activities, and enjoying the company of his tenants and neighbours whose interests were not so different from his own.

His town house was probably handsome enough, but he regarded it as a *pied-à-terre*; his home was his country seat. All down the social scale of gentry, from duke to backwoods squire, when he had the means to build ambitiously it was his country house on which he chose to lavish his money, and it was there that he entertained his friends.

To these enthusiastic countrymen and their love of their land we owe England's rich variety of great houses in all styles and sizes, from the traditional manor to the Georgian 'little big house', from the classical splendour of Holkham Hall or Burghley to the exuberant fantasy of Waddesdon Manor; from the house which stands as it was built 400 years ago to the hybrid upon which successive owners have imposed the fashions of their day. These are the houses which provided – and in some cases still provide – the setting for the country house parties which played such an important part in the social life of the English aristocracy during the nineteenth and early twentieth centuries.

The golden age of country house entertaining was the Edwardian era – by which I mean the whole period between the death of Albert, Prince Consort, in 1861 and the outbreak of the First World War in 1914. Strictly speaking, of course, most of these years were during Queen Victoria's

Opposite: A Royal shooting party at Lambton Castle, home of the Earl of Durham. Art is here allowed to outweigh reality. Would any sportsman shoot so low a pheasant while his loader stood nonchalantly in front of him?

reign, and the concluding few in the reign of George V; but the spirit of a society does not begin and end with the death of a sovereign, and during the years of Queen Victoria's widowhood society was dominated by Edward, Prince of Wales, and adopted the Edwardian code of values.

Since social history never proceeds in a straight line, but makes its advance in a series of zigzags with each generation reacting against the fashions and morals of the preceding one, the terms 'Victorian' and 'Edwardian' have come to mean very different things to the modern mind. To Victorians we tend to ascribe certain virtues – among them thrift, self-reliance, moral rectitude, and somewhat ostentatious piety – against which we mentally balance their undoubted vices of cruelty, self-satisfaction, and hypocrisy. The picture conjured up by the term 'Edwardian' is altogether more expansive, morally lax, liberal, philistine, and hedonistic. Thus, though the friends and companions of the Prince of Wales's generation lived most of their lives as subjects of Queen Victoria, their spirit was entirely Edwardian. While the select, rich, luxury-loving coterie known as the 'Marlborough House Set' dominated society, country house parties achieved a perfection never known before or since.

Entertaining in style is hard work, and has always required consider-able flair and showmanship. No matter what degree of muddle and mess a noble family might tolerate when it was alone, when guests were expected it was a different story, and the staff of a large country house collaborated eagerly in the matter of putting on a good show to impress visitors. Their pride was bound up in it as much as their master's was.

Entertaining Royalty is an area of particular delicacy: here the line between putting on a good show and vulgar ostentation is a fine one.

> Yet if his majesty, our sovereign lord,
> Should of his own accord
> Friendly himself invite
> And say, 'I'll be your guest tomorrow night',
> How should we stir ourselves, call and command
> All hands to work! Let no man idle stand . . . [1]

True enough: but it is also true that Royalty does not care to be upstaged by mere subjects. 'I have come from my house to your palace,' Queen Victoria once remarked to the Duchess of Sutherland, and one can read more than a hint of reproof into the words. Trying too hard is just as bad as not trying hard enough. All the same, Royalty expects to be comfortably lodged. The story of the hostess who spent thousands of pounds on redecorating her house for the Prince of Wales's visit, only to be gently reproved for the lack of a hook on the bathroom door, goes to show how difficult it is for even the most attentive host to be fully aware of a guest's needs. Most Edwardian hosts averted this danger by providing so lavishly that their guests were spoiled for choice. Staying with the Countess of Warwick at Easton Lodge, or Baron Ferdinand de Rothschild at Waddesdon Manor was more like stepping into a fairy tale than sharing a friend's home. Every imaginable comfort was provided, including hothouse orchids for the ladies' evening corsages and a choice of milk from three different breeds of cow for the early-morning tea. The sumptuous dinners that were staged every night consisted of a dozen rich and elaborate courses.

All this was very expensive. As the cost of entertaining in the Edwardian style rose in a matching spiral with the search for perfection, the inner circle of the Marlborough House Set suffered a number of casualties. Henry Chaplin, the jovial Squire of Blankney, who used to keep two packs of hounds so his friends could hunt six days a week, was eventually obliged to sell up and turn to his brother-in-law the Duke of Sutherland for support. Christopher Sykes – 'the Great Xtopher' – was narrowly saved from the bankruptcy courts after spending his fortune entertaining his Prince in style; and even the lovely Countess of Warwick – 'My own darling little Daisy wife', as the Prince fondly addressed her – was reduced to raising money by threatening to publish her Royal lover's letters.

But these troubles lay in the future. While their money lasted the Edwardians knew very well how to spend it. Glamorous clothes, food, wine, and entertainment ranked high on their list of priorities. It was not enough to feed and house your guests in beautiful surroundings. They must be kept amused as well, and here the English passion for country sports proved invaluable. Hunting and shooting could be arranged to occupy most of their guests' time in winter, while cricket, tennis, and boating filled long summer afternoons. On Sundays, when killing was forbidden, attendance at church was *de rigueur* and took up most of the morning, while an admiring progress round the hosts' estate accounted nicely for Sunday afternoon.

After-dinner entertainment was equally predictable. There would be dancing or cards; charades or amateur dramatics; and any guest with the slightest talent must be prepared to favour the company with a musical offering or 'turn'. True Edwardians were too secure in their own position to suffer from feelings of shyness or inadequacy, and indeed there were no uncomfortably high artistic standards to attain. Girls were taught as a matter of course to paint a little, sing a little, and play the piano well enough to accompany a drawing-room ballad with suitable embellishments. Rare cases of real talent, such as the Duchess of Rutland's for portraiture or Lady Randolph Churchill's concert-standard piano-playing, attracted astonished admiration in this most philistine of societies.

Only the little company known as 'The Souls' – among whose leading members were Arthur Balfour, Margot Asquith, and the Countess of Desborough – aspired to discussion of anything more elevated than food, ailments, and the social round, and their fellow Edwardians found these pretensions slightly ridiculous. *They* preferred not to argue or peer too closely into the dark workings of their psyches. The way society was ordered suited them very well, and they frowned on reformers within their ranks.

This attitude extended to their love lives. To Edwardians, the

Eleventh Commandment was more important than the sum of the other Ten. Their code demanded that brides should be virgins and wives faithful until they had presented their husbands with at least one, preferably two, male heirs. After that, the sole essential was discretion. Illicit liaisons were perfectly in order so long as they were not found out. Country house parties provided excellent opportunities for lovers to meet. Monitoring the progress of friends' affairs in conditions of absolute secrecy lent spice to the dullest gathering and contributed largely to a hostess's fun.

Edwardian house parties depended on an orderly, predictable pattern of events and behaviour. Hosts and guests were perfectly satisfied to follow the same tried and trusted pastimes year in, year out. The winter months were devoted to hunting and shooting; the spring to race-meetings; early summer was the time to don cricket flannels, and in late summer the migration of southerners north of the border to shoot grouse and stalk red deer was an immutable part of the sporting and social year.

It was only after the First World War threw this orderly society into confusion that a new generation began a restless quest for novelty which made country house entertaining at once more difficult and less satisfying. The importation of American fashions in music, dances, cocktails, and films all contributed to this general dissatisfaction with traditional pursuits; but undoubtedly the most pernicious influence was that of the motor car, which allowed guests altogether too much freedom to come and go as they pleased, and destroyed the unity of a country house party. Add to this a sharp decline in good manners, difficulties in recruiting and maintaining large staffs, and the opening of society's ranks to all sorts of people who would formerly have been excluded, and by the outbreak of the Second World War in 1939 country house entertaining had become a mere shadow of the glorious affair it had been in Edwardian days.

Worse was to follow. After the war, crippling taxation posed a more deadly threat to England's country houses than German bombs had done. Dry rot and death-watch beetle were at work in the fabric of these old buildings, and the owners had neither the money nor the skilled labour to repair their ravages.

Nevertheless, like all really adaptable institutions, the country house party has survived, and my last chapter charts the turning of what seemed an irreversible decline into a cautious revival. Today's week-end gatherings of the great and good would probably be regarded with amused contempt by those prolific writers of Edwardian memoirs to whom I am most indebted for the material in this book, but they would surely recognize the effort and sacrifice demanded of their successors in order to maintain England's great houses and breathe life into them by filling them with guests.

'Nothing,' wrote the Countess of Warwick, who had the knack of going straight to the heart of a problem, 'can be quite so dismal as a big suite of reception rooms perennially closed; nothing more depressing than a long corridor with rooms whose doors are never opened . . . '.

She was right. Without people, music, chatter, and laughter, even the most beautiful houses petrify into museums, as the immaculately restored yet lifeless palaces in Leningrad bear witness. So long as parties take place in them from time to time, the great houses of England need never fear such a fate.

I am grateful to the many librarians and archivists who suggested avenues of enquiry to me, in particular Mr Fuggles of the National Trust, and Mr Michael Pearman, Librarian and Archivist to the Trustees of the Chatsworth Settlement; to my father-in-law Sir Rupert Hart-Davis, who can be relied on to provide chapter and verse for any quotation, no matter how obscure; to Joan Dunn for memories of parties in the twenties, and to my husband Duff for tirelessly seeking out sources of Edwardian memoirs, all of whom have given me unstinting help in compiling this portrait of the English country house party.

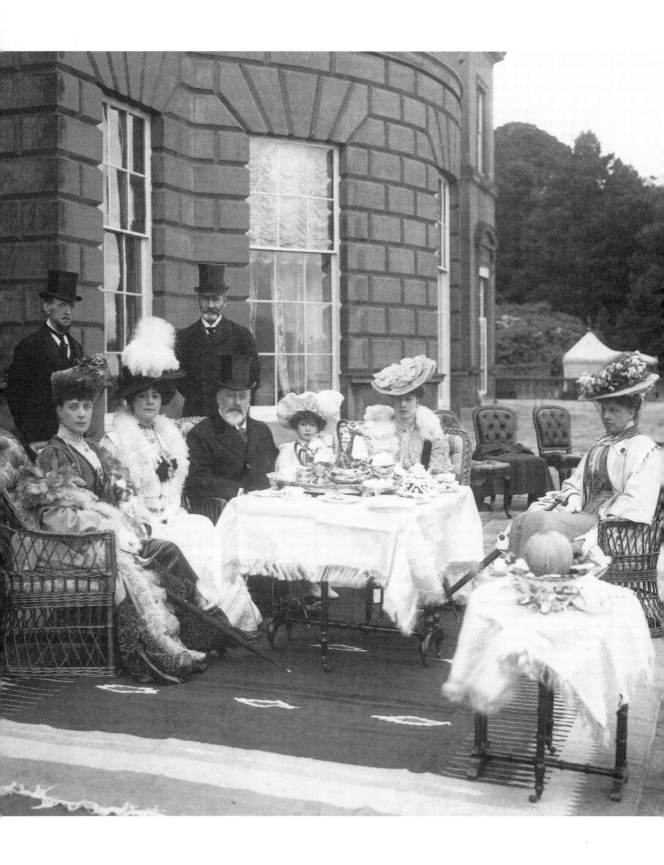

CHAPTER ONE

The Small World

Like the web of an industrious spider, the railway network was spreading across Britain, linking small local lines into a central system and stretching filaments into hitherto remote and inaccessible corners of the country, when Queen Victoria came to the throne in 1837. By 1861, when the Prince Consort died, it had made great changes in the social habits of England's great landowners.

No longer were they obliged to rely on neighbours within carriage-driving distance for company and entertainment during the months they spent on their country estates. From Sussex to Northumberland, Dorset to Norfolk, journeys which had formerly taken weeks could now be accomplished in days, or even hours. Within the snug enclosed comfort of a train carriage, where you could read or smoke or chat to your companions, stretch your legs or simply gaze from the window at the smoothly passing landscape, how different the view appeared from the one you used to see in glimpses through the fugged-up vibrating panes of a swaying, jolting, cramped, and icy coach!

It is amazing that people travelled as much as they did before the advent of steam, and when they reached their destination they deserved a rest. A guest who had endured five days' posting in winter from, say, London to the north of England, with all the attendant hazards and discomforts of rutted roads, lame horses, drunken coachmen, and bug-infested hostelries, could not be fobbed off with a mere week's shooting. He – and his wife and daughters – must have a period of recuperation before facing the return journey. If they did not get it, they were not likely to come again. Guests were the life-blood of country entertainment in those long dull winter months, and visits which lasted six weeks were not uncommon. Since no host, no matter how grand, could be expected to provide six weeks of sustained jollification, the guest's expectation of entertainment during such long visits was modest.

The visiting family and the servants they had brought with them – no one who was anyone travelled without servants – would become part of their host's household in a way no modern week-end visitor can hope to. They would learn the ways of the estate and the moods and foibles of their hosts; and as the weeks passed they would feel free to pursue their own interests without constant supervision.

Opposite: Come rain or shine, overloaded hats crowned even the youngest heads for a Royal tea on the terrace in 1900

A modern commuter's dream: no overcrowding on the new saloon carriage of the London, Brighton, and South Coast Railway in 1873

A guest – then as now – had always to be prepared to sing for his supper. He must be cheerful, attentive, admiring, and grateful – and keep any criticism strictly to himself. So long as he fulfilled these obligations, the eighteenth- and early-nineteenth-century visitor to some stately home felt entitled to stay as long as was convenient to himself, making free with his host's possessions and – in the case of the great and good – basking in his reflected glory.

This was all very well and certainly better than no company at all, but it made for straggling, uncoordinated house parties. Rail travel opened up possibilities for country entertaining on a very much grander scale for the rich and ambitious hostess, and in Victorian days the handful of women who, by virtue of birth, beauty, and intelligence, were the leaders of Society were very rich and ambitious indeed.

For them, entertaining their friends was both an art and serious business: not an afterthought tacked on to the end of a day's work, but an all-absorbing work in itself. Like generals they planned their strategy and deployed their troops. They spared neither effort nor expense and vied with one another to make their house parties memorable.

Their circle was a small one, but powerful out of all proportion to its size. Most of the country's political and social influence as well as its wealth was concentrated in the hands of six or seven hundred landowning families. From the 21 non-Royal dukes, in descending order of rank through earls and marquesses, viscounts, barons, baronets, and knights, this world of power and privilege was closely interconnected by marriage.

As in any society where virginity is demanded of a wife, girls married young, often straight from the schoolroom, before the excruciating dullness of a maiden's life led to their taking too close an interest in the muscular shoulders of the gardener's boy or paying untoward attention to James the understrapper's fascinating whiskers.

From time to time accidents occurred. There were elopements and pursuits and chastened daughters brought home in disgrace while the offending young manservant would be disposed of hastily – perhaps by recommending him to a position 100 miles away, where his employer had sons rather than daughters. But in general the vigilance of mothers and governesses kept the Victorian maiden fresh and innocent enough to please the most demanding husband on his wedding night, and this gave her a long breeding-span. Married at 17, she might have a dozen children by her mid 30s. Even allowing for the ravages of infant mortality, it was common for Victorian families to run into double figures. Since these families naturally tried to marry off their children at their own level of society, an immense *cousinage* resulted, as in the case of the 4th Earl of Durham, himself one of 13, who married one of the lively Bulteel daughters from Pamflete in Devon, who in turn had 12 siblings. The 2nd Earl of Leicester's two marriages produced 19 children of whom 15 survived, and the Dowager Duchess of Abercorn could, on her 82nd birthday, pose for photographs with 104 descendants.

Large families were usual among Society's upper crust. The Dowager Duchess of Abercorn's 82nd birthday is celebrated by 104 of her descendants

Interrelated though they were, few Victorian ladies suffered the mental confusion of Lady Clinton, whose convoluted family ties resulted in her being sister to one Lady Spencer, stepmother to another, and aunt to a third. She was also Lord Spencer's own aunt, and his stepmother's stepmother and his brother's grandmother.

Since a country house gathering of any size was almost bound to include cousins, in-laws, or other family connections, most members of this small society knew one another well and there was a familiarity among guests which struck some observers as delightful and others as distinctly cliquey. Private languages were developed for the double purpose of baffling outsiders and reinforcing a person's own sense of belonging. Fashionable society-speak was seldom witty, and leaned heavily on nursery and schoolroom for its inspiration.

In V. Sackville-West's novel *The Edwardians*, pretty Teresa Spedding, a doctor's wife, enjoying her first visit to a grand country house, listens with some disappointment to the inane conversation of her fellow-guests.

> She had expected their conversation to rival their appearance. She had expected to be dazzled by their wit and thrilled by their revelations . . . She did not know what it would be like, only that it would be wonderful. And now she found that it differed very little from the conversation of her own acquaintances, only the references were to people she did not know, and the general assumptions were on a more extravagant scale. They even talked about their servants. 'Yes, my dear,' Lady Edward was saying, 'I have really had to get rid of the chef at last. We found he was using a hundred and forty-four dozen eggs a week.' They went into screams of laughter at phrases that Teresa (reluctantly) thought quite silly . . .

This particular clique's private language was of the simplest:

> It consisted in adding an Italian termination to English words; but as that termination was most frequently the termination of Italian verbs of the first declension, and as it was tacked on to English words irrespective of their being verbs, nouns, or adjectives, it could not be said to be based on any very creditable grammatical system. Smartness, Teresa could not help thinking, was cheap at such a price.
>
>   'And after dinn-are, we might have a little dans-are,' said an anonymous lady; a suggestion greeted by exclamations of, 'What a deevy idea, Florence! There's nobody like Florence, is there, for deevy ideas like that?'
>
>   The critical faculty, raising its head for a second in Teresa, though immediately stamped on, suggested there was nothing very original or divine in the idea of dancing after dinner.[1]

Rather more mental ingenuity was displayed by the large marriage-linked tribe of Glynnes, Lytteltons, Gladstones, and Talbots whose conversation was peppered with expressions from the family language known as 'Glynnese'. This was sufficiently widely used for the scholarly Lord Lyttelton (who, when hunting, if foxes failed, amused himself by turning Milton into Greek) to compile a spoof Glossary:

Bathing feel: A significant description of the state of mind previous to some rather formidable undertaking, resembling that of a child about to fall into the arms of the bathing-woman. Mr Gladstone, so long ago as 1841, had so far advanced in the language that, on being asked how he felt on becoming Vice-President of the Board of Trade, he was able to reply, 'Bathing feel'.

Grub: A very vulgar expression for which we appear to be indebted to the Dean of Windsor. The Slang-Dictionary and Epsom-Downs meaning of this word is *food,* luncheon carried in a basket; from which service that dignitary has attempted to elevate it to mean food for the mind, information, etc.; but it has not reached a higher level than to mean 'gossip', 'news'. So if one of his nieces had been on an amusing visit, he might beseech her to come and sit close to him on the sofa, and say, 'Now, my dear, grub, grub.'

The Dean had a particular usage for the verb 'To Shoot'. This is, of course, a sporting or military metaphor. It means rapidly and suddenly to discover or hit upon, especially perhaps something at a little distance; from which definition a remote clue to its derivation may no doubt be gathered by the perspicacious reader. The Dean, as an agreeable piece of intelligence, wrote in a letter, 'Last night I shot the Bishop of London in a corner at the Queen's party.'[2]

Early Victorians indulge in homespun entertainment

Sociologists who claim that humans, like their monkey ancestors, only feel thoroughly at ease with members of their own tribe, whose habits and relationships they understand instinctively, would find plenty to support this theory in a study of the upper levels of mid-Victorian and Edwardian society.

Isabel Colegate, in her novel *The Shooting Party*, gives a revealing glimpse of the energy that high-flying members of this social circle were obliged to expend in keeping abreast of their fellows' activities, and how deep was their lack of interest in people outside their own small world.

During a shooting luncheon, Olivia Lilburn listens to her husband's conversation with their hostess, Minnie. They were

> running through the points of the Social Calendar they had jointly or severally most recently passed – so amusing or such a bore – and who'd been there (but everyone, of course) – and who was too beautiful for words, and who had quite lost her looks, and who was drinking too much and had made a frightful floater the other night in the House only luckily it was after dinner and no one had noticed – and she knew him to be doing no more than a kind of ritual checking of the points of the compass. He and Minnie were like two engines idling, keeping themselves turning over so that they should be ready to move the machine in a new direction when the exigencies of the occasion required it. Minnie was at the same time looking round the table to see whether everyone had finished eating and whether Sir Randolph was beginning to look impatient. Bob Lilburn was already mentally checking through his equipment for the afternoon's sport.
>
> 'The Barlows,' he nevertheless continued, 'at Rothermuir. Such views.'
>
> 'We were there with the Charlesworths. You and Olivia had just left.'
>
> Olivia had noticed that this checking of the compass points (or listing of names) seemed to constitute quite a large part of her husband's conversation, and that often when engaged in it with another such practised hand as Minnie, he could go on for what seemed to her a quite extraordinarily long time without feeling it necessary to extend his comments on the occasions or people mentioned beyond the most perfunctory kind of categorising. The object of the thing seemed to be enumeration rather than enlightenment. Once she had said to him, 'Supposing there are some other people somewhere, people we don't know?'
>
> He had looked at her seriously.
>
> 'What kind of people?'
>
> 'Perfectly charming people. Really delightful, intelligent, amusing, civilized . . . And we don't know them, and nobody we know knows them. And they don't know us and they don't know anybody we know.'
>
> Bob had thought for a moment and then he had said, 'It's impossible. But if it were not impossible, then I don't think I should want to know such people. I don't think I should find anything in common with them.'[3]

In such a climate of opinion, it was inevitable that any newcomer to a country house party would be subjected to careful inspection and cross-examination, none the less rigorous for being covert. It was essential to discover exactly where he or she fitted into the picture. Since fault-finding or the criticism of existing conditions were taboo, such

Far left: Philip de Laszlo's portrait of the 6th Duke of Portland, Master of the Horse to Queen Victoria. He inherited Welbeck Abbey from a distant cousin with a passion for tunnelling and subterranean building

Left: The Duchess of Portland, formerly the Scottish beauty Winifred Dallas-Yorke

interrogations were conducted in an atmosphere of smiling geniality that fooled no one. Both questioner and questioned knew that points were being added and subtracted in the light of each response. One ill-advised opinion, a whiff of Trade or suspicion of vulgarity, and the newcomer was damned.

On the other hand, much would be forgiven a person whose place in the social structure was beyond question. A Duchess might be a

> rough, downright old woman, who said what she meant and meant what she said, and who had no pretty or even civilised affectations of opinion or behaviour. She said quite frankly that she regretted the abolition of slavery. It irritated her that an offending servant could give notice. Her personal habits were equally primitive, and by virtue of her position she assumed an equal right to them: if she wanted to spit, she spat; and since she suffered cruelly from eczema, she scratched her back quite frankly with an ivory hand on the end of a long stick, plunging it down the opening of her bodice after dinner.[4]

Yet, despite her uncouth manners, the Duchess *belonged,* and Society closed its eyes to her failings.

Conversely, no amount of money, wit, or cultured charm could force an entry to this small privileged world for an outsider. Nor did it do to be too clever.

> We resented the introduction of the Jews into the social set of the Prince of Wales [explained Lady Warwick], not because we disliked them individually . . . but because they had brains and understood finance. As a class, we

A.K.T.
AFTER
D. MACPHERSON

did not like brains. As for money, our only understanding of it lay in the spending, not in the making of it.[5]

There was consternation at Chatsworth when the Duke of Devonshire, *plus royaliste que le roi*, announced that he had invited Joseph Chamberlain to stay, and gloomy predictions that he would eat peas with his knife. These predictions were confounded when the dangerous radical proved to be a charming and dignified guest.

Country house parties in those days played an important part in smoothing out political animosity. They provided a neutral meeting-place where any feeling of personal dislike had to be suppressed out of deference to the hosts. It is anyway difficult to maintain a high level of dislike for a man who has fished, shot, or hunted with you, whose wife you have flirted with at dinner, and whose bank balance you may have lightened by a few hundred pounds at cards. You may still abhor his policies, but you will probably admit at the end of a week that in most respects that matter he is remarkably similar to yourself.

Semi-formal contacts of this kind and friendships formed across political barriers did much to keep politics civilized even in an age where the social divides went far deeper than they do today. The Duchess of Devonshire welcomed all shades of political opinion at Chatsworth, and so did the Duchess of Marlborough, Lady Lansdowne and the Duchess of Buccleuch; but Lady Londonderry was a die-hard Conservative who would invite no Liberal or radical to share her table.

Politics were, though, only of minor importance when selecting a guest-list. Country house parties were built round country sports and pursuits; a man's ability to ride and shoot well, play a straight bat, tell a good story, entertain with a song after dinner, and be trusted not to cheat at cards was far more significant than his politics.

Inevitably in a society used to every luxury and able to indulge every whim, there were quarrels and jealousies, illicit liaisons and a few long-standing feuds.

> Our rule was No Scandal! [wrote the Countess of Warwick, who had been up to her beautiful neck in most of them]. Whenever there was a threat of impending trouble, pressure would be brought to bear, sometimes from the highest quarters, and almost always successfully. We realised that publicity would cause chattering tongues, and as we had no intention of changing our mode of living, we saw to it that five out of every six scandals never reached the outside world.[6]

Despite this insistence on discretion, the few scandals that did break publicly had the impact of depth-charges, shaking Society's foundations and sending shock-waves through the surface calm. The man most often called in to handle the delicate business of papering over the cracks – reconciling offender and offended, keeping the matter out of court and preventing any hint of trouble reaching the Press – was a solicitor named George Lewis, who used to claim that his head was so full of secrets that he dared not keep a diary for fear of it falling into the wrong hands.

Opposite: Sketches of scenes from the Prince of Wales's visit to Chatsworth in the 1890s, based on information supplied by a gossip-columnist among the guests

Right: Sir George Lewis, Society's discreet and adroit solicitor, who mediated in many potentially damaging scandals

Far right: Waiting about in the hall occupied much of a house party's leisure, but Edwardians seldom worried about wasting time

A skilful negotiator of great sense and discretion, Lewis was adept at sorting out the tangled affairs of cuckolded noblemen and card-sharps alike. Distraught ladies of fashion who had mislaid compromising love-letters found him a tower of strength. Though Lord Alington's daughter Winifred Sturt was young and naive enough to wonder at finding a mere solicitor a fellow guest at Sandringham, George Lewis was very far from being in awe of his noble clients: he knew their weaknesses too well. Indeed, he lectured them like a Dutch uncle, telling one indiscreet beauty:

> The trouble with you people, at the top of the tree, is that there is nothing left for you to climb. Worse still, you have nothing to do. Your responsibilities are few, and you can only get through the years by amusing yourselves. When you have humoured all your fancies, you tie yourselves up in knots, and here I step in, and have the pleasure and responsibility of loosening them.
>
> In my walk of life we are happier. The men must tackle their jobs and give themselves up to their work. Our womenfolk do not leave their children to nurses and governesses, but take an active interest in them and their education. When they meet their husbands at the end of the day, they are glad of companionship, and seldom suffer from the fashionable complaint of boredom. That is why, given the same weaknesses and temptations that beset people in your sphere, they live without the sort of troubles that I am called in to put right. If I were dependent on the middle classes, I could reduce my staff and move into smaller offices immediately.[7]

Human nature being what it is, George Lewis's business continued to flourish and he was eventually knighted by the King whose reputation he had done much to preserve.

There was a large element of hypocrisy in Victorian conduct. 'I will be good', the young Victoria said on realizing that she would inherit the crown; and with those simple words *Goodness* came into fashion. After the raffish, bawdy manners of society under the Hanoverian kings and the open scandal of Royal family life, it was high time for the pendulum to swing the other way; but, as usually happens, it swung too far. It was virtually impossible to be as good as the Victorians pretended to be, but the grim fate that had befallen the French aristocracy was still within living memory, and that was enough to convince their British counterparts that they should keep their own peccadilloes and extravagances well hidden. Fear that the Press would foment unrest among the labouring masses upon whom their income and comfort depended made them pretend to a quite unrealistic degree of piety and decorum, while secretly indulging their vices just as they always had done.

> At church on Sunday to attend
> Will serve to keep the world thy friend,

advised Arthur Hugh Clough's *New Decalogue*, and few Victorian socialites ignored the tip. The principal objective of their special brand of Christianity was to maintain the status quo.

> The rich man in his castle,
> The poor man at his gate,
> He made them high or lowly
> And ordered their estate,[8]

they sang, and prayed most fervently that this happy state of affairs might continue indefinitely. After all, the poor man and his brood had the Christmas party at the castle to look forward to, and when the sticky buns and lemonade were finished and the traditional games had been played, the children would line up in long rows to shuffle forward and receive a present from the two big heaps of gaily wrapped parcels. Each girl would bob a shy curtsey, and each boy duck his head with a mumbled, 'Thankee, sir. Thankee, m'lady', before stumbling out into the frosty night to begin the long trudge to the village.

A Victorian lady saw it as her Christian duty to set a good example to the lower orders. She was punctilious about calling on the old and sick among her estate workers, distributing coals or potatoes or calf's-foot jelly. But the beneficiaries of her charity had an equal duty to be grateful, and loud in their thanks. None of that nasty Socialistic nonsense about all men being born equal and with equal right to the good things of this world. The poor would get their reward in Heaven. But if her loyal estate workers were to find out just how much money their Lady Bountiful had lost at the baccarat table last week, or the sum their lord had spent on buying jewellery for a married woman who was not his wife, their thanks and blessings might not flow with the same freedom. They might, indeed, call them something disagreeably different. So it was best that they should remain in ignorance of things that really did not concern them at all.

Love-affairs were therefore conducted with discretion and dignity. No careless female hand must brush the shoulder of a man who had spent most of the previous night in her bed, nor were endearments permitted in public. There was, Lord Ernest Hamilton explains,

> a universal tendency to simulate a disbelief in the existence of those common-to-all-time delinquencies which the latter Georgian bucks had so shamelessly flaunted in the patched and powdered faces of their dames. But it was all a sham and a pretence. Under the regulation veneer of prudery which the social attitude of the day considered becoming, any number of most undesirable institutions flourished . . . The scandal of the Victorian streets; the scandal of the red blinds, where are they now? Gone, wiped clean off the dirty pavements. They are now no more than ugly memories; but in the straitlaced days of the good Queen they flourished most bravely and disreputably.[9]

Queen Victoria's influence was certainly powerful, and continued to be throughout her long widowhood. But from the date of the Prince Consort's death, it had a rival. A very different set of values was dangled temptingly under the noses of her subjects, enticing them into a very different style of entertaining. Edward, Prince of Wales, had inherited his mother's determination and his father's industry, without inheriting either parent's strong moral principles. After a lonely, unhappy, and closely supervised childhood, he was determined to have the freedom to enjoy himself, and tireless in pursuit of pleasure.

While the Prince of Wales and his circle dominated English Society, the country house party achieved its finest flowering.

CHAPTER TWO

The Widow and the Rake

Albert Edward, or Bertie, as the Prince of Wales was known to his family, had been the subject of an educational experiment that backfired. Determined that his eldest son, born in 1841, should be the very model of a modern monarch, Prince Albert – with the enthusiastic backing of his wife – set about the task of moulding the perfect king with Teutonic thoroughness. After much consultation with his confidant and mentor, Baron Stockmar, he devised a concentrated course of study and physical training for the young Prince which, by its sheer impossibility of fulfilment, might have given a more highly strung child a nervous breakdown.

Week in, week out, six hours a day, six days a week, Bertie was systematically crammed with knowledge as a Strasbourg goose is crammed with meal, and with equal indifference to how much of the force-fed information he could retain. The result was that he retained pitifully little, and that barely digested. He reacted to the stress by falling victim to sudden tantrums when he would attack his tutors or carefully selected playmates with a violence most unbecoming to a future king. Neither moral lectures nor corporal punishment had any effect beyond making him dejected and surly.

Intellectually, the Prince was a plodder, but his one sympathetic tutor pleaded in vain for him to be allowed more time to assimilate what he was taught. Prince Albert was determined to see his master-plan fulfilled, and responded by sacking anyone who tried to slow down the pace of Bertie's education. Yet to the Queen and her Consort's pained surprise and indignation, the magic regime had the very opposite effect to that which they had hoped for, and Bertie slid farther behind his contemporaries with every passing year. His writing was ill-formed, his spelling atrocious, his ignorance abysmal. He had neither physical energy nor intellectual curiosity. The rapid changes of focus as lesson succeeded unrelated lesson destroyed his power of concentration so effectively that for the rest of his life he was incapable of attending to any subject for more than a short time, and the fingers that fiddled with the cutlery or tapped the table became the terror of hostesses striving to amuse him.

It did not help that his sister, Princess Victoria, who was a year older, was a much quicker learner. Her achievements cruelly emphasized

*The Prince of Wales (left)
and Prince Alfred with
their tutor Mr Gibbs*

Bertie's lack of them. The Queen and her Consort, bitterly disappointed
by his failure to live up to their expectations, veered to the other extreme
and began to treat their eldest son as a moron who must be constantly
watched and advised. They refused to trust him with the simplest task.
His behaviour, dress, language, and comportment were the subject of
constant criticism. Wherever he went he was supervised by elderly
courtiers who were under orders to report everything the Prince said or
did.

No wonder the growing boy chafed at these restrictions and took
every opportunity to give his tutors the slip. Photographs of the period
show a lank-haired, heavy-featured, pale and moody-looking youth, with
bulging, dark-circled eyes and drooping mouth. He held himself badly
and was physically unimposing, but although far from handsome he had a
certain charm. His manners were engagingly frank and unassuming and
ladies, particularly, found him ready to be amused. When those prominent blue eyes lit up with interest, the Prince's whole demeanour changed.
It was noticed that the farther he was from his parents, the more readily he
came to life.

In 1856 he accompanied the Queen and Prince Consort on a State
visit to the court of Napoleon III in Paris. The French crowd cheered him
in his kilt, and the repressed, lonely boy began a lifelong love-affair with
France and her people.

More travelling followed: to Italy and Spain, Canada and America –

this last tour accompanied by a trio of well-behaved young men as companions and the grim Colonel – later General – Bruce to supervise and report on them all. The journal that Bertie was ordered to write for his father's perusal proved the usual disappointment: his comments on Old World and New were trite and as brief as possible. He had none of his mother's flair for vivid description.

Still, the tours were judged a qualified success. During his three brief stints at university – Edinburgh, Oxford for a year, then Cambridge – the Prince contrived to make a few friends of his own, despite being obliged to live with his Governor outside college, so that the danger of contamination by undergraduate high spirits was reduced to a minimum. He was a Knight of the Garter and a Colonel in the British Army, but there was nothing in the least dashing or military about his bearing. When Queen Victoria attended a review at Sandhurst, she recorded her surprise that her eldest son was even capable of marching in step.

'Bertie is my caricature', she wrote; and as often happens with mothers and sons who are too much alike, she regarded this distorted mirror-image of herself as a personal affront, and never felt easy in the Prince of Wales's company.

At an Army camp on the Curragh, where a last-ditch attempt to smarten up the Prince was proving no more successful than other efforts in that direction, a pretty young actress named Nellie Clifden was smuggled into his quarters by his brother officers, to the pleasure and satisfaction of all parties. It was unfortunate that the story should reach Prince Albert's ears some months later, and he travelled to Cambridge on a cold foggy November day to remonstrate with his son. When her beloved Consort succumbed to typhoid fever and died a few weeks later, Queen Victoria blamed his death on shock and sorrow as a result of the scandalous behaviour of the Prince of Wales.

'I shall never look at him without a shudder', wrote the distraught Royal widow; and at once proceeded to take the steps necessary to ensure that while she lived, her eldest son had as little opportunity as possible to meddle in affairs of state. Only on minor public occasions did she even allow him to represent her, giving as her reason that she did not want to 'put him in a position of competing for popularity with the Queen'. Since she virtually withdrew from public view after Prince Albert's death, this left a dangerous hiatus and can have done nothing to improve the Prince of Wales's self-esteem.

Other humiliations followed. Though a member of the Privy Council, the Prince was not shown State documents or Cabinet papers from the locked despatch boxes. In this instance, his mother's reason for excluding him was that she considered that he lacked maturity and discretion; but it must have been galling for the heir to the throne to have to glean scraps of information from gossip or the newspapers. He was no fool, and resented being treated as one. To see his brother, the haemophiliac Prince Leopold, 12 years younger than himself, trusted with the Queen's confidence and given a key to the despatch boxes must have been deeply wounding.

The widowed Queen's determination to mourn Prince Albert led to her virtual withdrawal from public life

Not surprisingly, he reacted by turning his back on public affairs and Queen Victoria's fossilized court alike, and bent his considerable energy to establishing a circle of his own, devoted to pleasure.

Society was ready and eager for change. To its younger elements, Victorian priggishness had begun to seem decidedly outmoded by 1861. The Sabbath, they argued, was made for Man, not Man for the Sabbath. To sit through two long, dull sermons every Sunday was asking a bit much. The idea of *wasting* time had not yet risen in the public consciousness. Gentlemen were not expected to work, so they had no feeling of guilt about spending their lives enjoying themselves. Landowners would probably have argued that they worked so hard they seldom had a minute to call their own, and in a sense this was true; but work undertaken voluntarily to support an individual's position is a very different matter from the work of the wage-slave. For the nobly born rich, each year still stretched ahead enticingly, with the gaps between the great sporting fixtures, the London season, and the summer and winter sporting seasons ready to be filled with visits to different great houses and a variety of entertainment. Imperceptibly the pace of life was increasing, but there was still no need to think in terms of days rather than weeks for country house parties.

Thus, for 40 years, from the death of the Prince Consort until Queen Victoria's long reign ended in 1901, two interlinked but very different circles dominated England's social world. As Victoria's court grew older and still more staid, hedged about with petty rules of protocol, its horizons bounded by the old-fashioned discomfort and hideous decor of Windsor, Osborne, and Balmoral, the Prince of Wales's circle of luxury-loving, rich, fast, 'chaffy' people provided a contrast that was both stimulant and irritant to the Widow of Windsor.

Where the Prince led, lesser hosts and hostesses followed. The dash and social prestige of his Marlborough House Set attracted numerous imitators, with the result that country houses became a great deal more comfortable, food improved, and amusements became ever more sophisticated.

This is not to say that Queen Victoria's own circle was disregarded. On the contrary, her strong personality and the almost mystic veneration with which even her longest-serving courtiers regarded her made her a figure to inspire awe. Her Master of the Horse, the Duke of Portland, spoke of a summons to Windsor Castle as

> a very high and particular honour. We were naturally rather overcome by the awe which was created by the intimate presence of H.M. It is difficult to understand why one should have felt this so intensely, for no one could have been kinder than H.M. in her manner, appearance, and speech. However there it is; and I believe the feeling was shared by almost everyone, even by Lord Salisbury and the other great statesmen of the period.[1]

Lady Frederick Cavendish, who had served, albeit briefly, as a Maid of Honour, and should have felt at home in the Royal circle, was thrown into a similar flurry.

> *15 April 1869*   An invitation to Windsor for three nights!! The dear Queen hasn't seen me since I married. She won't have Fred; I feel sure she has never forgiven him for standing on one leg and forgetting his manners that courting time at Osborne.[2]

That was the trouble. Queen Victoria noted every tiny irregularity, and she *never forgot*. Woe betide the wretch who tried to pull the wool over that all-seeing regal eye! Captain Frederick Ponsonby (known as Fritz), son of Sir Henry Ponsonby who had been Queen Victoria's private secretary for many years, was appointed an equerry when he was only 27, and his youthful high spirits sometimes led to trouble.

After dinner one evening at Osborne, on the Isle of Wight, while he and young Harry Legge were waiting in the hall for a carriage to drive them over to the equerries' quarters a couple of miles distant, Ponsonby took it into his head to demonstrate how statues are often mounted on a pivot so they can be displayed from the most advantageous angle.

> I went to the marble statue of Psyche about five foot high on a pedestal and gave it a twist [he recalled]. Apparently it was not on a pivot but it had a circular base which had the same effect. Instead of turning round it fell slowly forward on the top of me, and I put my hands up and tried to push it upright again. Harry Legge, who was no weakling, came to help me and we tried until we were purple in the face to save it from falling. I had no idea that a statue was such a heavy thing, but all we were able to do was to prevent it crashing down and being broken into a thousand pieces. I strained my back in my efforts and bruised my head, while Harry Legge hurt his hand and arm before finally letting it down gently on to the floor. We then found that although we had managed to prevent it being smashed, one of the wings of Psyche was chipped.
>
> Obviously the thing to do was to get it back on to its pedestal before anyone noticed the wing was chipped. We rang and eventually got two footmen, both of them big powerful men, but in powdered hair and red livery which was not intended for manual labour. We tried to raise the statue but all we could manage was to get it two or three feet off the ground.[3]

All hope of hushing up the incident was abandoned, and next morning a chastened Captain Ponsonby was obliged to own up to Princess Beatrice and ask her to tell the Queen. Next day he was in disgrace. The Queen sent a message to the household that 'they must not touch the statues and certainly not play with them', an instruction which puzzled Lady Lytton, who had heard nothing of Captain Ponsonby's accident.

There were other times when the young equerry was obliged to walk delicately in this household where most of the courtiers were in their late 70s or even 80s. They tended to react touchily to any suggestion that they might be becoming forgetful.

When the octogenarian General Sir Lyndoch Gardiner omitted to

*Jaunty and self-assured,
the Prince of Wales
succeeded in escaping from
his mother's domination*

order the band of the Life Guards to play during an important dinner, Captain Ponsonby acted with speed and efficiency, ordering conveyances on his own responsibility and rounding up stray bandsmen from all over Windsor. He also took the precaution of asking the gardeners for a number of ladders, since the terrace upon which the band played could only be reached through the dining-room.

Despite his efforts and fervent prayers that the Queen might be late, she entered the dining-room to silence instead of the strains of the National Anthem. Ponsonby glanced across at General Gardiner, whose face was the picture of woe. Then, through the window, he spotted shadowy figures climbing up ladders to the terrace, and before the Queen lifted her soup spoon, the band had begun to play. General Gardiner escaped with a mild reminder that the band should always play the National Anthem when the Queen came into the dining-room.

According to Mrs Montgomery, Fritz Ponsonby's sister, who was one of Queen Victoria's many godchildren, during dinners at the castle no one was allowed to speak, and if they had to ask for something, this must be in a voice not above a whisper.

> Dinners were interminable and dreadful. The Queen would address her family in German. The familiar phrase, *'Das ist shrecklich!'* haunts her. She once witnessed the Queen greeting Mr Gladstone, who had been summoned to dine. Gladstone was nervous about what his reception would be, and fumbled with his walking-stick. He was then over eighty. But contrary to expectation, when the Queen appeared she went straight up to him, leaning on a stick herself, and said, 'Mr Gladstone, you and I have known days when neither of us was lame,' and laughed very sympathetically.[4]

In general, however, the Queen paid little heed to her ageing household's frailty. Lord Colville of Culross was already old when the Duke of Portland became Master of the Horse, and greeted the newcomer thus:

> Well, young fellow, you've become one of us, and I hope you won't mind a very old courtier giving you a little advice. It is this. Sit down whenever you see a vacant chair, and always make yourself comfortable when you have the chance – for, I assure you, you will have very few opportunities of doing either![5]

Draconian though she undoubtedly was, Queen Victoria could be informal when she pleased. Before a concert at Windsor, she decided she wanted her chair moved to another part of the room, and as Fritz Ponsonby remembered,

> although there were hundreds of servants in the Castle, she did not want to ring for anyone but asked me to do this. She sat with her feet straight out and I took a firm hold of her chair and lifted it to the place she indicated. It nearly made me laugh to find myself staggering about with the chair and the Queen in it, but mercifully I did not drop her.[6]

Certain people had the knack of making her laugh, and with them she would allow a surprising freedom of speech. One of these favourites was the Earl of Rosslyn, stepfather to the Countess of Warwick, who admired his ability to

> tell a *risqué* story to Queen Victoria and go unrebuked. Even Lord Beaconsfield would not have dared address his 'Faery' in like fashion.
>
> I have been at dinner in Windsor Castle and heard Lord Rosslyn spinning a daring yarn to the Queen, while the Princess Beatrice looked as though she were sitting on thorns, and other guests were quaking. I have seen the Queen's lips twitching with suppressed laughter, and . . . I might go so far as to state that I have seen her most gracious Majesty shaking like an agitated jelly.[7]

At Balmoral on Deeside, the favourite home which she continued to visit twice a year in early summer and again in autumn throughout her long reign, Queen Victoria allowed a certain relaxation of formality. Though in the 1870s she no longer accompanied the stalkers to the hill, she kept in close touch with each day's events: an unlucky or inept sportsman was ill-advised to make excuses.

> Although the head stalker came in every night to tell her exactly what each person out stalking or fishing had done, she always pretended not to know the result of the day's sport and asked for information. Prince Francis Joseph of Battenberg, who was a very bad shot, unlike his brother Prince Henry, unfortunately didn't know this. Having been out stalking, he proceeded to give a rambling account of his day's sport, quite unconscious that the Queen knew every detail. All would have been well if he had left it at that, but he went on to say that it was a pity everything was so badly done and that the stalkers did not know much about stalking. Then the Queen turned on him and rent him. She asked him how many shots he had had, and when he replied he could not remember, she asked whether he had had seven, and had missed them all. She asked how far the stags were when he fired, and he replied that he was no judge of distance, whereupon she said, 'I suppose about a hundred yards.'
>
> It then dawned upon him that she knew exactly what had happened and he shut up like an umbrella.[8]

At Balmoral, too, there were moments of spontaneous gaiety, even

The Prince and Princess of Wales out riding in the early days of their marriage. The Princess was a dashing and elegant horsewoman

in the Queen's old age, as she records in her *Highland Journal*:

> *11 October 1890*   After dinner, the other ladies and gentlemen joined us in
> the Drawing-Room, and we pushed the furniture back and had a nice little
> impromptu dance, Curtis's band being so *entrainant*. We had a quadrille, in
> which I danced with Eddy!! [Her grandson, Prince Albert Victor] It did
> quite well, then followed some waltzes and polkas.[9]

At the age of 72, when she took to the floor one evening with Prince
Henry of Battenberg, her favourite son-in-law, old Sir Henry Ponsonby
admired her 'light airy steps in the old courtly fashion; no limp or stick
but every figure carefully and prettily danced'.[10]

Queen Victoria was naturally abstemious and had a blind spot about
the amount of whisky consumed by her servants and guests at Balmoral.

> Whenever anyone went out stalking, a whole bottle of whisky was given
> out, and whatever the guest did not drink became the perquisite of the
> stalker. It was quite a common thing for a stalker to come to the Castle and
> drink off a glass of neat whisky before he started. Of course if he went out
> stalking no harm was done, but when the weather was impossible and the
> mist came down he retired to his house and started the day slightly
> intoxicated. The amount of whisky consumed by the servants was truly
> stupendous. Whenever the Queen went out driving, a bottle of whisky was
> put under the coachman's seat and was supposed to provide stimulant to
> anyone who had had an accident. It was said that early in the Queen's reign
> a poor man had been found at the side of the road in a state of exhaustion
> and that Her Majesty had remarked what a pity it was that no one had any

stimulant to revive him. This was at once rectified and innumerable bottles of whisky must have gone astray in this way. But [observes Captain Ponsonby], the whole atmosphere was wrong. A drunken man was so common that no one ever remarked on it.[11]

On the anniversary of the Prince Consort's birthday, the Queen used to hold a small ceremony of remembrance around the statue erected to his memory in the Balmoral grounds. The ghillies, stalkers, and estate workers used to turn out in force, soberly dressed in dark clothes, and the Queen joined them for prayers. 'Then whisky was sent out as light refreshment at the back of the wood. The result was that the whole community was three parts intoxicated and when we went for a walk in the afternoon it was no uncommon sight to find a man in a top-hat and frock-coat fast asleep in the woods.'[12]

Still greater licence was usual on the night of the Ghillies' Ball, which the Queen made a point of attending, even postponing her departure from Scotland if necessary. At times it

was bacchanalian, but the hard drinking was supposed to take place so late that if anyone was the worse for drink no one should know of it. But as it began at seven and the Queen's dinner was usually about nine, those who had to wait at table had already been dancing for two hours. On one occasion it was a warm evening and, no doubt without being in the least drunk, some of the servants who waited were in rather a hilarious mood. The piper did not seem to mind whether he made a good shot at the glass when he poured out the wine, and some of the footmen were rather slapdash in their methods. The piper only made one or two really bad shots, but there were loud crashes when someone outside dropped the plates and dishes.[13]

Despite the uproar, Queen Victoria remained unruffled, telling stories and keeping the conversation going. It was part of her creed that anything was excusable on the night of the Ghillies' Ball.

Such exuberance was rare at Osborne, where courtiers found life dull and restricted. Their surroundings did nothing to lighten the gloom for the house was furnished in the worst Victorian taste. Lord Rosebery said that he had thought the drawing-room at Osborne was the ugliest room in the world until he saw the drawing-room at Balmoral.

Visitors to Osborne had difficulty filling the long hours between breakfast and dinner, and for the Royal princesses there was no escape from their mother's domination. While accompanying Princess Beatrice and another guest on their morning ride, Lady Frederick Cavendish could not resist speaking of forbidden joys. 'I could not help pitying all these Royal people who are never allowed to go out of their own domain,' she confided to her diary. 'Miss Bowater and I raving of country-house visiting. "I should like it!" said the Princess, half-hesitating. "Ah! That is one thing we are deprived of." Goodness! Life must be rather monotonous.'[14]

Queen Victoria kept firm control over her unmarried daughters, but the Prince of Wales had broken free. He was well aware that his mother disapproved of his friends and his way of life, and he regretted it; but in his own way he was quite as obstinate as she was, and determined to live as he pleased.

The only person to give the Queen any satisfaction in the Prince's entourage was the daughter-in-law she had so carefully selected from the crop of Royal princesses presented for her inspection. Though her mother was a rather flighty woman and her father a crashing bore, Princess Alexandra of Denmark appeared to have escaped these faults of heredity.

She was a slender, neatly made girl with a broad low forehead, large eyes under level brows and a classically chiselled profile. Luxuriant ringlets cascaded from a central parting and her colouring was fresh and delicate. She was endowed with natural elegance and moved gracefully, had pretty manners and plenty of common sense. She was also a Protestant, if somewhat High Church and, best of all, she appeared to have captivated the susceptible Prince at their very first meeting. What did it matter that she was slightly deaf, unpunctual, untidy, inclined to be stiff with strangers, and never opened a book?

Once she overcame her temperamental shyness, she could be very good company, even boisterous, and entranced Lady Frederick Cavendish (who was something of a hero-worshipper) one evening at Chatsworth. The Princess was

> a sight never to be forgotten for liveliness and fun as she whisked round the billiard-table like any dragon-fly, playing at 'pockets'; punishing the table when she missed, and finally breaking her mace across Lady Cowper's back with a sudden little whack. Likewise at bedtime, high jinks with all the ladies in the corridors; and yet through all one has a sense of perfect womanly dignity, and a certainty that no one could ever go an inch too far with her. She can gather up her beautiful bright stateliness at any moment. O, bless her for a vision of enchantment![15]

Queen Victoria was relieved to see her unsatisfactory eldest son so suitably married. He had recently spent over £200,000 on buying the Sandringham estate in Norfolk, after considering various properties with sporting potential. Now the young Royal couple set about remodelling the house to their own taste, replacing the existing building with a strangely ornamented and gabled hybrid with tall chimneys and a multitude of windows, built in a mixture of red brick and yellow Norfolk stone. Though large, it was never formidable, and though the proportions were odd, it suited its new owners very well. Inside, there was an oak-panelled hall where a stuffed baboon held out a tray for visiting cards, and the interconnecting long, light rooms of the ground floor, though narrow and cluttered with furniture and ornaments in claustrophobic profusion, had a friendly, informal atmosphere that invited guests to relax.

Outside, on the 8,000 acre estate, the Prince set his men to work planting up the coverts, which were poorly furnished with the shelter needed by game birds when he bought the land, and growing a variety of crops suitable for holding pheasants. Norfolk landowners were arguably the keenest shooting men in England, and the Prince had plenty of sporting neighbours to whom to turn for advice. Lord Leicester and Lord Walsingham were among those who helped him raise the estate's annual bag of game from 7,000 to 30,000 head.

Another of Norfolk's great advantages was that it was far enough from Windsor for the young Waleses to feel relatively free from Queen Victoria's censorious scrutiny, though when the Princess was rash enough to have herself whirled about the ice in a sleigh late in her first pregnancy, causing the premature birth of her son with no one but the village doctor in attendance, the Queen was quick to scold her fecklessness.

It is tempting to speculate whether this rough-and-ready reception into the world had a lasting effect on Prince Albert Victor, more generally known as Prince Eddy. Certainly he was a lethargic, slow-witted child, so simple-minded as to be almost unteachable. His early death on the eve of his marriage to Princess May of Teck was a considerable relief to the more objective of his future subjects. Prince George, his brother, was another 7-month child but brighter and more robust.

At Sandringham the Prince and Princess of Wales established a fashion for house parties that threw any former style of country entertaining into the shade. It soon became the model for every socially ambitious

Guns at a Sandringham shoot, 1867. (Left to right) The Marquess of Hartington; the Duke of Beaufort; Captain Ellis; the Duke of St Albans; the Prince of Wales; Christopher Sykes MP; the Earl of Chesterfield; Lord Huntingfield

hostess who could afford the expense of such a lavish style.

Guests were invited well in advance, and travelled in a special coach of the train from St Pancras to Wolferton, the nearest station, where they were met by a long procession of horse-drawn carriages and driven to Sandringham. Maids, valets, and loaders followed with the luggage and sporting equipment. As the early winter dusk gathered round the brightly lit long windows, the guests would descend from their vehicles and enter the hall where the Prince and Princess waited to greet them.

Despite the easy informality of his manner, the Prince was a stickler for punctuality – all the Sandringham clocks were kept half an hour fast – and much of his frustrated energy went into planning his parties. He chose the room each guest would occupy, approved the seating-plan for dinner, and gave precise directions on the clothes he expected his visitors to wear for each meal. Nothing annoyed him more than to see Orders incorrectly worn, or a black waistcoat on an occasion that called for a white one. His innate restlessness made him a demanding host. It needed stamina to keep up with his routine and, since he himself required little sleep, a few days at Sandringham left elderly guests exhausted.

The Prince did not like to see people idle and was ruthless about forcing activity upon anyone found unoccupied. Experienced guests learned to pretend to be busy, and invented pastimes that would satisfy the Prince that they were being properly entertained when all they really wished to do was skulk in the library with a book.

No one was allowed to cry off the serious business of sport. Wet or fine, gale or frost, during the shooting season the male guests must assemble outside the house on the dot of ten-thirty, Sandringham time, in their flat caps and thick tweed shooting-suits, heavy stockings and gaiters (looking so like their modern counterparts that 100-year-old photographs of shooting-parties give a strange sense of *déjà vu*).

Gamekeepers wore breeches, smart brass-buttoned, full-skirted coats with lapels cut high, and billycock hats with a twist of whipcord round the crown. While most of the loaders wore neat tweed jackets, stiff collars and ties, the Prince of Wales's loader was splendid in a kilt of Balmoral tartan.

Ladies were not required to put in an appearance before luncheon, and after breakfast they spent the morning as they pleased – reading, gossiping, or writing those voluminous letters which gave rise to a high proportion of the century's social scandals. Shooting is a sport of limited spectator-appeal, and standing in Norfolk's peculiarly penetrating east wind for an hour after lunch provided ample exposure to fresh air in the opinion of most ladies. Sometimes the Prince would summon a particular favourite to stand by him, but it was not advisable to distract him. On one occasion at Six Mile Bottom, after his accession, a lady's sudden exclamation caused King Edward to turn sharply while discharging his gun, and pepper a beater in the leg.

Ladies and luncheon arrived simultaneously, and the sit-down meal was a stylish affair, with snowy tablecloths, sparkling crystal and china set out on long tables in a marquee through which the wind whistled merrily

while the Prince and his guests ate quantities of chicken mayonnaise and
lobster salad, or tackled the appetizing hot dishes sent down from the
Sandringham kitchens in heated covered trays.

For entertainment, an equerry would read out the list he had
compiled of how many head of game each gun had shot, to the
accompaniment of polite clapping or jeers and laughter, which the less
successful sportsmen endured as best they might. More traditional
landowners thought it bad form to keep a tally of birds one had killed, but
the Prince encouraged competition among his guests, some of whom
became a bit too keen to win. It was with some justice that Lord Rosebery
complained, on finding himself between Lord de Grey and Harry
Chaplin, that the former would shoot all his birds and the latter pick them
up.

As dusk fell and the game-carts rumbled back to the larders with the
day's bag hung neatly in rows, the Prince and his guests would tramp
back to the house to shed their muddy tweeds and change for the
evening's entertainment.

Tea-time gave the ladies their first real chance to dress up, and they
made the most of it, emerging from their heavy tweeds radiant as
butterflies in elaborate flowing tea-gowns of chiffon, lace, or fur-trimmed
velvet.

Organized games of cards would be played after the tea-trolleys had
been wheeled out, but men whose heads were aching after the sustained
bombardment often preferred to slip away to the library to read or talk
until it was time to dress all over again for dinner.

These frequent changes of clothes occupied a great deal of time and
effort, not to mention expense, since ladies were not expected to wear the
same dress twice, and a four-day visit required at least twelve and

*Far left: Family card-
party: the Princess of
Wales with her sisters the
Tsarina of Russia and the
Duchess of Cumberland,
and their brother King
Christian IX of Denmark*

*Left: The absurd fashion
for crinolines caricatured in
Punch*

probably sixteen complete ensembles. Writing of a later period, in what
he calls the last posthumous fling of the polite nineties, James Lees-Milne
recalls that when he stayed at Cumberland Lodge with Lord and Lady
FitzAlan

> Not one of the guests was chic or fashionable. Not one of them, I am sure,
> took the least interest in what he or she wore. Certainly no single garment
> among the fourteen of us, except for one of Mrs Baldwin's hats, a
> confection of tulle and seven birds of paradise, is memorable. Yet the
> changing was incessant. We (and here I should exclude myself, lest it be
> thought I boast, for my wardrobe was then strictly limited) first assembled
> in breakfast clothes at 9 o'clock. We changed for church at 11. We changed
> for luncheon at 1.30. Those of us who went for an afternoon stroll changed
> at 3. We certainly changed for tea at 5. Thereafter I do not think we changed
> again until the dressing-gong went at 8. Then we changed to some tune, the
> women into long trailing gowns, and the men into tails and white ties.
> Some of us therefore put on six different garments that day as a matter of
> course, not vanity.[16]

Absurd as all this changing seems today, it did give both hosts and
guests a measure of privacy, so they were not continually in one another's
company. Staying in someone else's house for four or five days, constantly on one's best behaviour, imposes almost as much strain on the guest as
it does on the host. It is very important to be able to retire to territory
which is, however temporarily, one's own. Changing clothes provided
the perfect excuse for physical and mental recreation and was one of the
secrets of house party success.

Solitude, of course, did not exclude the company of the maid or valet
accompanying each guest. The elaborate ritual of dressing for dinner was
enlivened by fleeting glimpses of that other world behind the green baize
door, and information garnered from one's maid might be valuable at the
dinner table. Lord X was deaf in his right ear after shooting. Lady Y had
lost a lot of money on the St Leger and must not be allowed to sign IOUs.
Word of what other guests would be wearing that night flew up and down
the corridors between ironing-rooms and bedrooms. Even when the
Prince had specified how his guests should dress – with or without tiara
and Orders – there was still scope for individuality, and no lady wanted to
be outshone. If Lady A was wearing the famous A rubies, Lady B might
decide on emeralds; there were even occasions when a tip from a more
experienced lady's maid might solve a novice's problems.

> Cicely, dressed for dinner, was sitting in front of the mirror so that Ellen,
> her maid . . . might pin up her hair.
> 'It slips out so, doesn't it? Especially when it's just been washed.'
> 'I'm getting better at it, Miss. I'm using these very long pins at the back.
> They were all right last night, weren't they?'
> 'There were wisps after dinner, I know. I was tucking them in all the time
> I was talking to Count Rakassyi.'
> 'I know it was all right at dinner. I particularly asked John when he came
> out after the fish, and he said it was looking lovely . . .'

'You mean you hang about outside the dining room to ask the footmen if my hair's come down? Oh, Ellen, I'm sure that's not what proper lady's maids do.'

'I don't always do it. Just sometimes, when I'm extra worried. It was Hortense, you see, she showed me how to use these long pins and I wasn't sure if I could do it as well as she does . . . The things she can tell you, just about ironing. I could never be as good as that.'[17]

A lady's looks depended very much on the skill of her maid in those days of contrived and structured beauty. The mid-Victorian belle's snowy shoulders rose from a froth of lace or tulle perilously draped about a prow-like bosom which tapered abruptly into a handspan waist. As Lord Ernest Hamilton remarked, women could hardly be said to have contours.

The word seems to suggest smooth and gradual undulations and there was nothing gradual about them. They suddenly bulged in the most unexpected parts, without rhyme or reason and certainly without any effect of grace . . . It would seem as though the first consideration in their minds was that of puzzling mankind as to the shape in which women had been fashioned by Nature . . .

First [he continues] came a revival of crinolines on an exaggerated scale and, when this disguise was penetrated and man had made the discovery that the fair sex were not shaped like handbells, another brave attempt at deception was made by means of appliances known as 'bustles'. A more extraordinary distortion of the human form is not easy to conceive. As though in protest against Nature's niggardly dole, large wicker panniers were pinned on where, to the ordinary eye, any such addition would seem to have been least called for. The effect in profile was, of course, very striking, and was, at times, responsible for ribald comments on the part of street urchins.

In the craze for obscuring the lines of Nature, even the shape of the head was tampered with, first by means of sleek chignons pinned on behind, and then by means of fuzzy fringes pinned on, like birds' nests, in front.[18]

That shrewd observer Lord Ernest was not slow to realize why women decked themselves in such a fashion:

the great advantage of the standardised Mid-Victorian dress was that it gave nothing away. No matter how glaring might be Nature's defects, a woman could always bring herself up to the standard pattern with the aid of flounces, whalebone and staylaces. The main thing aimed at was pectoral protruberance, and anyone so endowed was considered to have a 'good figure', quite irrespective of any shortcomings in other directions.[19]

At Sandringham, at half-past eight, the ladies sailed down to the drawing-room to await the appearance of the Prince and Princess. Laced and boned, fringed and flounced, embellished with all the skill at their dressers' command and all the heirloom jewels their husbands could provide, their beauty owed everything to artifice except their complex ions which were, somewhat surprisingly, their own. Apart from a few notorious exceptions, the rule was that ladies did not paint. According to Elinor Glyn,

> None of the women would have used powder or lipstick, or had any kind of a bag. An ostrich feather fan was often carried, and long gloves were worn, being taken off at dinner and put on again afterwards. Those who did use powder made the most of the opportunity after leaving the dining-room to rush up to their rooms and put some on, but I never remember seeing anyone wearing lip rouge then, except old Lady Charles Beresford, who was considered quite a joke because of the way she would dab red grease on her face almost anywhere but near her mouth! She also had a pair of blackened eyebrows, put on nearly a quarter of an inch above her real ones![20]

Lady Charles was a notoriously slapdash dresser, and her eyebrows were only part of the story. Driving through Easton Park one day in company with Lady Warwick, she was sitting on the box when a gust of wind showed its indifference to persons

> in the grossest manner by lifting her smart hat, and her yellow hair, and carrying them along in one compact heap, first into the air, then on to the grass.
> I pulled up [Lady Warwick continues] in unbroken silence, and tried to keep a straight face. The two grooms at the back of the coach jumped down, in order to retrieve the rolling head-dress. They brought it back gravely to Lady Charles, who adjusted it with great care.
> 'How lucky we were not on the high road!' she remarked.[21]

More conventional ladies were proud that their complexions were shown as Nature made them. The Duke of Portland recalled

> a well-known beauty who was reported to use cosmetics, saying to the person she believed to have spread the rumour, 'Please be so good as to wipe my face with this clean handkerchief; and if none of my complexion comes off, you will kindly deny the report you have spread, and will send me an apology as well.[22]

No drinks and certainly no cigarettes alleviated the slight tension before dinner, and the assembled company would stand about stiffly, attempting to make conversation while at the same time keeping an eye on the door. Precedence was one of the Prince's favourite hobby-horses, and even on informal occasions he was meticulous about arranging his guests according to their rank. The Princess would lead the way to the dining-room on the arm of the foremost gentleman, followed by the Prince with the most distinguished lady. Their guests followed, carefully placed in descending scale of importance, and the long, sumptuous meal would begin.

The Prince was not a heavy drinker, but his appetite was immense and a delicious new dish would ensure his good humour better than the

wittiest lady's repartee. His talent was for listening, rather than holding forth himself. Sitting next to him could be nervous work as his interest flitted rapidly from one subject to the next, and the burden of sustaining the conversation always fell on his partners. The ominous signs of boredom were when the Royal fingers began to fidget with the cutlery, and his eyes to stray along the table as he murmured, 'Quite so, quite so'. The ingenuity of a lady called on to sit next to the Prince twice in a row was taxed to the limit, and she was usually thankful when the Princess gave the signal for withdrawal, and the Prince reached eagerly for a cigarette.

In the early days of his marriage – and, indeed, before it – baccarat was the Prince's favourite after-dinner pastime, though he played for modest stakes. Many of his closest friends were much richer than he was. The Duke of Sutherland, with his million and a quarter acres, for instance, lived in so grand a style that the visiting Shah of Persia murmured confidentially to the Prince of Wales, 'Much too powerful for a subject! When you are King you must have him executed.'[23]

With a mere £40,000 a year voted by Parliament, and the revenues from the Duchy of Cornwall, the Prince of Wales had to be moderate in his gambling if he was to indulge all his other expensive tastes, and the stakes at Sandringham were therefore not high. Still, they were enough to raise certain eyebrows. Winifred Sturt was shocked to see the Royal family playing an illegal game, every night, with a real table, and rakes, and everything like the rooms at Monte Carlo.[24]

Whist was another favourite game, and card-tables were set out in the drawing-room, but the Princess of Wales, as befitted someone brought up in one of Europe's poorer Royal houses, had simpler and cheaper ideas of fun. With engaging high spirits she would dragoon her guests, no matter how old or distinguished, into playing nursery favourites such as Hunt the Slipper, General Post, or Blind Man's Buff. On one occasion she was seen helpless with laughter, egging on her sons in a battle with soda-water siphons.

Soon after midnight she would sweep the women off to their rooms, where there would be more giggling and running about the corridors before all were settled for the night. Mrs Baldwin remembered affectionately how the Princess offered to help her undress, and ended by tucking her into bed.

Downstairs some of the men would be stifling yawns as the Prince settled down to gamble the night away. They were not permitted to go to bed until he did, and he was well known to need little sleep.

'The usual practice for those who didn't play,' records Fritz Ponsonby, 'was to go to sleep in the billiard-room with a footman specially warned to wake them when the baccarat was over.'[25] It was not unknown for the Prince to count heads in the early hours and summon any man who had tiptoed off to bed to attend him downstairs.

Such hours were tiring for guests and hard on the servants who had to stay up and put the rooms to rights when the Prince at last retired for

The Princess of Wales was devoted to her mixed pack of pet dogs who had their own kitchen at Sandringham

the night. A good deal of grumbling went on, though this was never directed at the Princess, who was generally loved. The farmer's wife who described her as 'some exquisite little being wafted straight from fairyland to say and do the kindest and prettiest things all her life and never, never grow old or ugly', may have allowed enthusiasm to carry her away; but it was astonishing how enduring the Princess's fresh complexion and slender figure proved.

In the 1890s, photographs show her looking young enough to be the Prince's daughter, and like an elder sister to her own daughters – an impression she made no attempt to counteract. Though she grew increasingly deaf, with a right knee so stiff that she limped a little, her rather childish sense of fun lasted all her life.

The Prince of Wales neglected and deceived her, but it must be said that he tolerated her scatterbrained behaviour, untidiness, and unpunctuality in a way he would not have with anyone else. The Princess was a special case and allowances must be made. In the same generous spirit she accepted his infidelities with dignity and even agreed to receive certain of his mistresses provided, as in the case of Daisy Warwick and the sympathetic Alice Keppel, they knew how to behave.

Sandringham house parties usually lasted four days and included two days' shooting. Sunday had its own routine. Breakfast was half an hour later; attendance at church obligatory, though the Prince was careful to time his own arrival to coincide with the beginning of the 10-minute sermon.

After a leisurely luncheon, the afternoon was usually spent in making a tour of inspection of the grounds and buildings. Accompanied by a pack of assorted dogs belonging to the Princess, the Royal house party would progress briskly round the model farm, visit the kennels and stable-yard, and throw crumbs to the birds on the ornamental ponds. Visitors were expected to be lavish with praise and comment on improvements made since their last visit, and certainly there was much to admire, with no expense spared to keep garden and grounds in apple-pie order. Even the dogs had their own kitchen, with cauldrons of stew simmering on the range; and here the Princess, girded in a large white apron, would fill the bowls for distribution to her pets.

There was no gambling on Sunday evening, and even the Prince retired soon after midnight, ready for the morning's shoot. On Tuesday morning the house party would disperse. Flourishing signatures were inscribed in the Visitors' Book; with thanks and compliments on their lips, the guests would troop out to the carriages waiting to drive those London-bound to the Wolferton station, while country neighbours drove home in their own carriages.

With greater or lesser variations, this routine came to be repeated in country houses up and down the land during the second half of Queen Victoria's reign. Guests might expect to be entertained with a ball, and a more informal evening party; sport according to season; some gambling, a little music, with perhaps an evening of amateur theatricals thrown in for good measure.

Not only must they arrive properly equipped for such amusements, they must also be able to make a fair showing in some or all of them. Pleasure was a serious business. The host who had gone to the trouble of organizing hunting for his guests did not want to be told at the last moment that one of them had pulled a riding muscle. Nor must the man who had shot until his barrels were red-hot suppose that the splitting headache he was suffering as a result would excuse him from charades that night.

Guests had to show a smiling face at all times, and look as if they were enjoying themselves even if they were not – particularly at Sandringham. In a society with nothing more important to gossip about than one another, word of a guest's shortcomings would spread like wildfire, with the inevitable result that he or she would receive no further invitations. Some people went everywhere, did everything: their names appear in every Visitors' Book. Others, apparently just as well qualified, stayed at home.

Who, then, were the stars of this specialized firmament, and what made them shine? Some requirements were obvious: beauty for a woman; sporting prowess for a man; breeding and riches for both. Yet these were not the only assets needed by those who wished to climb to the top of the social tree. Getting there, and staying there, demanded a particular flair, the most important element of which was to attract the roving fancy of the Prince of Wales.

CHAPTER THREE

Four Hostesses

*I*n an age when every mother's ambition was to marry her daughter to a duke, netting two of that rare species in succession may be seen as the feminine equivalent of winning a bar to your VC. It must have been exasperating for the ladies of Queen Victoria's circle to watch as the German-born Countess Louise von Alten – fascinating, fast, but no great beauty – carried off two of England's most eligible bachelors: first, the rich and raffish Duke of Manchester; then, two years after his death, capturing the handsomest matrimonial prize in the country – the Marquess of Hartington, soon to become the Duke of Devonshire, heir to Chatsworth and member of the Cabinet, one of the largest, richest, and most highly regarded landowners.

There was something very special about the Double Duchess, as Louise inevitably became known. Among her contemporaries she excited strong opinions, ranging from 'Too beautiful and winning, with the most perfect manners – high-bred, gentle and intelligent'[1] to 'a grim personality who never relaxed or displayed emotion. She could be strident, emphatic and persistent'.[2]

Between these extremes, what was the truth? The judgements are surprising in themselves. Lady Frederick Cavendish, who had her share of Victorian priggishness, might have been expected to disapprove of Duchess Louise's fast ways and the disreputable company she and 'Kim' Manchester invited to Kimbolton Castle; while Lady Warwick who, though a good deal younger, belonged to the same set, is less than admiring and for one whose view of her contemporaries is usually generous, this verdict seems uncharacteristically harsh.

Louise von Alten's rapid rise to prominence in English society began when the Duke of Manchester decided that his heir Lord Mandeville who, in his late 20s, showed disturbing signs of instability, would benefit from the steadying effect of a course of German studies, and despatched him to stay with Count von Alten. History is silent on how the German studies progressed, but very soon young Lord Mandeville was bewitched by his host's vivacious daughter Louise, and determined to marry her.

Though far from a classical beauty, she had dash and high spirits and her fair share of brains. Portraits show a compactly built, plumpish young woman with strong features rather closely grouped. Her heavily marked

Above: The Double Duchess: German-born Louise von Alten became Duchess of Manchester and later Duchess of Devonshire

Above right: The Marquess of Hartington, later the 7th Duke of Devonshire, a shrewd and respected statesman, sportsman, and pillar of Society

eyebrows nearly meet across her commanding nose as, with an air of unassailable superiority, she gazes from her frame. Though such portraits give little hint of the sparkle and vitality that must have captured the affections of both her dukes, it is easy to sense the energy that made her one of Society's most successful and longest-serving hostesses.

She was a few years older than the Prince of Wales, and must have seemed the epitome of sophistication and glamour. Glimpses of her early married years convey an impression of a devil-may-care contempt for convention and determination to grasp power. With barely concealed glee, Lady Eleanor Stanley describes a paperchase at Kimbolton, and the spectacular tumble taken by the Duchess who,

> in getting too hastily over a stile, caught a hoop of her cage in it, and went head over heels, alighting on her feet with her cage and whole petticoats over her head. They say there was never such a thing seen – and the other ladies hardly knew whether to be thankful or not that a part of her underclothing consisted of a pair of scarlet tartan knickerbockers (the things Charles shoots in) – which were revealed to all the world in general and the Duc de Malakoff in particular.[3]

An even more public tumble laid the – by then – Double Duchess low some 40 years later at the Coronation of King Edward VII when, in her haste to reach the Peeresses' lavatory ahead of anyone else, she pushed past the line of Grenadier Guards who were keeping back the crowd in the Abbey in the wake of the Royal procession, tripped over her robes, and measured her length down a flight of steps, her coronet rolling ahead of her.

Both incidents seem entirely in character. Whether in pursuit of a 'hare' or bodily relief, the Double Duchess was determined to be first.

Quick-witted, quick-tempered, no sufferer of fools or weaklings, she had none the less great charm when she chose to exercise it, was faithful to her friends, and could be both kind and practical, whether helping young Margot Asquith to pin up her rebellious hair before a dance, or tearing up the IOUs of friends who lost too much money to her at cards.

As the present Duchess of Devonshire puts it:

> When Louise arrived at Chatsworth there had been no Duchess of Devonshire for eighty years (because the 7th Duke had been a widower and the 6th a bachelor) and her love of society made a cheerful impact on the place, from the grand set-piece of a week-long shooting-party to the Christmas treat for the schoolchildren of Edensor, Beeley, Pilsley and Baslow held in the Theatre and still remembered with pleasure by two octogenarians . . .
>   Louise Duchess brought Chatsworth back to life.[4]

A distinguished audience for amateur theatricals in the private theatre at Chatsworth. Front row includes the Duke of Devonshire, Marchioness of Ripon, Duchess of Devonshire, Prince of Wales, and Mrs George Keppel

Her brisk practicality made an excellent foil for her brilliant, dreamy husband, who allowed her to boss and manage him while going his own sweet way. The faint German accent she retained gave her speech a piquant attraction. Like the Prince of Wales, she rolled her Rs, and according to Lord Clarendon, her conversation had the same charm as her letters. The intense interest she took in people – particularly powerful people – contributed to her success as a hostess, and though by degrees the gambling parties and midnight excursions to Covent Garden that had scandalized Queen Victoria in the 1860s gave way to more dignified political or sporting gatherings, she never lost her zest for entertaining and liked nothing better than to welcome 50 guests at a time.

A party of 50 guests meant well over 50 extra servants, especially if it included Royalty. The Prince of Wales's retinue included two valets, an equerry, two loaders and a groom, and if the Princess accompanied him there were still more mouths to feed. Nor was Royalty alone in thinking its own staff essential to comfort in a friend's house. The 6th Duke of Portland recalled that when Lord Dudley visited Welbeck Abbey he brought with him 'among others, Andrew Kirkcaldy, the famous golfer from St Andrews, his Austrian haircutter, the head keeper from Witley, his wife's footman, and two chauffeurs'.[5]

The great hostesses of mid to late Victorian days fell into two categories, social and political, with a certain amount of overlap. Supreme in the political class was Theresa, Marchioness of Londonderry, conservative to the backbone and the most obdurate die-hard of her generation. She would never have opened her doors to a radical such as Joseph Chamberlain, and her parties included no dissenting voices.

Right: The Marchioness of Londonderry, whose liaison with Harry Cust caused a bitter rift with her husband

Far right: The Marchioness of Ripon, patron of the arts and Lady Londonderry's rival

Harry Cust, political journalist, sportsman, and dilettante with an irresistible attraction for married ladies of rank. Large blue eyes like his might be found in many a stately nursery

She had been born Lady Theresa Chetwynd-Talbot, daughter of the 19th Earl of Shrewsbury, and married in 1875. Lady Warwick described her as

> short, and her head seemed to be a little too large; but her features were beautifully moulded, and she would have seemed even fairer to look on had it not been for her haughty expression.
>
> Hers was a remarkable personality, for she was amazingly shrewd and far-seeing. She was a born dictator, and loved to encounter opposition, so that she might crush it. As is often the case with those who are born to rule, her temper was that you might call brief, and she made a host of enemies.[6]

Yet even this powerful character had her Achilles' heel, and among her contemporaries the bitter rift between Lady Londonderry and her husband was an open secret. In *Edwardians In Love*, the historian Anita Leslie tells the strange story of how the passionate love-letters written by Lady Londonderry to her lover Harry Cust, younger brother of Lord Brownlow (whose many illegitimate children are supposed to have included Lady Diana Cooper), fell into the hands of another of Cust's mistresses named Lady de Grey, who later became Marchioness of Ripon.

This unscrupulous rival first amused herself by reading extracts from the letters to friends, then sent the incriminating bundle to Lord Londonderry himself. His response was to return them to his faithless wife with a note attached: *Henceforth we do not speak . . .*

For the rest of his life he avoided addressing a word to her, communicating always through a third party. He became Viceroy in Ireland, and held a number of official appointments. She was the leading political hostess of the day. But they received their guests standing a little apart, and he never spoke to her.

Lady de Grey, the cause of all the trouble, was a very different character from the proud domineering woman she had betrayed. In an outstandingly philistine society, where the arts attracted even less social patronage than they do today, Gladys de Grey was remarkable for her love of music, particularly opera. Dark-haired and white-skinned, her dramatic looks were said to make other women look vapid, and her entry into a room drew all eyes.

She was a Herbert by birth, daughter of the Earl of Pembroke, and was briefly married to Lord Lonsdale – whose brother and successor, Hugh, was one of the finest horsemen of the day. Lonsdale grumbled at his young wife's love of Society and forbade her to accept invitations to fast house parties – a double standard which was laid bare when, only two years after his marriage, he died in dubious circumstances in the house where he entertained actresses to supper.

Freed from his restrictions, his young widow cut a considerable swathe through Society for the next two years, earning herself Queen Victoria's disapproval and the Prince of Wales's admiration in much the same way as the Duchess of Manchester had done.

By April 1886 she had decided to marry again, and wrote to Henry Chaplin, the corpulent and convivial Squire of Blankney,

> I have been laid up with my eyes, or would have written sooner to tell you that I am going to marry Lord de Grey. You are such a true friend that I believe you really will be glad when I tell you that I have at last found peace and comfort, for you know how much trouble I had all my life, though I am afraid it was mostly of my own making.[7]

That last sentence tells us a good deal about the impulsive – even erratic – Lady de Grey. When she saw a pot of mischief brewing, she could not resist giving it a stir, even though she knew it would bring trouble. No doubt the same imp that prompted her to steal Lady Londonderry's love-letters was again at work when she caused her footman to drop a whole tray of specially bought china behind her porcelain-collecting husband's chair; but Lord de Grey's iron nerves were equal to the shock.

He was the best shot in England and one of the best billiard-players, and he took his virtuosity seriously. Though he liked to pretend his skill was inborn, he was not above a little private practice, as Mrs Balfour observed when, slipping into Lord Desborough's library late at night in search of a book, she was startled to find Lord Ripon there, practising changing guns with his two loaders. He was, she noted, not too pleased at being discovered.

Though Lord and Lady Ripon were poles apart temperamentally, their shared interest in the arts was rare in their generation and Covent Garden owed much to their patronage. The musical parties they gave on Sunday afternoons at Coombe, their house on Wimbledon Common, included such famous singers as Melba, the two de Reszke brothers, Edouard and Jean, and the great Caruso. Queen Alexandra was often a guest.

As the house party routine became firmly established, with its own ground rules, private jokes, and languages, hostesses introduced new refinements of entertainment and luxury. Great country houses had never, in centuries past, been noted for their comfort or their food. Generally speaking, the bigger the house, the farther the dining-room was from the kitchen, so food would arrive either stone cold or baked to a cinder. On one occasion, after course upon course of congealed lumps had been placed before him, champagne was served to the Earl of Beaconsfield, and he was heard to exclaim, 'Thank God for something warm at last!'[8]

But now the Prince of Wales's revolt against the solitary spartan regime he had endured as a child took the form of an almost pathological craving for rich food, pretty women, soft beds, and, of course, the huge cigars so detested by Queen Victoria. Many stories are told of her aversion to tobacco. No one was allowed to smoke in any part of Osborne where the smell might possibly drift to the Royal nostrils – this was odd, as Fritz Ponsonby remarked, because all her family smoked like chim-

The smoking-room was an all-male preserve adorned with sporting trophies and sometimes risqué picture·

The Cotillon. Knots of coloured ribbon added dash to sober tailcoats, and men wore kid gloves to avoid making fingermarks on expensive ball-gowns

neys. It made life difficult for foreign diplomats. There is the pitiful tale of Baron Hatzfeldt, who could not live without a cigarette, and was discovered one evening lying in his pyjamas on his bedroom floor at Windsor Castle, blowing cigarette smoke up the chimney.

The Prince of Wales swept away such petty restrictions. In great houses up and down the land new standards of comfort were now demanded, and nowhere could the discerning guest be more sure of living in the lap of luxury than at Easton Lodge, home of Lady Brooke, who later became the Countess of Warwick.

Frances Maynard, generally known as Daisy, inherited a handsome fortune at the age of three and grew up with the confidence of a girl who knows that everything in her immediate surroundings – the estate, park, deer, and house in which she lived with her mother and stepfather – actually belonged to her. Nor did the fairy godmother's gifts stop at wealth. Far from having the proverbial heiress's squint, Daisy was enchantingly pretty, slim, and intelligent, spoke three languages, and looked a dream on a horse. Small wonder that Queen Victoria considered Miss Maynard a suitable bride for her favourite son, the haemophiliac Prince Leopold; but Daisy was, in Disraeli's phrase, a *femme maître* who preferred to choose her own husband. The lovely eyes which Elinor Glyn described as 'smiling with the merry innocent expression of a Persian kitten that has just tangled a ball of silk', fell on the Prince's equerry, Lord Brooke, heir to the Earl of Warwick, and two years later they were married.

One of Daisy's most engaging characteristics was her strong attachment to her own home, and over the next twenty-odd years she raised the business of entertaining there to a fine art, sparing no expense to make her friends happy and supremely comfortable. Even when her husband succeeded to the Earldom, she continued to spend most of the hunting season at her beloved Easton.

Elinor Glyn, the romantic novelist who before her own marriage had known what it was to make her own clothes and live on a shoestring, was particularly well placed to appreciate the fun and luxury of Daisy's house parties, and it is worth quoting at length from her description of a winter visit.

> Easton in the 'Nineties was the centre of all that was most intelligent and amusing in the society of the day. Its hostess, Lady Warwick, was literally a Queen, the loveliest woman in England, of high rank, ample riches, and great intelligence . . . Her immense prestige made every invitation an honour, not lightly refused by those fortunate enough to receive it.[9]

Elinor described how she and her husband Clayton Glyn used to drive from their own home at Sheering in a brougham drawn by a fast pair of horses called Paire and Impaire in memory of their engagement at Monte Carlo. Spanking through the park as dusk was falling, they would see the shadowy shapes of deer grazing under the noble trees. They would pass

Far left: Grace and elegance in a Royal waltz: the Prince of Wales dances with Baroness Bolsover in the Honourable Artillery Company's Armoury at Finsbury. Note fan attachment and sweeping train which required dextrous management

Left: Frances (known as Daisy), Countess of Warwick, one of the brightest stars of the Marlborough House Set

the cricket ground and follow the great sweep of lawn up to the front of the house. The red-brick wing to the left of the drive was reserved for their hostess's own use – an excellent device to ensure a measure of privacy – and the whole house had been redecorated when Lady Warwick's husband came into the title. Although cluttered by today's standards, it then represented the last word in elegance.

> For a winter visit, you arrived at about five o'clock, and were greeted at the door by a superb Groom of the Chambers, 'Mr Hall' who . . knew everyone in the world and where to place them. I am sure he would have disposed of the body without fuss had any of the guests been careless enough to commit a murder on the premises!
>
> Never were there such servants as at Easton: all the footmen were the same height, six feet tall, and they seemed to fulfil every want before you were aware of it. To see four housemaids 'doing' a bedroom in about ten minutes was quite an experience, so perfect was their drilled efficiency, while if you wanted a telegram sent to Timbucktoo, or your train and boat connections worked out to Hades or the moon, you had only to ask the magnificent Hall, who would instantly make all the arrangements for your journey![10]

On being ushered into the saloon, the new arrival would find her hostess

> and any lady-guests who had arrived earlier in the day, arrayed in the most exquisite tea-gowns of sable-trimmed velvet or satin brocade. These garments were fitted to the figure and were not loose as became the fashion later. They showed low V-necks, and had elbow or open sleeves and were of splendid materials, or else of seductive silk gauzes and lace, in either case terribly expensive and very luxurious.

Skill was needed to balance cup and saucer while wearing an elaborate tea-gown

An appetising tea was laid out on a big round table which was removed by footmen as soon as the meal was over. There would be every kind of lovely muffin, crumpet, scone, cake, sandwich, jam, honey, and Devonshire cream as well, and the guests sat round and joked and chatted and had a delicious meal, like children in a schoolroom . . .

The parties at Easton consisted of about twenty people, sometimes more, composed of the *crème de la crème* of England's aristocracy, Tory politicians, ambassadors, sportsmen and distinguished men of this type, with or without their wives . . . and King Edward VII, then Prince of Wales, was often among the guests. In the 'nineties, not any artists, musicians, actors and actresses, or 'bohemian' society types ever came, nor people in business of any kind, but later, after the South African War, these barriers were broken down.

In those days no introductions were made, the assumption being that everyone would already know each other . . . The result was a pleasant informality, but there were drawbacks about the plan for a newcomer like myself, and if it had not been for my husband, who knew everybody and told me about them afterwards, I should never have learnt the names of most of my fellow-guests.

Girls did not often come to these parties unless there were girls in the family, and the average age of the men seemed to be older than it is at similar parties today.[11]

When tea was over, Lady Warwick would show the new arrivals to their bedrooms.

These were the height of luxury, such as is now quite common, but was then rare. Exquisite furniture and hangings, big comfortable armchairs and sofas, heaps of down cushions, great white bear hearthrugs, the finest linen, and shaded lamps in the right places to make reading as you rested a joy – these were the commonplace of every room. On little stands within easy reach of the sofa lay books of travel, biographies, and the talked-about new novels. The provision of such luxuries for each guest was an expensive but much-appreciated attention. The writing-tables were wonderful. No known article was missing from them, from books of reference to stamps in a box. Every new device brought out by the Aspreys and Finnegans of that time was sure to be there almost before it was obtainable in London. You could not wish for a special pen, but you discovered it in your pen-tray.

The whole house was beautifully warmed and lit – another rarity at that time, and a very welcome blessing. Ladies did not wear little coatees or scarves over their evening dresses in those days, and often in other houses you became absolutely frozen by draughts in passages, even when the rooms themselves were not horribly cold.[12]

Nor did Lady Warwick's generosity stop there: while the ladies were dressing for dinner,

Lady Warwick's eldest son, Guy, Lord Brooke, then about eleven, used to bring round to each lady's room a magnificent spray of gardenias, stephanotis or orchids, as it was the fashion to wear long sprays in those days. The cost of providing all these quantities of expensive flowers must have been fantastic, and the fruit at dinner was of the same order of rare

A formal dinner-table setting was often a work of art, with hot-house fruit and flowers, fan-folded napkins, individual menus, and an impressive array of silver

perfection. Even the men were all provided with buttonholes, and the flowers on the dinner-table, which were changed for every meal, were truly magnificent, and arranged most elaborately, sometimes in high vases round which you could only peep at your opposite fellow-guests.[13]

Newcomer though she was, Elinor Glyn's spectacular looks and glorious chestnut hair ensured that she would never be ignored. After dinner on the first night of an Easton party, she wrote,

When the men joined the ladies, whichever of them had been admired would be singled out for the attentions of the most dashing and adroit of the men, but good manners were such that no lady was ever left alone, and all of them would find that some man had come and sat down beside her. Men did all the chasing and contriving to see the ladies of their choice in those days. Etiquette was observed, in spite of the appearance of ease, and no one ever 'lolled' on sofas, or behaved in an undignified manner. Above all, there was *no* touching of each other even in seemingly accidental ways. It might be a lovely lady's own lover who was sitting beside her, but he would never lean over her or touch her arm to accentuate his speech, for all touching in public was taboo. The modern trick of 'pawing' only came in after the Great War, and would have been considered 'servants' hall behaviour' in those days . . .

By the end of the first evening, you usually knew which member of the party intended to make it his business to amuse you – in a discreet way – during the visit, in the hope of who knows what reward?[14]

Many and various were the stratagems then adopted to provide opportunities for privacy for the interested parties, always with the spice of secrecy and the tacit complicity of their beautiful hostess. An admirer might whisper a suggestion for a rendezvous as he bent to light a candle. A note might be passed from valet to maid, and discovered nestling unobtrusively under the napkin on the breakfast tray, or an accidental-on-purpose meeting on the stairs might decide the time and place. Lady Warwick's smiling eyes would note every move in the game, and if an unwanted third party showed signs of wishing to accompany the lovers on their morning stroll to Stone Hall, the little Elizabethan pleasure house in the grounds, she was quick to engage him or her in conversation until the pair had made their escape.

Distance lends enchantment: was it with the rose-tinted spectacles of nostalgia that Elinor Glyn remembered

The charming man you had met – in my experience they were all experts at pleasing women – would do his utmost to be agreeable, discovering your tastes, and talking to you about the things which he thought would interest you, not merely about his own occupations and hobbies as they do today

Pretty arms and a classic profile might be displayed to advantage at billiards

. . .Gracious words and apt phrases still meant something in those days, and cultivation of mind was admired and not laughed at as it is today.[15]

Eheu fugaces! In our own anti-heroic age, we find it hard to accept that Edwardian males could have been as chivalrous, brilliant, witty, and charming as Elinor Glyn would have us believe. In fact, we know they were nothing of the kind. There were just as many bullies, bores, cheats, perverts, and egocentrics in that society as there are in our own. The 'parfait gentil knights' she described existed only in her imagination – and in the nineteenth-century convention that decreed any fault-finding or adverse criticism to be wrong. It was, according to Lord Ernest Hamilton,

worse than wrong. It was not good form. Indiscriminate praise of all things and all people became the fashion. It was, of course, not always easy to put this admirable precept into practice, especially in the case of people, but it was made easier . . . under a system by which everyone's admitted good qualities were pigeon-holed or docketed, so to speak, for public use.

If Lord Augustus Binks's name was mentioned, everyone who had been well brought up knew at once that his two official good points were his poetry and his teeth; and the little party clustered about the hearth would at once start making pleasant allusions to these two assets which, in the ordinary nature of things, became, in the end, worn a little threadbare; but as they were well-known to be the only two items on the credit side of his balance-sheet, it was hopeless to try to praise him in any other direction, and praised he must be. The rules of polite conversation demanded it.

Now this was all very Christian and nice and charitable . . . but it necessarily imparted to all small talk a note of insincerity which everyone who took part in it was secretly conscious of. When Lady Georgiana burst into smiling ecstasies over Lord Augustus's teeth and poetry, every member of her audience knew perfectly well that she was really thinking all the time what a greedy, selfish, cross, ill-mannered old bore he was, as indeed they all knew him to be, but they were not allowed by the rules to say so.

If, as occasionally happened, a name slipped into the conversation to which no single good quality could be attached, it became necessary in the interest of convention to postulate at least one with which to raise him out of the mire of absolute unworthiness, e.g. –

'Sir Marmaduke Brown was staying with us last week,' Lady Charlotte would remark.

'Oh, yes, what an interesting man he is,' would be Lady Clara's comment.

'Yes, and he *really* is very kind-hearted, you know,' the stressed 'really' being an heroic attempt to explain away the outstanding fact that, to the ordinary senses, Sir Marmaduke Brown was about as mean, ill-natured, and disagreeable an old beast as ever snarled biliously across the dinner-table.[16]

Even considered in this rather cynical light, it is clear that Daisy Warwick's house parties had a special enchantment which was largely due to the impulsive charm of the hostess. Few people who attended those glamorous gatherings in the eighties and early nineties could have

Opposite: The talented accompanist was a treasured guest for musical evenings

A sporting house party outside Easton Lodge, Essex, home of the Countess of Warwick. She stands (back row, second from right) between the Prince of Wales and the Duchess of York. The Marquis de Soveral, known as the Blue Monkey, is seated, far right

predicted the amazing change that came over the frivolous Daisy a few years later; yet for those with eyes to see, the seeds of her concern for the poor had outstripped that of her most charitably minded contemporaries long before her dramatic conversion to Socialism.

In the eyes of those contemporaries, her change of political allegiance was as strange and shocking as Saul's conversion on the road to Damascus. Nevertheless, the signs had been there long before. The fires had been laid in her childhood as she rode about her estate and saw how hard were her farm-workers' and servants' lives compared to her own. Only a spark was needed to set her compassion ablaze.

That spark came in the unlikely form of an article in a radical journal called the *Clarion*, which scathingly attacked the waste and extravagance of a large fancy-dress ball Daisy had just given at Warwick Castle during a winter of severe weather when farm-workers and their families were sick and hungry and cold. Such criticism put a whole new slant on the ball in which Daisy had taken such pride, and she reacted with characteristic impulsiveness. Other ladies in her position might have ignored the article or consulted a lawyer, but Daisy believed in taking the bull by the horns.

Hurrying to London, she sought out the offices of the *Clarion* and confronted its editor, Robert Blatchford, who was considerably taken aback by the sudden appearance of an angry Countess in his threadbare sanctum. He rose to the occasion, however, and seized the opportunity to lecture her on social economics to such effect that she travelled home in a very thoughtful mood. As she joined her puzzled guests who were about to go in to dinner, she said nothing of the day's strange encounter; but the fire in her heart had been lit and had taken hold.

Through all the vicissitudes of the years that followed, through unhappy love-affairs and financial difficulties, when Daisy's reckless generosity at last reached the bottom of what she had always imagined was her inexhaustible fortune, neither the disapproval nor the ridicule of her friends ever managed to extinguish her blazing compassion for the poor and needy.

Trade union officials joined her guests at Easton and Warwick Castle. She campaigned tirelessly for better education, free school meals, and careers for women. Her proselytizing fervour often exasperated former friends, but if she cared she did not show it. Even the murky episode when she considered raising money by threatening to publish the love-letters addressed to *My own darling little Daisy wife* which the Prince of Wales had, with a lamentable lack of discretion, written during the nine years of their affair, shows Daisy's resource and enterprise. She ran rings round the various seedy agents commissioned to recover the damning letters.

Lady Randolph Churchill, born Jennie Jerome, daughter of an American millionaire and mother of Sir Winston Churchill

Of all the great hostesses of her generation, Daisy Warwick is the most attractive character and probably the only one who will be remembered for anything more than her social skills.

It was inevitable that there were some leaders of Society whose position required them to entertain large house parties, but who grew to dislike the whole exhausting, time-consuming business. Consuelo Vanderbilt, the rich and elegant American heiress whose fortune had provided a welcome injection of money to the Marlborough coffers, was forthright about her resentment of the work involved in entertaining 20 or 30 visitors at Blenheim Palace.

> My round of the thirty guest rooms, accompanied by the housekeeper, was apt to reveal some overlooked contingency too late to be repaired; a talk with the chef more often disclosed an underling's minor delinquency; orders to the butler invariably revealed a spiteful desire to undermine the chef – a desire that, if realised, I knew would jeopardise the culinary success of my party. Menus had to be approved and rooms allotted to the various guests. I had, moreover, spent hours placing my guests for the three ceremonial meals they would partake with us, for the rules of precedence were then strictly adhered to, not only in seating arrangements but also for the procession in to dinner. Since it was then considered ill-bred not to answer all letters oneself, I had no secretary. There was therefore a considerable amount of purely mechanical work to be done – dealing with correspondence, answering invitations, writing the dinner cards and other instructions which appear necessary to ensure the smooth progression of social amenities . . . which took up a great deal of my time.[17]

This reluctant hostess failed to engender any great sense of gaiety in her guests. A letter from Arthur Balfour describes the party travelling by special train to Blenheim as 'rather cross most of us', and continued: 'Today the men shot and the women dawdled. As I detest both occupations equally I stayed in my room until one o'clock and then went exploring, joining everybody at luncheon. Then the inevitable photograph . . .'[18] It hardly sounds the liveliest of house parties, and one is inclined to blame the hostess's own disenchantment for the guests' lack of enjoyment. Even the quality of Blenheim food was variable. Lady Randolph Churchill remembered the night when the snipe, which are plentiful thereabouts, ran short and 'The Lord Chief Justice, to his annoyance, was given only half of one. On leaving, he wrote in the Visitors' Book some lines to the effect that he would share almost everything in life, even his wife, but *not* a snipe!'[19]

The success of a house party and the memories, agreeable or disappointing, borne away by the guests, depend very much on the hostess's attitude to the whole affair. A sense of enjoyment, boundless zest, and an insatiable interest in human affairs were the essential qualities shared by such diverse characters as the Double Duchess, imperious Lady Londonderry, mischievous Lady de Grey, and the impulsive, courageous Lady Warwick, which made them outstanding in that golden age of country house entertaining.

CHAPTER FOUR

Sporting Parties

'Come for some hunting,' the invitation would entice. 'For a few days' shooting – fishing – tennis – cricket . . .'

Sport was the foundation upon which country house parties were built. The winter sports usually involved killing something and the summer ones hitting a ball. A good shot, a bold man across country, or a chap with an eye for a ball never lacked invitations, and though hostesses were careful to include a sprinkling of 'lap-dogs' – non-sporting men who would amuse the ladies during daylight hours and warble duets with them after dinner – most of the visitors were expected to take part in whatever sport was on offer.

Foreign diplomats were much in demand as lap-dogs. Few of them played cricket or had been properly instructed in sporting etiquette, and hosts usually preferred to see them flirting with their wives than ruining their horses, or firing at low birds to the peril of neighbouring guns. Even the equable Fritz Ponsonby was less than pleased to be assigned the grouse-butt next to M. Poklewski-Koziell for the purpose of discovering whether or not he was a safe shot; though in this case his anxiety proved groundless. There was, in fact, more to be feared from the short-sighted and sometimes absent-minded Duke of Devonshire, who once fired at a wounded pheasant on the ground and succeeded in killing not only the bird but the dog that was about to retrieve it, and at the same time peppering the dog's owner and the Chatsworth chef, who happened to be watching.

But the sport which men and women, English and foreigners could all enjoy with perfect safety (except to their pockets) was racing, the sport of kings; and house parties were regularly arranged to coincide with the major race-meetings at Newmarket, Ascot, Sandown, Goodwood, Doncaster, and Epsom.

Race-meetings in those days had a peculiarly intimate charm.

There was [recalls Lady Warwick] no crowd in the modern sense of the word. Remembering the absence of motor-cars, the infrequency of trains, the comparatively small attendance is easy to explain. Who can defend the over-crowded social gathering, whether it is a race-meeting, dance, or political reception?

At Newmarket there was a set with which one was on the best of terms. All our intimate friends appeared to be either patrons or real lovers of the turf. The group included Henry Chaplin and Lord and Lady Bradford – the last-named and her sister, Lady Chesterfield, being the two ladies to whom Lord Beaconsfield was so devoted. Others always in evidence were the Duke of Devonshire, then Lord Hartington, Lord and Lady Cadogan, whose entertainments at Chelsea House were part of the pleasures of the London Season; Lord Derby, always a sportsman, accompanied by most of the considerable Stanley family; the old Duke of St Albans, who married the daughter of that sometime wit of the House of Commons, Bernal Osborne, and Lord Falmouth.

The Prince of Wales never missed Newmarket, and would frequently ride out with the rest of us in the mornings to see the horses exercised. Generally he drove to the meetings.[1]

The Duke of Portland revelled in the Newmarket meetings, too. With a party of friends he would rent a house in the little town and keep open house.

We were called at seven o'clock in the morning. At eight, our hacks were waiting at the door, and, in the full enjoyment of the usual cold east wind – I hardly ever remember Newmarket at any time of the year without that doubtful blessing – we rode to the Heath to see the horses at exercise. Having done so, and perhaps tried some of them . . . we returned, either uplifted or downcast but in any case terribly hungry, to breakfast on prawns, poached eggs, bacon and muffins.

After breakfast the newspapers arrived, and much discussion – most of it foolish, took place on the prospects of the ensuing day's sport. For an hour or more before the races, a constant procession of acquaintances and friends passed our house, which was in the High Street, and we greeted

Keen racegoers rented houses in Newmarket for the prestigious Spring Meeting, which was attended only by the racing cognoscenti

them through the open windows. Our hacks were again brought to the door, and we then rode to the races. At luncheon, during the Spring Meeting, there were plovers' eggs and more prawns.

After attending the races . . . we rode home to tea, at which there were usually still more shrimps and prawns, but alas, no plovers' eggs. At six we went to the stables, for the evening inspection of the horses. When this was over, it was usually time for dinner, either at home or with our friends. When we dined out, we often finished the evening in the Jockey Club Rooms, where billiard matches took place.[2]

Looking back a quarter of a century later, Lady Randolph Churchill lamented the passing of those exclusive, convivial race-meetings.

Newmarket has become very different from what it was in the early eighties, when I first went there. Then, only the old stands existed, some of which date back quite two hundred years. The ladies who came were habituées, and did not muster a dozen at the outside. Among them were Caroline, Duchess of Montrose who was a large owner of horses, the Duchess of Manchester (now Duchess of Devonshire), and Lady Cardigan, who would drive up in an old-fashioned yellow tilbury, in which she sat all day. Lady Bradford and Lady Cadogan were always there, as were Lady Castlereagh (now Lady Londonderry), Lady Gerard and a few others. It was the fashion to ride, those who did not appearing in ordinary country clothes.

Nowadays velvet and feathers are worn by the mob which throngs the stands, many not knowing a horse from a cow, but coming because it is the fashion. I have heard amusing tales of the ignorance displayed on these occasions. One lady was overheard declaring that as she had not been to Newmarket for years, she had quite 'forgotten the names of the horses', and another, that someone had told her the name of 'the yearling which was going to win the Derby at the next Newmarket meeting'. A charming duchess, who cares only to see her friends at the races, generally brings her needlework, and takes no heed of the strenuous efforts of the horses and jockeys as they race past her.[3]

Lord and Lady Randolph Churchill kept their own horses in training with Mr Sherwood, and had some notable successes.

The shining star of our stable [she continues] was the Abbesse de Jouarre, for which Randolph gave £300 at the Doncaster sales, eventually selling her for £7000. I had been reading 'L'Abbesse de Jouarre', written by Renan in order, so it is said, to disprove the assertions of his friends that he could not write some imaginative work. I suggested the name as a fitting one for the beautiful black mare, which was by Trappist out of Festive.

She was a gallant little thing, with a heart bigger than her body, and her size made the public so sceptical that she invariably started at long odds. When she won the Oaks those who backed her got 20 to 1. Neither Randolph nor I witnessed her triumph. He was fishing in Norway, and I was with some friends who had a house on the Thames. On that day we happened to reach Boulter's Lock shortly after the hour of the race. Asking the lock-keeper which horse had won the big race, he replied, to my great delight and amusement, 'The Abscess on the Jaw'.[4]

Ascot was the social highlight of the flat-racing season. Here the Royal house party assembles for the drive from Windsor Castle

Racing had its murky side and attracted even more villains then than it does today. Chief among them was the money-lender Padwick, who raced under the pseudonym 'Mr Howard', and whose delight it was, according to Roger Mortimer in his definitive *History of the Derby Stakes*, 'to encompass the ruin of rich young men, whose wits were not in equal proportion to their bank-rolls'.[5]

Twenty years earlier, before the crusading Lord George Bentinck and forthright Admiral Rous declared war on crooks and defaulters, racing had been a very dirty business indeed. Roger Mortimer says unequivocally, 'Turf morals have never stood at a lower ebb than they did between 1820 and 1860. There was romance and excitement in plenty, but there was also an unwholesome air of suspicion and chicanery, and time and again the great races were marred by some calculated act of villainy.'[6]

Then, as now, there were strong links between all forms of gambling. Prize-fighters and keepers of gaming houses often owned racehorses, and mingled with the traditional owners among the aristocracy. Nor was it always among the lower orders that skulduggery originated.

As Charles Greville the diarist wrote in disgust, 'It is monstrous to see high-bred and high-born gentlemen of honoured names and families, themselves marching through the world with their heads in the air, living in the best, the greatest and most refined society, mixed up in schemes, which are neither more nor less than a system of plunder.'[7]

An account of Mr Francis Popham's experiences in the 1855 Derby demonstrated the lengths to which the criminal fraternity was prepared to go in order to nobble a good horse. Mr Popham was a country gentleman who lived at Littlecote, near Hungerford, and he named the first thoroughbred foal born to his mare Ellen Middleton after a notorious former owner of the estate, Wild Dayrell. The story goes that one dark night in the sixteenth century a midwife was summoned, blindfolded and, with the utmost secrecy, taken to a room where a woman lay in labour. On her way, the midwife counted the stairs; and when in the room, contrived to cut a snippet from the bed-hangings. After a long and difficult labour, the baby was delivered; but, as the midwife attended to the dying mother, the child was snatched from her by Wild William Dayrell, and flung on the fire which was burning in an antechamber.

On the midwife's evidence, backed up by the snippet of curtain material, Wild Dayrell was tried and found guilty of murdering the child born of his incestuous relationship with his sister. He escaped the gallows, it is said, by bribing Judge Popham with a gift of the Littlecote Estate, which had remained in the Popham family ever since. Although he did not hang, Wild Dayrell came to a bad end, dying after a fall from his horse, which shied at the ghost of the burning baby and – so legend runs – he has haunted Littlecote ever after.

Though this unsavoury blackguard could in some sense be regarded as the founder of the Popham family's fortune, his was not, perhaps, the happiest choice of name for Mr Francis Popham's Derby hope 300 years later.

Roger Mortimer tells the story of Wild Dayrell's preparation:

> He was entered for the 1855 Derby and word of his speed spread so widely that he was heavily backed to win. Mr Popham, however, was alarmed to find that however much money was poured on to Wild Dayrell, his price never shortened, and the bookmakers displayed an ominous desire to lay him at generous odds. Suspicion that villainy was afoot was confirmed when Mr George Hodgman, a professional betting man, was approached by a well-known racing character of singularly doubtful reputation, who strongly advised him to lay Wild Dayrell for all his worth as the horse was 'due to be settled' before the race. Hodgman at once passed the information on to a Mr Roberts, who had been entrusted with the backing of Wild Dayrell for the stable. Immediate precautions were taken and the only person in [his trainer] Rickaby's yard who could possibly be regarded as a suspect was sacked on the spot without a word of explanation.
>
> That, however, was not the end of the business by any means. First of all the indignant Mr Popham, who had been under the illusion that racing was purely a sport, was approached by an individual who offered him £5,000 not to run Wild Dayrell at Epsom. Finally, there was an attempt to interfere with the van in which Wild Dayrell was to travel. Rumours of this plot luckily reached the stable, and as an experiment a bullock was put in the van, which was then paraded past Mr Popham. As soon as the van moved, the wheels collapsed and the van topped over on its side, breaking one of the bullock's legs in the process.[8]

The failure of their plot left the gang of nobblers in a difficult position. They were compelled to back Wild Dayrell at whatever odds were available, with the result that the horse started at even money. He won by a comfortable two lengths, netting his owner £10,000; but it was

'The Road to Ruin –
Ascot' by W. P. Frith, a
road travelled by many rich
and foolish young
noblemen with the help of
the villainous money-
lender, Mr Padwick

hardly surprising that Mr Popham declared that he never wanted to own a
Derby horse again.

One of the Turf's larger-than-life patrons in the 1860s and 1870s was
the Squire of Blankney, Henry Chaplin, a parson's son who inherited a
large estate and fortune from his uncle. He made the Prince of Wales's
acquaintance during his Oxford days, when hunting with the South
Oxfordshire Hunt, and they became lifelong friends. Though Chaplin
was a heavyweight, he went well to hounds, riding enormous horses, and
kept two packs at Blankney so that his friends might hunt six days a week.

His racing operations were on the same generous scale. He was said
to buy horses as if he were drunk, and back them as if he were mad.

In 1864 he was engaged to marry the diminutive and beautiful Lady
Florence Paget – nicknamed 'The Pocket Venus' – daughter of the
Marquess of Anglesey, but shortly before the wedding she left him
waiting outside an Oxford Street shop while she went in to buy some
gloves, and walked out by the other door on the arm of the wild young
Marquis of Hastings. They eloped, and married by special licence; and
though Chaplin was generous enough to say he bore neither of them any
ill-will, by a strange quirk of fate it was the victory of Chaplin's horse
Hermit in the 1867 Derby that finally drove Hastings into the moneylen-
ders' clutches. He died, ruined, a year later at the age of 26.

This was another drama-packed Derby, run on a bitterly cold June
day when the snow fell heavily both before and after the race. Hermit's
stamina was suspect. In a trial at Newmarket he had broken a blood
vessel, and he started at odds of 1,000 to 15. The story goes that his trainer
packed his hoofs with butter to prevent the snow balling and hindering his

action. Whatever the truth of the matter, he beat the favourite to win by a neck, increasing Chaplin's fortune by £120,000 while Hastings lost a similar sum.

It was the beginning of the end for Hastings, though he hid his feelings and was the first to step forward and pat the winner on his return to the enclosure. For a further year he struggled to retrieve his fortunes, but another heavy loss on the Middle Park Stakes obliged him to go to Padwick for a loan. He had already sold his Scottish estates to Lord Bute, and given a reversion on his home at Donington, besides disposing of all his hunters and racehorses except a single high-class filly and colt, Lady Elizabeth and The Earl.

Both were entered for the 1868 Derby, which in those days was open to 3-year-olds of both sexes. Although The Earl – had he run – would have had an outstanding chance of winning and clearing Hastings's debts, Lady Elizabeth had been raced too hard and too often as a 2-year-old. She had tired of the game and was no longer thoroughly sound, though her trainer was careful to conceal this from Hastings.

The Prince and Princess of Wales at the National Hunt steeplechases at Cottenham, 1870. Jockeys rode with long reins and stirrups and plied their whips freely

The villainous Padwick, who held bills of sale on a number of Hastings's assets, including The Earl, now demanded that the colt should be scratched from the Derby, the reason being that Padwick himself had laid so much money against him *before* Lady Elizabeth lost her form that he could not afford to risk The Earl winning.

Hastings had no choice but to obey. As Admiral Rous wrote in a furious letter to *The Times*, exposing the whole sorry business: 'you will ask, "Why did he scratch him?" "What can the poor fly demand from the spider in whose web he is enveloped?"' Thus Hastings lost his last chance to win the Derby, and in November that year he died. His brother-in-law, Lord Berkeley Paget was sitting by Hastings's bedside, as he lay very ill at Donington Hall, when he distinctly heard the sound of wheels and hoofs drive up the house. 'Who is coming, Harry?' he asked. 'If you are expecting guests at this late hour, I had better go down and receive them.' 'Don't bother, Berkeley,' replied Hastings calmly. 'It has only come for me.'[9] He died a few hours later, fulfilling the legend that when the owner of Donington is about to die, a horse and carriage drives up to the house to fetch him.

Lady Florence Paget had jilted Harry Chaplin in favour of Harry Hastings. Chaplin consoled himself for the loss of Lady Florence Paget by marrying Lady Florence Leveson-Gower, sister of the Duke of Sutherland. As the years rolled on, the Squire of Blankney's extravagant style of entertaining proved too much even for his handsome fortune, and in a

However wet or windy, Gold Cup Day at Ascot demanded the height of fashion among spectators

period of agricultural depression he was forced to sell up. His brother-in-law the Duke came to his rescue by providing him with a roof over his head, while his many friends rallied round to find him suitable employment. After some debate, it was decided to revive the long-defunct Board of Agriculture in order to elect him President. He had a special talent for making rousing speeches to farm labourers, and the post left him plenty of time for huge gourmet meals, which were his other consuming passion.

House parties for Newmarket and Epsom races were given only by the racing cognoscenti. Ascot had a wider appeal, and even 100 years ago it attracted a large and fashionable crowd. Daisy Warwick might pour scorn on those 'stilted, expensive, extensive and over-elaborate garden parties that made up Ascot, and lasted for four days on end',[10] but for most members of Society, Ascot was the high point of the racing calendar. The pretty pageantry of the Royal landaus' state drive from Windsor Castle, complete with postilions in gold-laced liveries and outriders in scarlet coats, always delighted the crowd, though from the point of view of the mounted equerries who jogged beside the carriages it was a tedious six-mile ride.

Fritz Ponsonby vividly remembered the occasion when, one cold, rainy afternoon, King Edward VII kept the carriages and horses waiting over an hour before deciding to drive back to the castle. When the procession did at last move off, Ponsonby's bored and restive mare put her head between her knees and began to buck. The more the crowd waved and cheered, the higher she humped her back.

> A tall hat and frock-coat, however dignified they may look, are obviously unsuited for riding difficult horses [he recalled], but there I was with the hat at the back of my head and the tails of my frock-coat flying in the wind, nearly unseated and quite unable to control the animal who bucked away until she was level with the leading pair of horses in the carriage . . . Queen Alexandra said something which I did not catch, but Hawkins, the sergeant footman, who was seated in the rumble of the carriage, explained: ''Er Majesty says you must 'ave got a pin in your saddle, sir.'[11]

For the St Leger meeting at Doncaster in the autumn, the Prince of Wales liked to stay with his old friend Christopher Sykes – 'the great Xtopher', as he referred to him – at Brantingham Thorpe. The tall, distinguished-looking, long-suffering Sykes was a natural butt for teasing and practical jokes that sometimes descended into horseplay. Brandy was poured over his head, soapsuds substituted for whipped cream on his pudding, his hands burned by the Royal cigar as he watched obediently to see 'Smoke coming out of my eyes'. His pained yet courteous, 'As Your Royal Highness pleases', while enduring these indignities always provoked gales of laughter from the ungrateful guests who, like the fabled pelican's brood, were systematically draining his life-blood. They ate and drank him out of house and home. It was only the intervention of his plain-speaking sister-in-law, Jessica Sykes, who informed the Prince bluntly of Sykes's impending ruin, that saved him from bankruptcy: yet another casualty of lavish Edwardian hospitality.

With the great Xtopher *hors de combat*, the Prince changed his routine in 1890 and accepted the invitation of Mr Arthur Wilson, a rich ship-owner, to stay at Tranby Croft for Doncaster Races. It was a grand house party, with no expense spared, but rather surprisingly in view of the Prince's well-known fondness for baccarat, they played after dinner on a makeshift table formed by pushing three whist tables together.

It was the son of the house, young Stanley Wilson, who first noticed that Sir William Gordon-Cumming was cheating by surreptitiously increasing or decreasing his stake *after* looking at his cards. In Stanley Wilson's words: 'When Lord Edward Somerset, who sat immediately to the left of Sir William, was taking up the cards, I saw that Sir William had one £5 counter at the top of the notepaper (which lay in front of him) and he was sitting with his hands clasped over the counter.'[12]

Sir William Gordon-Cumming was an easily recognizable type: one of those brave, aggressive, cocksure men who so often make excellent soldiers but are rather a menace in ordinary life. Certainly he gave offence freely and made enemies more easily than friends. One glance at his narrow, obstinate, strong-boned face with its jutting nose and chin and air of impregnable self-satisfaction gives the game away. Here is a man who thinks he can get away with anything. In the words of a contemporary: 'If England had always been at war, or if Bill had always been in pursuit of dangerous big-game, everyone would have thought, quite rightly, that no better soldier, or finer fellow in every way, ever existed . . . But he had one serious fault: he could not play fair at cards, even when the stakes were extremely small.'[13]

This judgement makes one think that his cheating at Tranby Croft was no isolated instance and his failing was fairly well known. On this occasion, he and Lord Edward Somerset were playing together, so were entitled to see one another's cards, but it was against the rules to alter the stakes once the cards had been dealt. As young Stanley Wilson continued in evidence:

> Sir William leaned over to see what cards Lord Edward Somerset had got. I was also looking, and whilst doing so I saw something red in the palm of Sir William's hands, which I knew could be nothing else but a £5 counter. Lord Edward had a natural – a nine – and a Court card. Immediately Sir William saw this he opened his hands and let drop on to the notepaper three more £5 counters, and he was paid £20 for the coup.
>
> After this I saw him again sitting in the same position as before . . . The cards were bad, and I think our side were nothing. Sir William was sitting with his hands advanced over the table as before, and when he saw the cards were bad he withdrew his hands and let some counters which were in his palm fall back on his own pile. I could not see how many.[14]

Shocked, young Stanley Wilson nudged his neighbour Berkeley Levett, a subaltern in Sir William's regiment, the Scots Guards, and whispered, 'By God, Levett, this is too hot!' After first protesting that Wilson must be mistaken, Levett also watched Sir William's play more closely, and agreed he was cheating.

What was to be done? That night, there was scandalized discussion in several bedrooms. Before they retired to sleep, five people knew Sir William was under suspicion, and were pledged to watch every move he made the following evening.

The most urgent concern for Mrs Wilson, the hostess, was to prevent any scandal ruining her house party. She and her son took the sensible precaution of providing a proper baccarat table for the next night's play, with a white chalk line drawn round it, across which the stakes had to be placed. In theory this should have made cheating impossible, but once again Sir William Gordon-Cumming hunched forward over the table, his hands hovering across the line, surreptitiously adding to and subtracting from his stake after looking at the cards. All five of the covert observers saw further instances of cheating.

Within the house party, the story spread further. General Owen Williams, a friend of Gordon-Cumming, was consulted and it was he, together with Lord Coventry, who undertook to speak directly to the suspect.

Not surprisingly, Sir William hotly denied the accusation; but in the face of so many witnesses, he was later persuaded to put his name to a pledge drawn up by General Williams and signed by 10 people, including the Prince of Wales, vowing that he would never again play cards for money. In return, he demanded that the whole affair should be kept secret; but already the scandal was too widespread for this promise to be practicable.

To the dismay of his hostess, the Prince left Tranby Croft next day,

Lord Annaly's luncheon party at the Pytchley Hunt and Grand Military Point-to-Point Races in March 1912

never to return, and thereby fuelled the rumours that spread from mouth to mouth on Doncaster racecourse. Soon the matter was common knowledge and Sir William, in a last desperate attempt to retrieve his reputation, brought an action for slander against the five people who had accused him of cheating. He lost the case, resigned his commission, and withdrew in disgrace to his Scottish estate at Gordonstoun. His blameless wife and children suffered years of ostracism as a result, and unfair though it seems, the reputation that suffered most from the whole sordid affair was that of the Prince of Wales. Thundering editorials condemned his frivolous, extravagant way of life, and demanded that he, too, should be made to swear he would never play cards for money again – a promise which Queen Victoria eventually extracted from her unwilling son.

Doncaster was the last of the season's fashionable race-meetings. As the autumn drew on, the thoughts of the English gentry turned to the shooting of partridges and pheasants, overlapped by five solid months of hunting. It was, says Lord Ernest Hamilton, 'an almost universal pursuit. The Midvics hunted as religiously as they went to Church. Whether they liked it or not, they did it. A man who did not hunt, in one form or another, was looked at sideways. He was not quite "one of us".'[15]

A century ago, England was a hunting man's paradise. Today's beleaguered foxhunters, following nose-to-tail round muddy headlands or hammering down the hard high road, can only sigh with envy at the memory of a time when there was neither wire nor motorways, no antis or electric fencing and very little spring corn; when the stoutly fenced pastures of the shires were cleared of stock in the autumn, and railway companies were happy to transport horses from one part of the country to another in comfortable, well-designed travelling-vans hitched to passenger trains, so you and your horse could arrive together at meets which were too far from home for hacking.

It was a thrilling sport which brought life and gaiety to the winter months, besides providing a whole host of craftsmen and tradesmen such as saddlers, farriers, tailors, hatters, corn-merchants, and kennel staff with gainful employment. For the sporting guest in a country house party, it provided unsurpassed entertainment since nothing is more exciting than hunting a new country, and the ladies enjoyed it as much as the men.

An entry in Lady Frederick Cavendish's diary for 1862 conveys the authentic post-hunting euphoria.

> *Newnham Paddox, Friday, 31 January 1862* A delightful and memorable day! I went hunting!!! Ld Denbigh and his sons and 2 daughters went and when they offered to mount me, and supply me with habit, etc., and old M [her sister Meriel] encouraged me, could anyone refuse? No! so off I went on a glorious old hunter of 21, called Marmion, his action free and beautiful and his gallop like the South Wind, so easy, yet so rapid and strong. I saw the fox break away, I heard the music of the hounds, and horns and halloos, I careered alone to the sound of the scampering hoofs with the delicious soft air blowing in my face. I flew over 2 or 3 fences, too enchanted to have a moment's fright; in short I galloped for ½ an hour in all the glory of a capital run . . . really I think it was the most glorious exciting enjoyment I have ever had; and that says a good deal.[16]

Lady Randolph Churchill, who had quite undeservedly become tarred with the same brush as her cantankerous husband when he fell out with the Prince of Wales, soon discovered the delights of Irish hunting during the six years they spent abroad in social exile. High-spirited Jennie Churchill was always one to make the best of any job, however bad.

> Hunting [she wrote] became our ruling passion. Whenever I could 'beg, borrow or steal' a horse I did so. We had a few hunters of our own which we rode indiscriminately, being both of us lightweights. Some of my best days with the Meath and Kildare Hounds I owed to a little brown mare I bought from Simmons at Oxford, who negotiated the 'trappy' fences of the Kildare country, and the banks and narrow doubles of Meath as though to the manner born. Many were the 'tosses' I 'took', as the Irish papers used to describe them, but it was glorious sport, and, to my mind, even hunting in Leicestershire later on could not compare with it. With the exception of the Ward Union Staghounds and the Galway Blazers, I think we hunted with nearly every pack of hounds in Ireland.[17]

Hunting sidesaddle had its dangers, chief of which was the difficulty of dismounting in an emergency. As Jennie negotiated a heavy gate during one run, it swung back, knocking her horse into the adjoining deep ditch.

> Luckily I fell clear [she remembered], but it looked as if I must be crushed underneath him, and Randolph, coming up at that moment, thought I was

killed. A few seconds later, however, seeing me all right, in the excitement of the moment, he seized my flask and emptied it. For many days it was a standing joke against him that *I* had had the fall, and *he* the whisky![18]

Most glamorous and most fanatical of all the hunting ladies was the Empress Elizabeth of Austria, the beautiful narcissistic wife of the Emperor Franz Josef and mother of the doomed Crown Prince Rudolph. After two seasons' hunting with the Grafton in England, she rented a handsome Palladian house in County Meath for the winter of 1879.

The whole country was agog [wrote Jennie Churchill], and crowds used to flock to the meets to catch a glimpse of her. The Empress, although her reputation for physical endurance and love of riding was great in the sporting world, astonished everyone by the indefatigable life she led.
     Arriving at Summerhill, from Vienna, without a break she donned a habit in the train, got on a horse, and before going into the house went for a school over a small course which had been specially prepared by her orders. Lord Langford, the owner of Summerhill, had, with much care and at considerable expense, furnished a boudoir for her, which was hung in blue damask and decorated with pictures and china. However, before the Empress had been there twenty-four hours, disdaining such feminine frivolities, she converted it into a gymnasium, in which to exercise daily

before going out hunting. With a wonderful figure and a beautiful seat on a horse, she rode gallantly and knew no fear, but her riding was of the *haute école* order, and like most women she could seldom make a horse gallop. This was a source of perpetual worry to her hard-riding pilot, Captain Bay Middleton, whose 'Come on, Madam, come on!' was constantly heard in the field.

The Empress wore the tightest of habits, buttoned down and strapped in every direction, the safety skirt not having as yet made its appearance. She found herself in many a ditch, and whether she fell clear of the horse or not, it was impossible for her to stand up until the buttons and straps had been unfastened. Under the circumstances it was a marvel that she did not hurt herself.

It was her invariable custom to ride with a large fan, which she held opened between her face and the crowd, whether against the rays of the sun or the gaze of the people I never made out. Another curious habit of hers was to use small squares of rice-paper in the Japanese fashion instead of pocket-handkerchiefs; by these she could be traced for miles, as in a paperchase.[19]

The skin-tight habits that Lady Randolph refers to were, in fact, sewn on to the Empress, whose demanding routine on hunting mornings bears out the adage *Il faut souffrir pour être belle.* In his biography *The Sporting Empress,* John Welcome describes the task of dressing her:

If a meet were at a private house, and almost all were in those days, a room in it was by arrangement set apart for her. Early in the morning a carriage would drive up to it carrying a 'dresser', usually Frau von Feyfalik, and a footman carrying Her Majesty's carefully packed hunting clothes and other

The Prince of Wales attending a meet of foxhounds at Easton Neston, Northamptonshire, in 1887

The Empress Elizabeth of Austria hunting with the Meath Hounds in Ireland. A beautiful rider of the haute ecole, *she was sewn into her habit and invariably piloted by England's finest man to hounds, Captain 'Bay' Middleton (right)*

accoutrements which included Her Majesty's personal chamber pot, made of gold and bearing the Imperial arms. A little later, still long before the meet [the Empress] would leave . . . in a single-horse brougham with an equerry in attendance. Before she set out she would have taken a bowl of soup, a special mixture of her own consisting of game, beef and chicken boiled together, and nothing else. This would constitute her entire nourishment for the day . . .

When she arrived in the brougham at the chosen house she would be wearing walking dress. At the entrance the owners met her and escorted her to the room made ready for her. Then would come the business of dressing for the chase. With the assistance of the dresser she was sewn first into the chamois undergarment and then into her habit. She had brought no less than sixteen habits with her and others were ordered from London during her stay. When she was satisfied – and this often necessitated changes of habit and much stitching and unstitching – and not before, she made her appearance. In this respect the Empress had a truly regal disregard for the convenience of others and moving off was frequently delayed.[20]

The Empress Elizabeth undoubtedly looked a picture on a horse, but she was often tactless as well as vain, and excited almost as much jealousy as admiration in the hunting-field, particularly from her own sex. Piloted as she invariably was by 'Bay' Middleton, renowned as the best man to hounds of his generation, she could be sure of a good start and, barring a fall, would be in the first flight throughout any hunt, however fast. Ladies who took their own line without the benefit of a pilot thought the Empress's reputation exaggerated and her affectations absurd – but then foxhunters are a jealous lot and the Bitch Pack was no more charitable 100 years ago than it is today.

Any man who rode outstandingly well had a passport to social success. The presence of dashing young officers like 'Doggie' Smith, 'Chicken' Hartopp, 'Sugar' Candy or 'Bay' Middleton gave cachet to any house party and, though seldom in a position to return the lavish hospitality they received, their names are found in Visitors' Books all over the country. Other fine horsemen of the day were Hugh, Earl of Lonsdale, Master of the Woodland Pytchley, and then the Quorn; Lord Willoughby de Broke; the brothers Hugh and Roddy Owen, 'Buck' Berkeley, and yet another of the sporting Greys, Lord Grey de Wilton.

Margot Tennant, sixth daughter of a rich Scottish ironmaster, who in 1894 became the second wife of the rising politician Herbert Asquith, was another of the dashing girls who accepted hunting invitations wherever they offered. In her lively autobiography she describes the day she was lent a horse by her beau of the moment, Peter Flower, brother of Lord Battersea, and the mixture of alarm and exhilaration with which she discovered that she could not ride one side of him.

At the meet I examined my horse closely while the man was lengthening my stirrup. Havoc, as he was called, was a dark chestnut, 16.1, with a coat like the back of a violin and a spiteful little head. He had an enormous bit on and I was glad to see a leather strap under the curb-chain.

When I was mounted, Peter said, 'You're on a topper! Take him where you like, but ride your own line.' . . .

It was a good scenting-day and we did not take long to find. I stuck to Peter Flower while the Bicester hounds raced across the heavy grass towards a hairy-looking double. In spite of the ironmonger's shop in Havoc's mouth I had not the faintest control over him, so I said to Peter, 'You know, Mr Flower, *I* can't stop your horse!'

He looked at me with a charming smile and said: 'But why should you? Hounds are running!'

MARGOT: 'But I can't turn him!'

PETER: 'It doesn't matter! They are running straight. Hullo! Look out! Look out for Hydy!'

We were going great guns. I saw a man slowing up to the double so shouted at him.

'Get out of my way! Get out of my way!'

I felt certain that at the pace he was going he would take a heavy fall and I should be on the top of him. While in the act of turning round to see who it was that was shouting, his willing horse paused and I shot past him, taking away his spur in my habit skirt. I heard a volley of oaths as I jumped into the jungle . . .

I had no illusions! I was on a horse that nothing could stop! Seeing a line of willows in front of me, I shouted to Peter to come along, as I thought if the brook was ahead I could not possibly keep close to him, going at that pace. To my surprise and delight, as we approached the willows Peter passed me and the water widened out in front of us; I saw by his set face that

Breakfast on a hunting morning. It took good nerves and a strong digestion to tackle devilled kidneys, ham, and kedgeree while the horses were led on to the Meet

it was neck or nothing with him. Havoc was going well within himself, but his stable-companion was precipitate and flurried; and before I knew what had happened Peter was in the middle of the brook and I was jumping over his head.

On landing I made a large circle round the field away from hounds, trying to pull up; and when I could turn round I found myself facing the brook again, with Peter dripping on the bank nearest to me. Havoc pricked his ears, passed him like a flash and jumped the brook again; but the bank on landing was boggy and while we were floundering I got a pull at him by putting the curb-rein under my pommel and, exhausted and distressed, I jumped off. Peter burst out laughing.

'We seem to be separated for life,' he said . . . 'Hullo! What is that spur doing in your skirt?'

MARGOT: 'I took it off the man that you call 'Hydy', who was going so sticky at the double.'

PETER: 'Poor old Clarendon! I advise you to keep his spur, he'll never guess who took it; and, if I know anything about him, there will be no love lost between you even if you do return it to him!'[21]

With its thrills and spills, obstacles surmounted and dangers shared, hunting induced a camaraderie between the sexes that often took a more tender turn. At the end of an exciting hunt, many a man shared the emotions with which Surtees's Mr Sponge presented the fox's brush to the ravishing Miss Lucy Glitters.

The fair lady leaned towards him, and as he adjusted it becomingly in her hat, looking at her bewitching eyes, her lovely face, and feeling the sweet fragrance of her breath, something shot through Mr Sponge's pull-devil, pull-baker coat, his corduroy waistcoat, his Eureka shirt, Angola vest, and penetrated the very cockles of his heart. He gave her such a series of smacking kisses as startled her horse and astonished a poacher who happened to be hid in the adjoining hedge.

Sponge was never so happy in his life. He could have stood on his head, or been guilty of any sort of extravagance, short of wasting his money. Oh, he was happy! Oh, he was joyous! He was intoxicated with pleasure. As he eyed his angelic charmer, her lustrous eyes, her glowing cheeks, her pearly teeth, the bewitching fulness of her elegant *tournure*, and thought of the masterly way she rode the run – above all of the dashing style in which she charged the mill-race – he felt something quite different to anything he had experienced with any of the buxom widows or lackadaisical misses whom he could just love or not, according to circumstances . . .

'Twopence for your thoughts,' cried Lucy . . . touching him gently on the back with her light silver-mounted riding-whip. 'Twopence for your thoughts!' repeated she, as Mr Sponge sauntered leisurely along, regardless of the bitter cold, followed by such of the hounds as chose to accompany him.

'Ah!' replied he, brightening up; 'I was just thinking what a deuced good run we'd had.'

'Indeed!' pouted the fair lady.

'No, my darling; I was thinking what a very pretty girl you are,' rejoined he, sidling his horse up and encircling her neat waist with his arm.

A sweet smile dimpled her plump cheeks, and chased the recollection of his former answer away.[22]

Decidedly, as Lord Ernest Hamilton remarked, 'Hunting was always a useful ally in the matrimonial campaign.'[23]

CHAPTER FIVE

Fine Feathers

t's really remarkably pleasant [wrote A. P. Herbert in 1930]
To wander about in a wood
    And kill an occasional pheasant
    Provided the motive is good.
And one of the jolliest features
Of killing superfluous game
Is the thought that you're saving the creatures
From a death of dishonour and shame.

Every bird has to die
By-and-by, by-and-by,
And they're lucky to die as they do,
For if they do not
They are probably shot
By someone who's not in *Who's Who*;
And I give you my word
Any sensitive bird –
A point for our foolish reproachers –
Prefers his career
To be stopped by a peer
And not by unmannerly poachers.[1]

Such mockery would have been considered blasphemous before the First
World War. Shooting pheasants – and partridges and grouse, for that
matter – was a serious business, almost a religion. Anyone who dared
poke fun at such sport or suggest there was anything reprehensible about
parties of over-fed, self-indulgent men using beautiful and perfectly
harmless specially reared birds as living targets would soon have felt the
weight of Establishment disapproval.

As in sexual matters, a Victorian double standard operated with
regard to shooting. The traditional *tir aux pigeons* on the French Riviera,
for instance, where diners in a restaurant shot at doves on the rocks below
them, was considered by all right-thinking Englishmen to be a nasty,
sadistic, foreign pastime that could hardly be called sport. Shooting
driven partridges, grouse, and pheasants in their thousands was quite
different: clean, manly, healthy – a sport at which every gentleman should
strive to excel.

Opposite: Lord de Grey, later the Marquess of Ripon. Renowned as England's finest shot, he was not above a little late-night practice with his loaders in his host's library

Unlike hunting, shooting makes no inconvenient demands on courage or physical fitness. So long as his eyesight is unimpaired, a man can continue to shoot driven birds until he is moribund. Driven to the stand, assisted to his peg, propped on a shooting-stick with a loader ready to hand him his guns, all he has to do is aim and fire.

As muzzle-loading guns gave way to the improved breech-loaders, and the tiring business of walking up game was exchanged for the new system of driving the birds over the guns, tall hats and cutaway coats were replaced by comfortable baggy tweeds, and shooting enjoyed a popularity it had never known before.

During the years between the death of Albert, Prince Consort, and the First World War, landowners vied with one another to produce the biggest bags of game on their estates, and the number of head killed each year went up by leaps and bounds. It culminated in one never-to-be-forgotten day at Hall Barn, in Buckinghamshire, in 1913, when Lord Burnham's guests shot 3,937 pheasants – a total which prompted King George V to remark on his homeward journey, 'Perhaps we overdid it today.' Perhaps. At Wilton, home of the Earls of Pembroke, three consecutive days' shooting in 1899 realized respectively 1,236 head, 1,142 head, and 2,276 head, and these bags were considered no more than normal.

A shoot was judged not only by the abundance of birds but on the way they flew. Connoisseurs demanded a sporting – that is, difficult – shot. One frequent visitor wrote:

> It would perhaps be an exaggeration to say that, at Wilton, there was never a low bird, but it is certainly true to say that the great majority of birds were high and, in some cases, very high indeed. That this was so was . . . mainly [due] to the exuberant genius of McKellar, the head-keeper who, in the art of bringing birds high over the guns, may truly be said to have stood alone in his profession. McKellar, in fact, could make birds fly at any height he chose.
>
> During the winter which followed on the death of the thirteenth Lord Pembroke, the Wilton shooting was let for the season to a syndicate of ambitious sportsmen determined to equal, if not to surpass, the achievements of former shooting-parties, as recorded in the game-book. Before the first drive of the first day, McKellar went up to the spokesman of the syndicate and, in his own quiet, courteous way, asked if the guns would like the birds brought to them high, medium or low.
>
> 'Oh, high, of course,' was the unanimous reply.
>
> McKellar smiled to himself and walked away. After a certain interval, the birds came as the guns had elected that they should come, with the result that, though there was a prodigious expenditure of cartridges, there was next to nothing on the ground in response. Thenceforward the members of the syndicate, after a short and gloomy conference, decided in favour of 'medium' birds for the rest of the day, and did better.[2]

East Anglia was famous for its shooting. Holkham, home of Lord Leicester, Merton Hall, where Lord Walsingham ran one of the best shoots in the country, and – of course – Sandringham where, as

Christopher Hibbert writes in his biography of King Edward VII:

> the light and sandy soil was particularly suited to the rearing of partridges and pheasants; where there were also woodcock and wild duck to be had, where hares and rabbits abounded; and where his game-keepers were as efficient and smartly dressed as any in Germany. They turned out on shooting days wearing green velveteen coats and bowler hats with gold cords, accompanied by regiments of beaters in smocks and black felt hats decorated with blue and red ribbons. Formed up in a vast semi-circle, the beaters advanced, driving the birds into the air towards the fence behind which the guns were concealed. Behind them, rows of boys waving blue and pink flags prevented the birds from flying back.[3]

As a neighbouring farmer recalled:

> On they come in ever increasing numbers, until they burst in a cloud over the fence . . . This is the exciting moment, a terrific fusillade ensues, birds dropping down in all directions, wheeling in confusion between the flags and the guns, the survivors gathering themselves together and escaping into the fields beyond. The shooters then retire to another line of fencing, making themselves comfortable with camp-stools and cigars until the birds are driven up as before, and so through the day, only leaving off for luncheon in a tent brought from Sandringham.[4]

'. . . a terrific fusillade ensues, birds dropping down in all directions, wheeling in confusion . . .' The Prince of Wales shooting at Sandringham, 1871

The vexed question of when and where to lunch exercised the minds of hosts then just as it does today. Is it better to stop for a little warming something out of a flask at noon, then continue shooting until the light begins to fade around three o'clock; or to stop for a full-scale, slap-up, sit-down meal at one, and then desperately try to squeeze three drives into what is left of the daylight after getting your guests on the move once more? Both systems have their merits and their disadvantages. A long luncheon-break is inclined to find beaters chilled and mutinous, their faces sour when the guns emerge, rosy with port and sloe-gin; while a mere bite at noon makes it hardly worth the ladies' while to join the party, and luncheon postponed until three plays havoc with the time-schedules of tea and dinner, besides leaving the women to their own devices for most of the day.

Then, as now, the problem was solved in different ways on different estates, according to the relative importance placed by the host upon sport and sustenance. The Prince of Wales loved his food and had a full-scale meal at Sandringham, carried to wherever the guns happened to be, and ladies were required to attend. At Holkham, on the other hand, Lord Leicester offered his guns a spartan snack of beer and sandwich – in the singular.

At Eaton Hall, the Duke of Westminster's amazing pinnacled Gothic pile in Cheshire, there was often a degree of uncertainty about the sporting arrangements. The Duke was a man of

The day's bag at Sandringham laid out beside the luncheon tent, 1904

quiet, attractive manner in which dignity was tempered by an ever-present but submerged sense of humour. He had a number of quaint idiosyncrasies . . . gave away more in charity than any other man in England but, at the same time, kept the eye of frugal scrutiny on the issue of such homely commodities as candles, soap, and sugar for, as he himself would put it, he

liked giving, but particularly disliked being 'done', and he was fully alive to the melancholy fact that dukes with large incomes and half-closed eyes are, as a rule, most whole-heartedly and systematically done.[5]

The Duke's invitations never included the magic formula 'Come for some hunting', or 'a few days' shooting'. Nor were the sporting prospects for the visit discussed either at dinner on the night of arrival or breakfast the following morning. A first-time guest who had arrived hopefully equipped with his guns and all the paraphernalia required to cut a respectable figure in the hunting field, might find himself hanging about disconsolately in the hall next morning, wondering why he had come.

Lord Ernest Hamilton was in this situation when the Duke

strolled up to me and said: 'Brought a gun?' I replied brightly that I had. As a matter of fact I had brought two.

'Care to come out and see if we can pick up a pheasant or two?' he continued.

I said that I was even prepared to do that.

'Then we will start from the front door in a quarter of an hour,' he said, and walked away.

I had visions of myself and the Duke poking about in the hedgerows with a spaniel and coming proudly home with a couple of cock-pheasants in our hands. But what actually happened was very wide of this. At the appointed hour I found a large brake waiting at the door in which the Duke and five other guns besides myself took their seats, and off we set at a very fast trot. After a short drive the brake pulled up some two hundred yards distant from a fair-sized wood out of which pheasants were flying in considerable numbers. Keepers were in attendance to guide us to our allotted posts, which were all marked and numbered and stamped, so to speak, with our names.

The organisation was perfect. The moment I had disclosed my name, the keeper attached to me told me that I was No. 3 and pointed to a spot some two hundred yards distant which was marked by a cleft stick bearing a card and over which an uninterrupted stream of pheasant were making their hurried and, so far, uneventful exit. I snatched up a gun and did that two hundred yards in fairly good time . . .

We went home to luncheon having shot a thousand pheasants in two hours, and that concluded the day's sport. Such was then the custom at Eaton. The Duke never shot after luncheon but, while he was shooting, he liked to be busy. I learned afterwards that the keepers had orders to start driving the pheasants at eleven o'clock to the minute, irrespective of whether the guns were in their places or not.[6]

Meanwhile, what of the ladies? As a spectator sport, shooting lacks charm and few of them pretended to any great enthusiasm for standing in a bitter wind amid the deafening bombardment, watching dead birds rain down from the skies. Though it was the done thing to put in an appearance at luncheon and stand with the guns for at least one drive after it, most ladies returned to the house as soon as they decently could.

That left the long empty hours between breakfast and luncheon to be filled, usually by making a great parade of catching up with correspond-

Kaiser Wilhelm II (centre row, third from right) with his upswept moustaches seems to dominate a shooting party at Windsor in November 1907. Seven years later England and Germany were at war

ence and retiring to the well-equipped writing-desk in one's bedroom to write those voluminous soul-searching screeds that so often led to trouble. Sometimes these even ended up in the hands of that most discreet of solicitors, Mr George Lewis. By the simple method of holding used blotting-paper to the looking-glass, or examining the contents of the waste-paper basket, the groom of the chambers might – if he felt so inclined – read the latest instalment in a dozen torrid love-affairs. It was not unknown for an unscrupulous hostess to make use of this rich source of information.

In V. Sackville-West's novel *The Edwardians*, Lucy, the widowed and worldly Duchess, mistress of Chevron during the minority of her son, visits her guest Lady Roehampton in the Chinese Room for rather more than a cosy chat. Their conversation centres on Romola Cheyne, mistress of a Very August Personage. 'Wasn't she here last week?' asks Lady Roehampton.

Lucy knew from her tone that some revelation was imminent, and when she saw Lady Roehampton take up the blotting-book she instantly understood. 'How monstrous!' cried Lucy, moved to real indignation; 'How often have I told the groom of the chambers to change the blotting-paper, in case something of the sort should happen? I'll sack him tomorrow. Well, what is it all about? It make's one blood run cold, doesn't it, to think of the hands one's letters might fall into? I suppose it's a letter to . . .' and here she uttered a name so august that in deference to the respect and loyalty of the printer it must remain unrevealed.

'No,' said Lady Roehampton, 'that's just the point: it isn't. Look!'

Lucy joined her at the mirror, and together they read the indiscreet words of Romola Cheyne. 'Well!' said Lucy, 'I always suspected that, and it's nice to know for certain. But what I can't understand is how a woman like Romola could leave a letter like that on the blotting-pad. Doesn't that seem to you incredible? She knows perfectly well that this house is always full of her friends,' said Lucy with unconscious irony. 'Now what are we to do with it? The recklessness of some people!'

The two friends were both highly delighted. Little incidents like this added a spice to life.

Lady Roehampton carefully tore out the treacherous sheet. 'There's no fire,' she said laughing; 'for the moment I'll lock it up in my writing-case. I daresay I'll find some means of destroying it safely tomorrow.'

Lucy laughed too, and agreed, knowing well that Lady Roehampton had no intention whatever of destroying it. She might never use it, but on the other hand it might be useful.[7]

The ladies' morning correspondence might well be more prosaic; instructions to their men of business to make more money available; gossipy epistles to married daughters or homilies to unmarried sons. My own great-grandmother Lady Trevethin, wife of the Lord Chief Justice,

King Edward VII's passion for shooting lasted to the end of his life. Sandringham, 1909

was a devoted mother and tremendous letter-writer. Her son-in-law George Barstow wrote in Tennysonian parody:

> Letters of good advice I send
> To Clive, and Geoff, and Trevor,
> At twenty sheets some mothers end,
> *But I go on for ever!*

Foreigners tended to mock this English habit.

> The amount of scribbling which goes on in a country house, and in which Englishwomen in particular indulge [wrote Jennie Churchill, who had been brought up in France], is always a source of astonishment and amusement to our Continental neighbours. I have heard them exclaim, *'Mais qu'est-ce qu'elles écrivent toute la journée?'* No foreigners, indeed, can understand the Englishwoman's busy life, full as it is of multitudinous occupations, ranging from household duties to political gatherings, and all necessitating correspondence.[8]

Idle mornings afforded opportunities for other business of a private nature between ladies. In Isabel Colegate's novel *The Shooting Party*, Lady Hartlip seizes her chance to touch her amiable hostess for a loan. Gently she leads the conversation round to the subject of money. Minnie, shrewd and obliging, takes the bait.

Ladies endure the noise and try to look interested at a pheasant shoot at Coombe Abbey, 1890s

'Bills?'

'My confounded bookmaker mainly. I've never known a man so stingy with credit. He knows he'll get it in the end.'

'I could probably let you have a little something for a few weeks if it would help.'

'My dear, you are too sweet, I couldn't possibly. I can't bear looting my friends. If only I hadn't had such a rotten Cesarevitch. I can't tell Gilbert because I promised to give it up. I could let you have it back very soon, that's the only thing, because he pays me part of my dress allowance on the first of December.

'Of course I can let you have something till then. It's so horrid having to worry about money.' Minnie reached for her cheque book, wiped her pen on the green leather pen-wiper, dipped it into the ink and held it poised.

'One? Two?'

'You're too sweet. If you could make it two.'

Minnie filled in the cheque for two hundred pounds, saying as she did so, 'What about a hand of whist? We shall get quite enough fresh air this afternoon and we've plenty of time before we need to change.'

'Divine. As long as you don't make it double or quits.'

'No, no, no,' said Minnie, ringing the bell for someone to put out the card table. 'Gambling at cards before lunch? What immorality. Certainly nothing over sixpence a point.'[9]

However ingenious a hostess might be in devising entertainment for her female guests, a party without men soon begins to seem a flat affair and 'lap-dogs', no matter how amusing, are seldom suitable material on which to build romantic or matrimonial plans. Soon after noon the ladies would be ready in their stout walking shoes, ankle-length tweed skirts and fitted tweed jackets topped with furs, broad-rimmed hats anchored under the chin by a scarf. They would climb into the brake and drive to join the guns in some woodland glade, rustic pavilion, or cottage specially converted for use during shooting lunches.

The flutter and bustle of their arrival, their eager enquiries as to how the morning's sport had gone and simulated interest in the number of head killed, would lighten the mood of the men who might, by now, have become a little over-competitive. In deference to the ladies, bad shots would put aside their gloom and stop brooding over missed birds, while good shots were given an opportunity to display becoming modesty when congratulated upon their scores. A female presence might even prevent the smouldering resentment of crusty old Lord X from flaring into an open quarrel with pushy young Sir Jasper Y, who had been shamelessly poaching his neighbour's birds all morning.

Ladies at luncheon had their uses, but when the meal was over they reverted to supernumerary status, with nothing to do but stand (preferably without coffee-housing) by their chosen gun, and coo admiration as the birds tumbled from the sky. Those eager to impress with their devotion to sport might opt for a second drive, but soon the warmth and comfort of the house would beckon, and they would return to the brakes and pony-traps, leaving the guns to their final *grande battue* in the fading light.

As darkness fell, the men would trudge back to the house, but even then the ladies could not be sure of their company. Shooting without ear-protection often gave a man a splitting headache, and there was a strong temptation to skulk away to read in peace until it was time to dress for dinner, instead of joining the ladies for cards and gossip.

In this hiatus, lap-dogs came into their own, enlivening the whist-tables with a presence which, if not sporting, was at least male. This was the moment to lay plans for the evening's entertainment. In the 1850s, after-dinner amusements were homespun, with each member of the party required to provide a 'turn'. Those who could sing sang, in sentimental or humorous vein. Those who could not recited, danced, or played the piano.

Staying in Yorkshire, Lady Frederick Cavendish records:

7 October 1858   For the evening came Mr and Mrs Duncombe and her two sisters, who made most beautiful music, singing Italian together in such harmonious unison, with soft full voices. There were also two comic songs, and to wind up, the most capital jig, performed by Lord Boyle and Cousin Bick. Oh, the fun of the former![10]

The following evening the performers repeated their success:

8 October 1858   or rather the 9th, for it must be past two. – We have all sat up to this unconscionable hour at Lord Boyle's earnest request to Cousin Ebbett, put in irresistible Irish, under the promise of something amusing at the end of the evening. So we had playing, the Miss Grahams' glorious singing, three comic songs, a round game, from whence I was 10s. richer,

and finally a jig by Lord Boyle, in a coat with one tail, tucked-up trousers, and all etcs, to make him a perfect tipsy Irish post-boy. He kept us dying with his brogue for some time: amazing fun, but perfectly gentlemanlike all the time, and looking too absurd.[11]

By degrees, such entertainments became more sophisticated as society exploited the talents of recognized star performers in its ranks. Lady Bolsover was renowned for her fine contralto voice, and the adventurous Mrs Ronalds was semi-professional. She was a beautiful Bostonian endowed with a good soprano voice, who ran away from her rich American husband to live in Paris. There she embarked on a love-affair which eventually left her stranded, penniless, in North Africa. English friends came to her rescue and she was assisted by the Duke and Duchess of Edinburgh to set up house in Sloane Street, where she often entertained a select gathering with her singing.

Lady Maud Warrender was another who would burst into song at the least provocation, though she was not universally admired. Fritz Ponsonby remembered her nearly blowing the audience from their seats at Chatsworth.

> One night we had theatricals. Lady Maud Warrender sang, but she seemed too big for the tiny stage and certainly her voice was too powerful for the room. Princess Daisy of Pless sang some songs and looked lovely. After each song she quickly changed her dress, beginning as a geisha and ending in white fur, short skirts, and red-brown boots, while snow fell on her.[12]

Other talented amateurs were Lady Henry Grosvenor, Lady Folkestone, and Lord Northampton; while if Lady Maud Lyon could be persuaded to play her violin, the evening's success was assured. In fact, her whole family loved music. Staying at Glamis Castle, Lord Ernest Hamilton remembered,

> It was at part-singing that, as a family, the Lyons chiefly excelled and chiefly delighted. At any moment they would suddenly start, just as the spirit moved them, on some madrigal or sextet – during dinner, out walking in the park, sitting round the fire in the billiard-room, or driving to the station in the family omnibus – it didn't matter where; one note was given – with a tuning-fork or otherwise – and off they started. Their voices, being all made according to one pattern as it were, blended most delightfully, and the effect was fascinating beyond belief.[13]

The Countess of Warwick, of course, took entertainment to new heights of sophistication. Sometimes, she wrote,

> Ellen Terry would come to our Barn Theatre, in the Park at Easton, and recite. On one memorable occasion she played the role of Hubert in *King John,* and on another equally unforgettable night she took part in a scene from *Romeo and Juliet.*
> One evening, after dinner in H. G. Wells's house, the Glebe, I saw Charlie Chaplin, as most of us know him. There were charades, those

inevitable charades in which all visitors, no matter how old or how distinguished, were compelled to play their part at 'The Glebe'.

On this occasion, 'The Flood' was the subject of the charade. H.G.'s eldest son G.P. was perched on the top of the bookshelves, distinguished in a long beard, to represent the Deity. Charlie Chaplin was Noah, and when he came out of the impromptu Ark his antics with his umbrella were absolutely irresistible. Those quick movements to see whether the rain was at an end and the umbrella could be laid aside – I shall never forget them! How we seemed to forget that there was anything but laughter in the world!

Charades at 'The Glebe' in those days must have been devastating to poor Catherine Wells's wardrobe. The demand for hats and clothes was only equalled by the indifferent treatment that was meted out to them. So far as the furniture was concerned, it was a customary thing for the village carpenter – a very skilled and clever carpenter too – to call on the morning after charades and take away pieces of furniture for prompt repair.[14]

Once the necessary preparations had been made for the evening's entertainment, props collected and turns rehearsed, the ladies were free to devote themselves to that major undertaking of the day: dressing for dinner.

First came the agreeable ritual of the bath. Even at luxurious Easton Lodge, bathrooms were still rare, but, says Elinor Glyn,

behind a screen in each room, tipped against the wall, was a huge, flat but deep tin tub, painted to match the colouring of the curtains and with a lovely woolly bath-mat of the same tone and a specially big bath-towel as well. Housemaids set out this bath and brought immense cans of hot water . . . so that baths, really quite adequate ones, were available for everyone. How the poor creatures carried the great cans, I don't know. Men-servants brought them to the bedroom doors, I believe, but the business of emptying the baths and carrying away the water must have been tremendous, as well as that of preparing them.[15]

In more primitive houses, hip-bathing could be a chilly business.

In the absence of the modern stew-bath, the Ladies Laura, Victoria and Georgiana were driven to perform their periodical ablutions in their bedrooms with the aid of a hip-bath, by the side of which were placed a can containing hot water, and a can containing cold water, side by side with a complete equipment of sponges, soap and flannel. The actual operation of washing, I was always given to understand, was not unduly protracted for, as everyone knows who has made the experiment, three parts of the anatomy of anyone using a hip-bath are out in the cold, cold blast and any attempt to raise the water-level to more enveloping heights results in the flooding of the room upon the slightest movement of the body.[16]

Of course, some bathrooms existed, but the hot-water system was seldom reliable and they were usually situated in some inaccessible corner of the house. In his autobiography *Silken Dalliance*, H. J. Bruce remembered that

Opposite: Lady Frederick Cavendish, born Lucy Lyttelton, was one of the large marriage-linked tribe of Glynnes, Gladstones, Lytteltons, and Talbots, and served as Maid of Honour to Queen Victoria. Portrait by Sir William Richmond

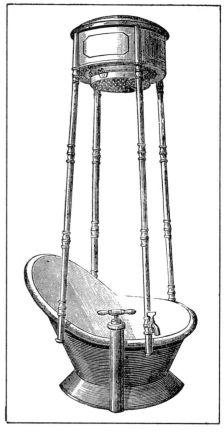

Above: In the absence of bathrooms, hot water for guests to wash in was carried to their bedrooms in brass cans by the maids

Above right: A curiosity: the problems of operating this combined shower and hip-bath can be readily imagined

When we came to Clifton there was not a single bathroom in the house . . . Later my father did import one big bath from his London house. This was an apparatus after his own heart, for he dearly loved what are now called 'gadgets'. It had at one end a kind of sentry-box fitted with about as many controls as a modern bomber. Their use was no longer indicated by any distinctive denomination. Age and steam had obliterated the indications. The result was that an amateur tampering with the controls never knew whether he was just going to turn on the bath in the ordinary way, to get an icy jet in the ribs, a tepid showerbath or a boiling eruption from the floor. It remained the only bathroom in the house during my father's lifetime, and only privileged persons were encouraged to try their luck in it. I was not among them, and anyway it was a long walk from my bedroom to the servants' wing.[17]

At Chatsworth, even at an earlier date, the 6th Duke's bathing arrangements were much more satisfactory.

The two smaller baths are convenient [he recorded with some complacency], and much frequented when I have company. The other is the most luxurious and enjoyable one that I know. The water for it is heated by retorts over the fire in a vault underneath, from which it is conveyed by a slanting pipe to the *coiled* pipes, that fill the entire space under the perforated tiles of the floor, by which the water is circulated and cooled to the temperature required. By this contrivance, steam in the bath is avoided.[18]

Men were more liable than women to appreciate such ingenuity, while children were adept at finding alternative uses for the bathroom. Lord Ernest Hamilton again:

> Every big country house boasted one or more large iron tanks encased in mahogany, evidently designed to do duty as baths and – judging from their size – designed to accommodate several people at once. At one end of these tanks was a brass dial on which were inscribed the words 'hot', 'cold', and 'waste', and a revolving handle manoeuvred an indicator into position opposite such of these inscriptions as a prospective bather might be attracted to. When the indicator pointed to 'cold', there was a free response in the shape of a flow of clear, clean water, which made its appearance through a small circle of perforated holes in the bottom of the bath. A call on the hot water supply, however, did not meet with an effusive or even warm response. A succession of sepulchral rumblings was succeeded by the appearance of a small geyser of rust-coloured water, heavily charged with dead earwigs and bluebottles. This continued for a couple of minutes or so and then entirely ceased. The only perceptible difference between the hot water and the cold lay in its colour and in the cargo of defunct life which the former bore on its bosom. Both were stone cold.[19]

Neither at Eastwell nor Baron's Court, where the Duke of Abercorn lived during most of Lord Ernest's childhood, were the bathrooms used for the purpose of bathing. But they were admirably suited to the trial trips of toy boats, and from time to time the children found them useful as aquariums.

By and large, ladies preferred the hip-bath, whatever the cost in toil to the servants. Consuelo Yznaga, a Cuban beauty who married the Double Duchess's son Lord Mandeville, used to recount in her husky, attractive drawl the story of how, when she was taking a bath in an hotel, the door opened and in walked a man.

> 'How awful! What did you do?' everyone would ask.
> 'My dear, I just covered myself with soapsuds, and sat down in the water as deep as I could. Such, however, was the good feeling of the man that he turned round, opened the door and, as he went out, said, 'I beg your pardon, SIR, for my intrusion!'[20]

Ablutions completed, the serious business of dressing could begin. In a splendid set-piece, V. Sackville-West describes the ritual she must often have watched in her mother's bedroom. Duchess Lucy, Lady Sackville's fictional counterpart, sits at her dressing-table and issues a stream of orders.

> 'Give me a wrap, Button. You can start by doing my hair. Sebastian, give me the plan of the dinner-table. On the table there. No, silly boy. Button, give it to his Grace. Now, Sebastian, read it out to me while I have my hair

done. Oh, George Roehampton takes me in, does he? *Must* he? Such a bore that man is. And Sir Adam the other side. Don't pull my hair like that, Button; really, I never knew such a clumsy woman; now you have given me a headache for the rest of the evening. Do be more careful. Well, I am not going to enjoy myself very much, I can see: Sir Adam and George Roehampton. However, it's inevitable. Or no, let me see for myself. That Miss Wace is such a fool that she may quite well have made a muddle of the whole thing. Come and hold the plan for me to see, Sebastian. Button! You pulled my hair again. How many times must I tell you to be careful? Once more, and I give you notice, I declare I will. Tilt it up, Sebastian, I can't see.'[21]

Her son watches as she rearranges the seating-plan, at the same time wiping cream from her face. Her maid, meanwhile removes the pads upon which her coiffure will be built.

'Rats', her children called them. They were unappetising objects, like last year's birds'-nests, hot and stuffy to the head, but they could not be dispensed with, since they provided the foundation on which the coiffure was to be swathed and piled, and into which the innumerable hairpins were to be stuck. It was always a source of great preoccupation with the ladies that no bit of the pad should show through the natural hair. Often they put up a tentative hand to feel, even in the midst of a most absorbing conversation; and then their faces wore the expression which is seen only on the faces of women whose fingers investigate the back of their heads . . .
    'Why are you staring like that, Sebastian? You make me quite shy.' Her hair was about her shoulders now, and Button was busy with the curling-tongs. She heated them first on the spirit lamp, and then held them carefully to her own cheek to feel if they were hot enough. 'Bless the boy, one would think he had never watched me dress before. Now about that dinner-table, yes, it's all wrong; I thought it would be. She has clean forgotten the ambassador.'[22]

Still talking, the Duchess vanishes into her dressing-room leaving her son, who has now been joined by his sister Viola and Miss Wace, the social secretary, to wrestle with the seating-plan.

For a while there was silence, broken only by irritable exclamations from within. These inner mysteries of his mother's toilet were unknown to Sebastian, but Viola knew well enough what was going on: her mother was seated, poking at her hair meanwhile with fretful but experienced fingers, while Button knelt before her, carefully drawing the silk stockings on to her feet and smoothing them nicely up the leg. Then her mother would rise, and, standing in her chemise, would allow the maid to fit the long stays of pink coutil, heavily boned, round her hips and slender figure, fastening the busk down the front, after many adjustments; then the suspenders would be clipped to the stockings; then the lacing would follow, beginning at the waist and travelling gradually up and down, until the necessary proportions had been achieved.
    The silk laces and their tags would fly out, under the maid's deft fingers, with the flick of a skilled worker mending a net. Then the pads of

pink satin would be brought, and fastened into place on the hips and under the arms, still further to accentuate the smallness of the waist. Then the drawers; and then the petticoat would be spread into a ring on the floor, and Lucy would step into it on her high-heeled shoes, allowing Button to draw it up and tie the tapes. Then Button would throw the dressing-gown round her shoulders again – Viola had followed the process well, for here the door opened, and the duchess emerged.

'Well, have you done that table? read it out. Louder. I can't hear. Yes, that's better. I'm sorry, Sebastian, you'll have to take in old Octavia Hull again. Nonsense, she's very amusing when she's not too fuddled with drugs. She'll be all right tonight because she'll be afraid of losing too much money to Sir Adam after dinner. Now, Wacey, off you go and rearrange the cards on the table, And you too, Viola. There are too many people in this room. Oh, all right, you can stop till I'm dressed if you like. Button, I'm ready for my dress. Now be careful. Don't catch the hooks in my hair. Sebastian, you must turn round while I take off my dressing-gown. Now, Button.'

Button, gathering up the lovely mass of taffeta and tulle, held the bodice open while the Duchess flung off her wrap and dived gingerly into

Tight-waisted dresses and enormous meals caused problems for the fashion-conscious

the billows of her dress. Viola watched enraptured the sudden gleam of her mother's white arms and shoulders. Button breathed a sigh of relief as she began doing up the innumerable hooks at the back. But Lucy could not stand still for a moment, and strayed all over the room with Button in pursuit, hooking.

'Haven't you finished *yet*, Button? Nonsense, it isn't tight. You'll say next I'm getting fat.'[23]

Arrayed in all her magnificence, the Duchess's mood improves. She smiles at her daughter.

'Now, Viola, my darling, I must run. Kiss me good night. Go straight to bed. Do I look nice?'

'Oh, mother, you look too lovely!'

'That's all right.' Lucy liked as much admiration as she could get. 'Now you'll run away to bed, won't you? . . . I shall want you to wait up for me, Button, of course. You go in front, Sebastian, and open the doors. Dear, dear, how late you children have made me. Sebastian, you must apologise to old Octavia at dinner, and tell her it was all your fault. My fan, Button! Good heavens, woman, what are you there for? One has to think of everything for oneself.'[24]

Most women welcomed company during the lengthy and elaborate ritual of dressing, though sometimes people got in the way. Entering his wife's room to wait for her to finish dressing, the Duke of Portland threw himself into the nearest chair – 'Both she and her maid gave a scream,' he recorded ruefully, 'and so did I, for I had sat down upon the very sharp points of her diamond tiara. Naturally the tiara was broken to bits, while the lower part of my poor person resembled the diamond mines of Golconda, so full was it of precious stones!'[25]

A generation earlier, men had dressed for dinner with almost as much care. On his first night at Jawleyford Court, in the 1850s, that dressy sporting man, Mr Sponge, was out to impress, and

put on a desperately stiff starcher, secured in front with a large gold fox-head pin with carbuncle eyes; a fine, fancy-fronted shirt, with a slight tendency to pink, adorned with mosaic gold tethered studs of sparkling diamonds (or French paste, as the case might be); a white waistcoat with fancy buttons; a blue coat with bright plain ones, and a velvet collar, black tights, with broad black-and-white Cranbourne-alley-looking stockings (socks, rather) and patent leather pumps with gilt buckles – Sponge was proud of his leg.[26]

But by the 1880s knee breeches and buckled shoes had nearly vanished from the social scene, and men's legs were for the most part anonymously shrouded in trousers which gave little indication of whether or not their owner rejoiced in a good calf. The Prince of Wales took a keen interest in clothes and was considered the final authority on all questions of what should be worn when. He was genuinely horrified when his groom-in-waiting proposed to attend a wedding wearing a black waistcoat instead of a white one, and to see the ribbon of an Order worn upside down was enough to put him off his food.

As the nineteenth century drew to a close, men's clothes lost their individuality and declined into the neutral, dateless uniformity which has been their chief characteristic ever since. Well cut, perfectly fitted, of excellent quality – but deadly dull. If Mr Sponge had appeared in the drawing-room at Chevron where Duchess Lucy's party was assembled before dinner, he would have been damned, even before he opened his mouth, as a flashy ill-bred fellow, definitely not One of Us.

Even with the men dressed more like penguins than peacocks, a grand country house party gathered in full evening dress in an English stately home was a dazzling spectacle. Under the soft radiance of spermaceti candlelit chandeliers – no harsh electric glare to accentuate the wrinkles – diamond tiaras winked and glittered and plump bare shoulders gleamed enticingly. Luxuriant moustaches of every shade from black to pure white adorned all but the youngest male lips, and Lord Lathom's snowy beard – which he used to wear divided into two plaits and tied behind his neck while shooting – would now be brushed out in its full chest-sweeping magnificence.

Exotic corsages, fresh from the hothouse, adorned the ladies' well-upholstered bosoms; in their long white gloves, enormous skirts, and tiny tight-laced waists they managed to combine stateliness with a degree of kittenish high spirits. The Prince liked his women dignified yet lively, and all strove to achieve this delicate balance.

Among the crowd whose groups constantly reformed like a kaleido-scope as they waited for their host's signal to take their dinner-partner's arm, one might pick out Lady Randolph Churchill, vivacious and sparkling, her dark hair piled in a high chignon in the French style;

In 1868, no party seemed complete without a few hands of whist

glimpse the handsome, sensitive features of Mr Arthur Balfour wearing, as usual their air of faint disdain; hear the langorous drawl of Consuelo, Duchess of Manchester, and the booming laugh of England's favourite foreign diplomat, the Marquis de Soveral (known affectionately as the 'Blue Monkey'), as some lady playfully corrected his pronunciation.

At Chatsworth, small parties would assemble in the ante-library for, as the 6th Duke explained:

> I find that most formal, weariest, hungriest moment of life less painful when the patients are squeezed together in a small compass; there is less space for their ceremonies, their shyness, their awkwardness. When more than twenty-two, we congregate in the Library, and on very great occasions in the Drawing-room – from which the march is awful.[27]

The real headache, over which even the most experienced hostesses spent many anxious hours, was the question of precedence when the procession eventually formed. Forgetting that difficulties might arise, the Countess of Warwick once invited a Russian Grand Duke at the same time as the Minister of a foreign country.

> The question suddenly confronted me – who was to take me in to dinner? As hostess, if I went in with the Grand Duke, the foreign Minister would be affronted, while if I went in with the Minister, the Grand Duke might be offended.
>
> It seems absurd among friends, and at a house party that had no political significance, that such a situation should arise, but I realised that a mistake might lead to a great deal of mischief. I made my choice with the greatest trepidation. Later I discussed the matter with a personage whose tact amounted to genius. He wrote to me:
>
> *As S. is not an Ambassador, it was right that the Grand Duke should take you in to dinner; but such complications are best avoided, and I advise you in future to scan your list of guests more critically.*[28]

It is not difficult to guess the identity of Lady Warwick's adviser. The Prince of Wales had the enviable knack of reducing questions of ceremonial to their simplest terms; when he was asked if a visiting African chief should take precedence over the German Crown Prince, he replied robustly: 'Either the brute is a King, and precedes a Prince, or else he is an ordinary black nigger.'

The order of precedence into the dining-room was decided by the hosts, and guests had to submit to it, whatever their private estimate of their own importance. When the ladies withdrew it was another matter.

> Very gracefully and genteelly had they trailed into dinner on the arms of their appointed partners – not always quite satisfied with the appointment but concealing under light smiles such rancour as they secretly nursed . . .
>
> Lady Eva may have been sent in with Lord Bloomsbury instead of Lord Bayswater, to whom she considered that her rank entitled her. That slight she had no option but to swallow smiling, but she inwardly vowed

that she would burst her stays before she let that minx Lady Marion who consciously or unconsciously had usurped her right, to get out of the dining-room before her. No, indeed! One or the other of them should leave a flounce or two on the floor before that happened. The exact moment for action had, of course, to be nicely timed. There were probably present two or three ladies of such outstanding eminence that their order of going was firmly established. These stalked out first with the air of smiling superiority which was their right. Then it was that the fun began. Lady Eva, with a straight left elbow, followed by a quick hook to the right, broke through Lady Marion's guard and sent her reeling to the sideboard . . . She passed through the door an easy winner and practically unmarked.[29]

As the American-born Duchess of Marlborough complained,

The seating arrangements caused endless trouble but were greatly facilitated when I discovered a Table of Precedence and against the name of every peer the number of his rank. I was glad to know my own number, for, after waiting at the door of the dining-room for older women to pass through, I one day received a furious push from an irate Marchioness who loudly claimed that it was just as vulgar to hang back as to leave before one's turn.[30]

When entertaining a large house party, host and hostess often sat opposite one another across a long table, rather than take the ends as we do today. The table setting was a work of art. Bare polished tables had not come into fashion then, and pure white damask cloths of the loveliest designs were in use.

At Chatsworth, writes the present Duchess of Devonshire in *The House*:

The table was laid with ornate pieces of silver, like silver pilgrim bottles and six silver vases adorned with eagles, filled with exquisite orchids from the greenhouses, which were nightly admired by the guests . . . On Sundays, if there was a shooting party, the table was laid with gilt decorations, and in the centre a large oval gilt container filled with fruit, sometimes cantaloupe melons and grapes grown in the greenhouses; rather like a harvest festival with so much fruit displayed.[31]

In Fanny Cradock's family saga *The Lormes of Castle Rising,* set a few years later, not one but two tables are handsomely arrayed to celebrate the heir's coming-of-age.

Above stairs, the table waited in the subdued glitter from the cherry logs burning under the huge marble mantelshelf. Behind the double doors which Le Brun had painted, and under his ceilings, a separate table was set for the service of dessert . . . the silver gilt compotes and tazzas were pyramided with Sawbridge's nectarines and pineapples, studded with little green figs and late-ripening Reine-Claudes, cascaded with grape tresses from the great vine. The Crown Derby and gold dessert knives and forks flanked the Stuart finger bowls on each gold plate, each held a miniature lake of rain water scented with orange and rose waters supporting a tiny flotilla of yellow rose petals.

Even in the fading light, the log flames caught the shimmer of silver gilt upon the great marble-topped table. The warmth of the room drew out the scent of the tuberoses; the firelight even shone a little in the dark green hedera and smilax. It flamed upon the polished crystal and made the formally folded napkins into motionless white birds, poised for flight.[32]

As the party settled into chairs round just such a beautifully decked table, the ladies would remove their long gloves and dispose of their fans. Each man took the chair to the left of his dinner-partner, and was supposed to converse with her throughout the first course, only turning to his neighbour on the other side when the plates were changed.

One would like to think that the splendour of the setting and the colossal expenditure of time, trouble, and money that had gone into achieving this moment would raise the tone of the conversation to match the occasion. What did the flower of England's wealth, wit, wisdom, and beauty discuss at such moments? Politics? Poetry? Philosophy? Metaphysics? The future of the greatest nation on earth?

Not a bit of it. When they were not drawing on their stock of anecdotes, we have it on the reliable testimony of Lord Ernest Hamilton that they

> talked mainly about their food, and a great deal about their health (or otherwise and, preferably, otherwise) of their friends. No one ever argued. To tell the honest truth, [they] did not argue particularly well. They were not mentally equipped for it. They didn't want to argue and they disliked people who did, so much so, in fact, that hostesses fought shy of asking any such to their luncheon-parties or dinner-parties. It was so very unpleasant when they disagreed with the Duchess or – even worse – when they put their meddlesome fingers on some weak spots in the dear Prime Minister's speech.[33]

There were times, particularly at shooting parties, when it was civil to invite country neighbours to meet the guests staying in the house. A backwoods peer with straw in his hair found it hard to keep up with the crossfire of allusion and reminiscence, in-jokes and character assassination which the Marlborough House Set found so endlessly entertaining, but there were ways of overcoming this.

In *The Shooting Party,*

> Minnie and Aline had Harry Stamp sitting between them, but they were old hands at keeping boredom at bay. They had invented an infatuation. Maisie Arlington, they said, adored him. Maisie, the most up-to-date and generally admired of young London hostesses, had stayed a night or two with her husband at Nettleby in September on their way back from Scotland and had been taken by Minnie to see the gardens at Corston.
>
> 'She told me about it,' Aline cried, clasping her hands excitedly as if she were recognising the description. 'She told me a divine man had shown her round and been too fascinating for words.'

'There you are,' said Minnie. 'That's exactly how it happened. I've never seen her so bouleversé. Maisie, of all people. It was a coup de foudre.'

'Oh I say – really? Do you mean it?' Harry Stamp turned from one to the other in high excitement. 'I must say I did think she was most charmingly – well, responsive, if you know what I mean – '

'Responsive? She was mad for you, mad for you, Harry,' said Minnie quite throatily. 'And she has all London at her feet. What a conquest for you.'

'Well, I don't know about that, I'm not sure you two ladies aren't pulling my leg.'

'How could you think that?' Aline looked hurt. 'I'm not at all that sort of person, am I, Minnie? Don't I simply hate ragging and all that sort of thing?'

'Of course, my dear. Aline would never tease. No, no, it's love at first sight. The truest love of all, I always think. Of course, you will have to follow it up. She will be in despair if you don't.'

'Follow it up? You really think so? You think I ought to follow it up? What, send flowers or something?'

'My dear man, not yet,' drawled Aline. 'Flowers come after, not before. You must call.'

'Call?'

'Of course. She's always at home in the mornings. About twelve is the best time. And if she says she's not at home you must persevere.'

'Call again the next day, sort of thing, what?'

'And the next and the next and the next,' said Aline, knowing that her friend Maisie simply detested being called on before four o'clock in the afternoon.

Minnie laid one soft, jewelled hand on his.

'I am so happy for you, Harry. Some people go all through life without it happening to them. The real thing, I mean.'

'Yes, but look here, you know, I'm a happily married man and all that.'

'So is she, so is she. But we are all of us helpless before the storm of passion. The real thing, Harry, the real thing cannot be denied.'

'It can't,' he cried, quite persuaded. 'It can't be denied. But I don't know when I'll next be in town, dash it.'

'You must make a special journey,' said Aline. 'Without any doubt at all. 38, Princes' Gardens. That's her address. What was it she said to me about small red moustaches? I wish I could remember – bruising one's lips on a fiery-blossomed cactus, was that it?'[34]

The Harry Stamps of the world were considered fair game. Fortunately rather more indulgence was extended towards young females. The transition from girlhood – where you spoke only when spoken to – and matronhood – where you were expected to hold your own in conversation with the greatest in the land – was an abrupt one, especially since girls married so young. Margot Tennant, later Asquith, who had never known a moment's shyness in her life and chattered away quite unselfconsciously to prime ministers, princes, and masters of foxhounds alike, was a favourite with such crusty old gentlemen, though her own sex considered her unbecomingly forward. It was difficult to please everyone.

Many girls were heavy going until they acquired their essential fund of dinner-table chitchat spiced with flirtation. With dismay one sociable young man found himself seated next to a pretty girl upon whom his conversational efforts fell, as he put it,

as raindrops on the Atlantic Ocean, with no appreciable effect. I went through the whole gamut of conversational topics, as laid down in the unwritten laws of dinner-table-talk: theatres, Royal Academy, weather, food, gardening and even religion but without raising even a momentary gleam of interest in the bright brown eyes of the sylph whom I had armed in to dinner. Just as I was on the point of throwing up the sponge and abandoning my official property to her right-hand neighbour, a footman approached and handed me, on a salver, a diminutive scrap of paper tightly rolled up. Very much mystified I opened it surreptitiously under cover of the table-cloth, and found scrawled on it, in pencil, the three words: 'Try the Zoo'.

I glanced up the long table with its fringe of distinguished and busily-engaged diners and, at the far, far end, caught for one second the laughing eye of Lady Meg (now Marchioness of Cambridge), the charming and understanding daughter of the house . . . I pocketed my scrap of paper and, with new hope in my heart, returned to the attack of my partner.

'Do you ever go to the Zoo?'

Instantly into the lovely but, so far, somewhat wandering eye of my neighbour there leapt a gleam of real live interest.[35]

What with keeping the conversational ball rolling as well as munching their way through eight or ten courses, jaws were busily employed during the next hour. At Blenheim Palace, writes Christopher Hibbert in *The English: A Social History,*

guests of the Duke of Marlborough sat down to dinners of alarming richness. First two soups, one hot and one cold, were served simultaneously; then two kinds of fish, again one hot and one cold. After the fish came an entrée, then a meat dish, followed by a sorbet. This was followed by game – grouse or partridge, pheasant, duck, woodcock or snipe. In the summer, when there was no game, there were quails from Egypt, fattened in Europe, and ortolans from France 'which cost a fortune'.

The Duchess of Marlborough herself takes up the tale:

An elaborate sweet followed, succeeded by a hot savoury with which was drunk the port so comforting to English palates. The dinner ended with a succulent array of peaches, plums, apricots, nectarines, raspberries, pears, and grapes, all grouped in generous pyramids among the flowers that adorned the table.

Hibbert again:

In some houses the meals served were even more elaborate than the dinners at Blenheim. Poached turbot and salmon mayonnaise would follow the hot and cold, clear and thick soups; two subsequent dishes – turkey and roast mutton, perhaps – would be accompanied by several entrées, such as cutlets, *vol-au-vent*, fillets of leveret or sautéed fillets of fowl. These would be succeeded by two roasts; as well as sorbet and game, there would be numerous *entremets* – lobster salad, maraschino jelly, truffles with champagne. Those with delicate appetites would merely pick at a selection of these dishes; but others might help themselves to all.[36]

Where did those tightly-corseted ladies put all this food? It is true that in later years most of them became extremely stout: such constant overloading over several decades made this inevitable. By the 1890s, the Prince of Wales measured 48 inches round both waist and hips, and it is a tribute to the skill of his tailor, Mr Poole, that his figure retains a kind of portly distinction, even in later portraits.

Dinners at Sandringham consisted usually of at least 12 courses. The Prince enjoyed simple food almost as much as rich fare and, says Christopher Hibbert,

would tuck into Scotch broth, Irish stew and plum pudding with as much zest as into caviare, plovers' eggs and ortolans. He was once noticed to frown upon a bowl of boiled ham and beans but this, he hastened to explain, was not because he despised such fare, but 'because it should have been bacon'. He would enjoy several dozen oysters in a matter of minutes, setting the fashion for swallowing them between mouthfuls of bread and butter; and then would go on to more solid fare, to sole poached in Chablis and garnished with oysters and prawns, or to chicken and turkey in aspic, quails and pigeon pie, grouse and partridge; and the thicker the dressing, the richer the stuffing, the creamier the sauce, the more deeply did he seem to enjoy each mouthful. He liked his pheasant stuffed with truffles and smothered in oleaginous sauce; he delighted in quails packed with *foie gras* and served with oysters, truffles, mushrooms, prawns, tomatoes and croquettes. He never grew tired of boned snipe, filled with forcemeat as

Game provided plenty of scope for culinary artistry. Boned birds of different species were frequently stuffed one inside the other like Russian dolls, with a truffle or foie gras at the centre

After the ladies withdrew,
it was time for cigars and
anecdotes as the port
circulated the table in a
clockwise direction

well as *foie gras* and covered with truffles and Madeira sauce. And, after
eating all this food for dinner, he would advise his guests to have a good
supper before going to bed, strongly recommending grilled oysters which
were his own favourite refreshment at that time of night. On his bedside
table was placed a cold chicken in case he became hungry during the
night.[37]

Over-eating continued down the social scale, and in the best circles it
was not considered polite to pick at your food, or plead a lack of appetite.
On the contrary, most diners had trained themselves to eat right through
the dinner-programme from end to end, commenting appreciatively on
certain dishes and eagerly scanning the menu to see what delights were
still to come. Not only were people openly greedy, but they talked
incessantly of what and where they had eaten. Host and hostess considered it a duty to keep a sharp eye on what their guests were eating, and
should they happen to let a dish pass untasted, would urge them to change
their minds.

In their search for novelty, some chefs went beyond the limits of
good taste or even legality. George Cornwallis-West, second and much
younger husband of Lady Randolph Churchill, remembered with amusement a dish that used to be served in July at Halton, country home of Mr

Alfred Rothschild. 'It was called *Poussins Haltonais,* and consisted of young pheasants who had had their necks wrung, quite illegal to kill, but excellent to eat.'[38] But Lord Fitzharding (nicknamed the Giant because he was so small) knew when enough was enough. 'He had a marvellous chef at Cranford, called François, who was no doubt partly responsible for Lady Fitzharding's increasing weight, for his cooking was irresistibly tempting,' recalled Elinor Glyn. 'Finally he had to leave because he used two thousand eggs in a week, and, "Damn it all, Milady," the Giant said, "That's too many!"'[39]

French chefs were much in demand. As Lady Warwick put it,

> The Victorians of my little world regarded food with an interest and an enthusiasm that have no counterpart today. They were connoisseurs, for whom the best was good enough after they had learnt to know it. I use this limitation advisedly, because good cooking, like original sin, undoubtedly came from Paris; and until the great world capital had exported some of its chefs for the benefit of English millionaires . . . dinners were often expensive rather than good.[40]

Lord Beaconsfield's friends, for instance, used to declare that only his conversation could atone for his cuisine.

Drastic measures had to be taken to counteract the effects of constant over-eating, though these were no more effective than modern fat-farms. Sitting at the head of his table, watching his mother's guests, the moody young Duke Sebastian observes them with a jaundiced eye.

> Those meals! Those endless, extravagant meals, in which they indulged all the year round. Sebastian wondered how their constitutions and their figures could stand it; then he remembered that in the summer they went as a matter of course to Homburg or Marienbad, to get rid of the accumulated excess, and then returned to start on another year's course of rich living. Really there was very little difference, essentially, between Marienbad and the vomitorium of the Romans. How strange that eating should play so important a part in social life! They were eating quails and cracking jokes. That particular dish of the Chevron chef was famous: an ortolan within the quail, a truffle within the ortolan, and pate de fois gras within the truffle; by the time all the disembowelling had taken place, there was not much left of any of the constitutents. From his place at the head of the table, Sebastian watched the jaws going up and down.[41]

Was this simply a young man's distaste for the gross appetites of his elders? Or could it have been the first uneasy stirrings of social conscience in one who had reason to know that below stairs stunted little scullery-maids aged 13 or 14 were scouring pans, up to their reddened elbows in greasy water; and yawning footmen stood in the passages, with no prospect of seeing their own attic beds until they had set fair the billiard-room in the early hours?

Or had his inner ear caught some ghostly pre-echo of the guns of August which would obliterate most of his generation?

Whatever the reason for his black mood, it was a fact that Sebastian and his contemporaries would never experience the same uncomplicated relish for life's pleasures – whether rich food, extravagant clothes, unbridled passion, or endless leisure – that true Edwardians had enjoyed. The pendulum was swinging back. Queen Victoria's generation had regarded luxury as sinful and frowned on sybarism. Her grandson's went further, questioning the social order itself.

It was only during the 50 years – a mere blink of historical time – that the Prince of Wales dominated the social scene, that pure self-indulgence was considered morally right. The very titles of Edwardian memoirs encapsulate this sense of feckless enjoyment. *What Fun it Was; Edwardian Hey-Days; Silken Dalliance; The Glitter and the Gold.*

Gorgeous as butterflies, carefree and conscienceless, they gorged and gambled, rode and revelled, flirted and fornicated as they pleased. A hundred years later, knowing how completely that privileged world would vanish, only the dourest of killjoys could grudge them their half-century of fun.

CHAPTER SIX

The Marriage Mart

When the London season drew to a close in July, it was time for mothers with daughters of marriageable age to consolidate the introductions and acquaintances their girls had collected at balls and assemblies by embarking on a round of country visits in the hope of bringing some eligible *parti* up to scratch. They would not have defined their objective so crudely, but everyone knew that was what it amounted to.

A marriage that unites great fortunes and estates must be carefully considered and planned; and it was important that the protagonists should see one another in their natural setting as well as in the artificial atmosphere of a London ballroom. If the young people found one another attractive, so much the better, but love came a poor second to suitability. It was rare, though not unknown, for an English heir to a great estate to throw himself away on a girl who brought nothing but her beauty to the family, though in France parents were harder-headed. Although Elinor Glyn's striking looks made her the toast of Paris, she later wrote ruefully, 'I did not realize until later that a girl may appear to have the greatest success in French society, and may seemingly break the hearts of all the charming and eligible young men, but she will never receive a serious offer of marriage unless she has a substantial dowry.'[1]

In her case, the lack of a dowry was an insurmountable obstacle in France; fortunately Englishmen were less cold-bloodedly mercenary.

> There are still old people in Devonshire [she recalled] who can remember a wildly exciting incident after the Walrond Coming-of-Age at Bradfield, when four responsible Englishmen (perhaps not quite sober at that hour of the November morning) jumped into the lake at Hillerston where we were all staying, in their full evening clothes, after quarrelling over me, and then came back to the house and had baths in our host's best champagne![2]

In the same spirit, the Duke of Portland remembered that at a ball given at Bestwood, near Nottingham,

> During the cotillon, Lancelot Rolleston and I raced through a paper hoop for the honour of dancing with Miss Grey, and I am proud to say I won the race. I also had the privilege of giving Miss Grey a mount on one of my

hunters on the following day, when she distinguished herself by jumping a five-barred gate. I am sure the horse was delighted to carry a featherweight instead of myself. I have retained a sentimental and very charming remembrance of that ball, the day's hunting, and of the whole party.[3]

Though he might indulge in such frivolous gallantries towards beautiful Miss Nobodys, every young nobleman knew he was expected to marry within his class, and when the time came, the canny family lawyers as well as his parents would insist that he chose a girl of suitable rank and fortune. It was his duty to his family.

Sometimes the heir to a dukedom came perilously near to flouting this rule, as in the case of Lord Hartington, eldest son of the widowed Duke of Devonshire, who neglected his dynastic obligations for so long that after his death a nephew inherited Chatsworth and the title. But then Lord Hartington – 'Harty-Tarty' to his friends – had always been a law to himself, and stories about him were a minor industry.

Brilliantly clever yet afflicted with chronic sleepiness, he was considered the sanest man in politics and his judgement so sound that on the occasion when it was noticed that he had slept right through a Cabinet meeting, his colleagues woke him up, repeated the whole discussion for his benefit, and then accepted his opinions.

He was a keen racing man.

It was said that Lord Salisbury never allowed anything to interfere with the transaction of public business [noted the Duke of Portland] except what he termed 'The Duke of Devonshire's holy days' – that is, days upon which the more important races were decided. When discussing dates for Meetings of the Cabinet, he was always careful to ask, 'Are you quite sure that isn't one of Devonshire's holy days?'[4]

Lord Randolph Churchill judged him 'Slow, but sure. If an important paper, requiring an early answer, was sent to him to read, it might be pigeonholed for weeks. But when he *did* read it, he would at once discover any flaw or weakness, and his verdict generally carried the day.[5]

Though he was careless about his clothes, his large, calm, patrician face and tall figure made him attractive to women, but he was in no hurry to marry, embarking instead on a long-running affair with the Duchess of Manchester, whose busy, managing nature perfectly complemented his dreaminess. When pressed by match-making mammas, he replied, 'I would marry tomorrow, my dear Ma'am, if I could be certain that the Duchess of Manchester was unfaithful to me'; an answer that effectively dashed any false hopes.

For a time his leisurely courtship of the Duchess was interrupted by a new enthusiasm. Pretty Catherine Walters, known as 'Skittles', was a courtesan who turned every male head when she rode in Rotten Row, a picture of grace and elegance on her well-bred hack. Lord Hartington set her up in a Chelsea love-nest and filled her stables with good-looking horses. It was even rumoured that they were secretly married, but that report proved groundless two years later when Lord Hartington re-

Far left: Miss Catherine Walters, known as 'Skittles', courtesan and horsewoman par excellence

Left: Consuelo Vanderbilt who married the taciturn Duke of Marlborough but grew disenchanted with life at Blenheim Palace

appeared to take tea with the Duchess of Manchester as calmly as if he had never strayed from her side. After 'Kim' Manchester's death they eventually married, though the Duchess was by then beyond child-bearing age, and he continued to support Skittles to the end of his life. In *Edwardians in Love* Anita Leslie tells us that some months after the death of the 8th Duke of Devonshire, the widowed Double Duchess was asked by the family lawyers if her late husband's allowance to the ageing Skittles should be stopped. To her credit, she ordered them to continue it.

Certain scions of great English families found new-made American fortunes as attractive as the lively uninhibited girls who came with them. The Duke of Marlborough made lovely Consuelo Vanderbilt his Duchess, though she grew disenchanted with her silent, sardonic husband and the tedious formality of life at Blenheim Palace.

Lord Randolph Churchill followed suit when he won the heart of dark-haired Jennie Jerome, one of three beautiful sisters brought up in Paris by their millionaire father, thus adding French polish and sophistication to her easy American manners – an irresistible combination.

The Cuban beauty Consuelo Yznaga and her sister Emily arrived from their father's home in Louisiana to take London by storm. Consuelo married Lord Mandeville, while Emily's conversational powers quite won the heart of Fritz Ponsonby on the occasion when he discovered, with some dismay, that since two players were missing from the bridge table, he and Emily were condemned to one another's company in the drawing-room for more than three hours after dinner until the King's steam pinnace arrived to release them from this enforced tête-à-tête.

> There was something so cold-blooded [he complained] in asking anyone to come and talk for three and a quarter hours with no possibility of escape,

American heiress Jennie
Jerome who married Lord
Randolph Churchill, with
her sons John (left) and
Winston (right)

and I therefore said to her that as we had to sit for so long I proposed we should each choose a book and read. She cordially agreed with me and we went round the drawing-room and selected books that might interest us. We sat down in two armchairs and we never stopped talking till one. It just made all the difference having something to fall back on, but as a matter of fact we never even opened our books.[6]

Few unmarried English girls could have held a man's attention so long. The stifling chaperoned monotony of most girls' lives had effectively blighted all precocity and originality by the time they left the schoolroom, leaving them swaddled in convention and as inert as the cocooned chrysalis. Their clothes seemed designed to make any form of activity difficult. In mid-Victorian days girls customarily wore three petticoats, two linen and one flannel, under their half-blown crinolines, and below the petticoats long linen trousers reached to the ankle. Square-toed, low-heeled boots and flat hats tied by ribbons under the chin were worn for the decorous morning walk with their governess, no matter how warm the day. A long-sleeved white blouse, buttoned to the neck, topped by a fitted jacket or possibly a shawl, further impeded their movements. While their brothers ran, jumped, fished, splashed in puddles, and climbed trees, the well-bred daughters of England's landed gentry walked slowly along the gravel paths surrounding their stately homes, and longed for the proposal of marriage that would let them burst the chrysalis and spread their wings.

Boys were not marketable products, but girls were and, as such, had always to be kept nice and cool and neat and unruffled . . . They were not allowed to do anything hot or violent because such rough exercises were held to be damaging to the complexion and so to rub a little off their market value. For it is sad to have to admit that the market value of daughters was considered a long way before their present happiness. They were reared like Pekinese pups for the market. The practical effect of this market-product rearing was that both mother and daughter looked forward to marriage as a kennel-bound spaniel looks forward to a day's shooting . . .

The idea was to keep daughters very conspicuously under glass cases as exhibits for eligible young peers, or eldest sons of peers, to examine and approve and select from, in full knowledge that what they selected always had been kept under a glass case. In common justice to the system it must be admitted that the exhibits which it offered for inspection were very nice, clean, fresh, docile exhibits, without a scratch or a chip on them anywhere. It is also not to be denied that it was productive of good matrimonial results, but it achieved these results at a very heavy sacrifice, for it made maiden life cruelly colourless and the maidens themselves cruelly dull. They knew well enough, poor dears, that they were mere exhibits, and the knowledge tended to knock all spontaneity out of them, and also had a tendency to make them artificial and affected and morbidly conscious of sex.[7]

Beside these bread-and-butter misses, American girls with their easy manners, their quaint drawling speech and, of course, their immense fortunes, seemed vividly alive and attractive. For their part the girls found – to begin with, at least – a title and a stately home a fair enough exchange for their loss of freedom. Some regretted it later, but by and large they blended easily with their adopted society.

If early marriage did not always bring quite what the adolescent maiden dreamed of, at least it freed her from the relentless supervision of mother and governess; and it ensured a long breeding-span. Year in, year out, more babies would be added to the overflowing nurseries.

Lady Frederick Cavendish, unhappily childless herself, revelled in big family parties at Hagley, the Lyttelton home.

The dear old house is choked, overflowing, echoing with children [she wrote in 1875]. The meals are the fun. Breakfasts are composed of two tables, a loaf and a half or two loaves, a plate of bread and butter, three or four good-sized pats of butter, two tea-pots, a dish of meat, a dish of bacon, and a toast-rack full. They are attended by Miss Smith presiding at the top of one of the tables, dispensing drinkables, me at the bottom, dispensing meat, bacon, and butter, and cutting hunches of bread like a machine; at the top of the other table, Meriel presiding. Round the table are little Mademoiselle, Albert, Nevy, Spencer, Winny, May, Agnes, Stephy, Mary and Lena. The four little girls are at Meriel's table, the rest at ours. The noise pervading the room, as much from scolders as scolded, from bellowers as bellowed at, from children, boys, women, girls, may be imagined, mingled with clatter of crockery, pouring of tea, hewing of bread, and scrumping of jaws.[8]

Twenty years later, Sonia Keppel, daughter of Mrs George Keppel, who was the most generally liked of all King Edward VII's mistresses since she was not only beautiful but kind, intelligent, and discreet as well, remembered an Edwardian house party from a child's point of view.

> At their Christmas parties, punctiliously the Alingtons catered for their friends' children, but more in the category of extra Christmas luggage than anything else. Where extra cupboard-space was allotted to the ladies for their numerous dresses, and to the gentlemen for their guns and cartridge cases, so rooms were allotted to their children. But their hosts' responsibilities to the children stopped there. What they set out to do was to give their own contemporaries a good time. Elaborate shooting-parties took up each day, and each night Lois and I would peer through the banisters to see the glittering cavalcade go down to dinner. Moving like Paris and Diana, eagerly I would espy my own beautiful parents and, no doubt, Lois viewed her mother's majestic progress with equal pride. (Poor Lord Alington's progress was less impressive as he had hammer-toes.) But the cavalcade was as remote from us children as a stage procession, and we were allowed to watch it only by courtesy of the management. It had nothing to do with our ordinary nursery lives. Occasionally, it passed near enough to touch us but, for me, always this was an alarming experience, like suddenly being called out of the audience to help the conjurer. It was much better at a distance, where it did not notice us.[9]

The average age of guests at summer house parties tended to be rather younger than for the grand shooting parties of the winter months.

Far right: The 4th Marquis of Hastings, a reckless gambler who got into the clutches of the moneylender, Padwick, and died, ruined, at the age of 26

Right: Lady Florence Paget, 'The Pocket Venus', eloped with the Marquis of Hastings while engaged to marry Henry Chaplin

This was for the simple reason that summer sports – generally speaking – required more physical strength and agility. Cricket parties were fashionable, and when her eldest son, Guy, showed promise at the game, the Countess of Warwick began to hold cricket weeks at Easton, during which she entertained large numbers of visitors.

> We used to put up at least two teams in the house, spread a big luncheon-tent, and invite the County to see the play. Various teams of the Guards, the I Zingari, and other well-known elevens would play on the ground. One summer, to the great delight and excitement of my son, W. G. Grace accepted an invitation to come to Easton . . .
>
> He was a genial, simple man, very kind-hearted, and one of his modest traits was his generous appreciation of other players. William Gilbert Grace gave me the impression of being surprised at his own popularity. He knew, of course, that he played a good game of cricket, but I do not think he ever quite understood why he should be a national hero on that account.[10]

The Lyttelton tribe were keen cricketers and could make up a side entirely composed of family members. On one occasion when they fielded an all-Lyttelton team, their sister recorded:

> *26 August 1867* Got to old Hagley before 12. The Bromsgrove side were in, hitting very well, Papa in flannels taking immense pains, fielding (I think) at short slip. Uncle Spencer, in magenta flannels, sitting on a bench as a distant long-stop, did two balls the honour of fielding them. Uncle B running about rather vaguely. All the boys fielding capitally, (except Bob who was no great shakes); little Edward really admirable, never missing a ball, and throwing them in as neatly and quickly as possible. Papa, to his infinite delight, caught out the last wicket, and we went in with 151 to get. Alfred's batting was truly excellent; his defence being wonderful. They began sending him slow balls out of kindness, but soon found he was up to anything. Arthur made two or 3 very fine slashing hits, especially a drive which showed great strength.[11]

Even the Lyttelton girls played cricket. The diarist records with glee: 'The H. Meynells came over and I had the honour and gratification of bowling him out twice with a scientific slow shooter!'[12]

One of her uncles, a bishop, used to say that he could never walk up a church aisle without bowling an imaginary off-break and wondering if the floor would take spin.

Given the nature of the English climate, as many matches must have been played under lowering skies, watched by shivering spectators, as there are today; yet the old group photographs of cricket teams and full-skirted, flower-hatted ladies seem bathed in perpetual sunshine.

H. D. G. Leveson-Gower summed up his idea of the ideal country house cricket party thus:

> People are asked to stay in the house who are all previously acquainted with one another, thereby removing any stiffness or undue formality. I do like a hostess to act as mother to the team, and for the old sportsman who

Beards and neckties were worn for cricket, lest the sight of a manly throat should alarm the ladies

entertains us to stand as umpire. A bevy of nice girls is needed to keep us all civilized, and the merriment then is tremendous . . .

Anyhow, there is a dance one night. On the others, songs, games, practical jokes, any amount of happy, innocent nonsense, as well as perhaps a flirtation . . . The cricket itself ought to be of sufficient importance to interest everybody, but not be allowed to degenerate into an infatuation and therefore a nuisance to the fair sex . . .

As for the cricket lunches . . . champagne lunches are being horribly overdone. Men do not play good cricket on Perrier Jouet, followed by Crème de Menthe, with two big cigars topping a rich and succulent menu. No, give us some big pies, cold chicken, a fine sirloin of English beef, and a round of brawn, washed down by good ale and luscious shandygaff. That is all cricketers want.[13]

True to their generation, cricketers dressed formally. After breakfasting in country clothes, they changed into flannels in a tent erected on the cricket-ground. 'Every player had to wear flannel trousers and a flannel shirt, buttoned at the neck and finished off with a small bow tie. Round the waist there had to be either a belt or a sash. A player appearing in a shirt open at the throat would have caused widespread consternation among the ladies.'[14]

While the men were busy on the cricket-field, the lively maidens of the party had ample opportunity to devise those practical jokes dear to the Edwardian heart. They were usually extremely simple: mustard substituted for custard or soapsuds for whipped cream; holly-leaves in pillows, or the classic apple-pie bed made by removing the top sheet and doubling up the lower one in its place, so the victim trying to slide wearily into bed would find his knees doubled up to his chin, and wonder sleepily what the trouble was until he saw bright eyes peeping round the door, and heard bursts of muffled laughter. Such jokes were usually perpetrated by men on men, or girls on men. In those chivalrous days to have made a girl the butt of a practical joke would have been considered poor form, like shooting a sitting duck.

Sometimes the joke rebounded, as on the occasion described by John Welcome when Captain 'Bay' Middleton, staying in a country house party,

> decided that it was not at all the thing for a member of the party to play pool after dinner in a tail coat, all the others having changed into smoking jackets. 'If you do that again tomorrow,' he warned the owner of the coat, 'I'm blessed if I don't rip it up.'
>
> No notice was taken of the warning, for the following night the coat appeared again. As its wearer was making a stroke at the billiard table Bay, taking the coat by the tails, tore it straight up the seam. The owner did not appear in the least put out. In fact, he roared with laughter. Puzzled, Middleton enquired the reason for the mirth.
>
> 'No harm done at all,' was the reply. 'This is your coat. If you go upstairs, you'll find mine on my bed.'[15]

A less deserving victim of a joke that misfired was Frederick Ponsonby when, during Queen Victoria's visit to Ireland, he took the opportunity to pay a call on the Duke and Duchess of Connaught.

> The Duchess of Connaught, pointing to an old black chair with a high back, said to me, 'That is the most comfortable chair. Do try it.' I ought to have suspected that there was some sell as it was most unlikely that she would wish to have my opinion on a subject like this. I at once sat down, when to my horror some spring worked and two iron clamps came out and closed with a snap, holding me fast. There were roars of laughter in which I joined, although I could not move. Then the Duchess explained that all she had to do to release me was to touch a spring at the back of the chair, and she proceeded to show how easily this was done.
>
> 'Come here, Patsy,' she said. 'You know how to do it better than I do.'
>
> Princess Patsy went to help and there was much fumbling behind the back of the chair, but still I remained pinned to the seat.
>
> 'I am afraid it is broken,' said Princess Patsy, and I had visions of remaining there for days.
>
> 'Nonsense,' said the Duchess, scarlet in the face from pushing at every likely place at the back of the chair, while I sat with an idiotic smile on my face pretending to be amused. By now the laughter had quite died away and I had become an extremely tiresome incubus.
>
> 'Ring the bell for the butler,' suggested someone; but no one came, the butler having gone out with the Duke. Where were the footmen? One had gone with the carriage, and the other had been sent off with a telegram. So we had tea, and as the Duchess and Patsy felt responsible for my detention, they brought me every sort of biscuit and cake to pass the time . . .
>
> Meanwhile Princess Beatrice was itching to go, feeling that she was

outstaying her welcome, but she hardly liked to leave me still imprisoned. Someone then suggested that the gardener knew the secret and we all cheered up. Princess Patsy offered to go and find him, but minutes passed, the conversation languishing when no gardener appeared. Again I felt like the skeleton at the feast, but after another twenty minutes the gardener appeared and at once touched the right spring.

I sprang out of the chair with alacrity in case anything should go wrong again, and when taking leave of the Duchess I said that never again would I sit down on any chair in her house.[16]

Rather more successful was the joke played on the Vice-Regal party in Dublin by mischievous Jennie Churchill, when she visited Lord and Lady Londonderry during Queen Victoria's Jubilee Year. Public enthusiasm had reached such a pitch that 'God Save the Queen' was heard until the tune became an obsession.

One morning, speaking of the Jubilee craze, I pretended that I had received as an advertisement a 'Jubilee bustle', which would play 'God Save the Queen' when the wearer sat down. This, of course, created much curiosity and laughter. Having promised to put it on, I took my host into my confidence. An aide-de-camp was pressed into the service, and armed with a small musical-box was made to hide under a particular arm-chair.

While the company was at luncheon, I retired to don the so-called 'Jubilee wonder', and when they were all assembled I marched in solemnly and slowly sat down on the arm-chair where the poor aide-de-camp was hiding his cramped limbs. To the delight and astonishment of everyone, the National Anthem was heard gently tinkling forth. Every time I rose it

Romping childish games like 'Sardines' or 'Blind Man's Buff' afforded a strait-laced Victorian youth a welcome opportunity for amorous horseplay

stopped; every time I sat down it began again. I still laugh when I think of it and of the startled faces about me. [17]

Few gentlemen managed to solve the perennial problem of where to put their legs at a picnic

So accustomed did house party guests become to practical joking that anything out of the ordinary became attributed to this special brand of tomfoolery. In her *Afterthoughts* the Countess of Warwick remembered the earthquake that shook the Midlands, and her guests' reactions.

We happened to have a large house-party at Warwick. I wakened at three in the morning, in response to a violent shaking, and found the whole room behaving incredulously, while I could hear china and crockery going the way of all household goods, but even more rapidly than usual . . .

The excitement that manifested itself during breakfast was indescribable, and the thing that amused me was that everybody reacted in a different fashion.

The Prince and Princess of Pless, suddenly jolted into wakefulness by finding that the bed had become a rocking-chair, concluded at once that Lord Herbert Vane-Tempest, their fellow-guest and noted for his practical joking, was responsible. The Prince was certain that Lord Herbert had got under the bed and was deliberately shaking it.

'Come out, Bertie – I know it's you!'

There was no answer, and for a moment or so the Prince and Princess suffered in silence. Then, determined to turn out the intruder, the Prince sprang out of bed.

'Bertie, this is awfully silly and annoying of you.'

It was only when he discovered that there was no Bertie beneath the bed, and that the walls had joined in the peculiar behaviour of the floor, that he realized what was happening. [18]

*Right: William Grenfell,
Earl of Desborough, a
brilliant all-round athlete
whose feats included
swimming Niagara Pool*

*Far right: Many and
ingenious were the
stratagems designed to
avoid the chaperone's all-
seeing eye*

Well-bred and well-fed, with unlimited leisure to practise their chosen sports, young men of the privileged class often became fine athletes, though they would not have considered it sporting to specialize in one sport to the exclusion of others as modern athletes do. A gentleman was expected to ride, shoot, play cricket, golf, and tennis at least well enough to make him a welcome team-mate.

William Grenfell, later the Earl of Desborough, was an outstanding athlete with a formidable record of sporting achievement. As a schoolboy, he was a first-class cricketer, playing in the Harrow Elevens of 1873 and 1874 against Eton and in the former match taking four wickets for 27 runs. He also won the school bowling and catching prizes; and won the school mile in 4 minutes, 37 seconds, setting a record that stood for 60 years.

On going up to Oxford, he ran in the 3-mile race against Cambridge and rowed in two successive Boat Races. He was also President of the Oxford University Athletic Club and the Oxford University Boat Club, and Master of the Drag Hounds. During his Oxford vacation, he climbed in the Alps, and ascended the Matterhorn by three different routes. He won the Punting Championship of the Thames in three successive years; he won the Foils at Harrow and at Oxford, also the Epée at the Military Tournaments in 1904 and 1906. He was chosen to represent Britain in four international competitions including the Athens Olympic Games of 1906.

Other feats included stroking an Eight in a clinker-built sliding-seat boat from Dover to Calais in 1885; and sculling 105 miles on the Thames in a single day, in a treble sculling boat with two companions. Most daring of all were his swims across Niagara pool, starting as near the Falls as practicable, in 1884 and 1888.

According to his friend the Duke of Portland, Willie Desborough's brains nearly equalled his strength and activity. Certainly the Grenfell sons who were killed in the First World War had shown exceptional promise. Julian achieved lasting fame with his war poem 'Into Battle', and his brother Billy won not only the Newcastle Scholarship at Eton as an Oppidan, but also the Balliol and Craven Scholarships at Oxford.

Apart from cricket, most summer amusements of Edwardian country house parties were of the unstructured, anyone-for-tennis variety. Croquet was a good leveller of the sexes, besides affording excellent opportunities for flirtation, or 'making love', as they preferred to call it. It gave equally good chances to the determined cheat.

In his first volume of autobiography, James Lees-Milne tells of a meeting with Stanley Baldwin.

> He recalled the croquet tournaments at my grandmother's house and my mother's astounding prowess at the game. Did she still play? No, and I was quite unaware that anyone so impatient could ever have done such a thing. (The next time I saw my mother, I passed on this meed of praise. Her comment was, 'So long as skirts were worn to the ground you have no idea how successful I was. Cheating the Baldwins was as easy as falling off a log.')[19]

With their sweeping skirts in light, summery colours, striped or ruffled high-necked blouses with leg-of-mutton sleeves and a cameo brooch at the neck, neatly belted waists and high-piled hair crowned with frothy confections of tulle and silk flowers – how deliciously fresh and

Sweeping skirts provided excellent opportunities for levelling up the scores at croquet

Opposite: A summer idyll: boating party by the Palladian bridge at Wilton House

romantic the ladies looked as they drifted about the croquet-lawn, swinging their mallets with pretty frowns of concentration!

Lawn-tennis was then a very different game from the sweaty, strenuous modern version. For me, the quintessential image of a summer house party before the First World War shows a ladies' four vaguely waving their large, square-headed racquets as they flit about the court marked out on a gently sloping lawn before a handsome Georgian house. Nothing so ugly or utilitarian as netting impedes the view of the admiring group of splendidly moustached young dandies in jaunty soft hats, boaters, blazers, and astonishing pale checked trousers who lounge at their ease to watch the girls at play.

Several of the sailor-suited children have been bribed into picking up lost balls and returning them to the players; the young men are far too comfortable to move. But as the hands of their half-hunters move towards five o'clock, the procession of footmen, preceded by the butler, bringing out trays piled high with food – triangles of brown or white sandwiches plump with egg and cress, jam, cucumber, or savoury Patum Peperium; seed-cake, fruit-cake, rock-cakes, gingerbread, and freshly baked scones, luscious with strawberry jam and whipped cream – will remind them that three whole hours have passed since they rose from the luncheon table.

Then they will get up and stroll across the smooth green lawn faintly marked with the felted hoof-prints of the mowing-pony, to the shade of the cedar or spreading copper beech, where older ladies in darker hats perch on deck-chairs, and their hostess, seated behind the table, silver tea-pot poised, asks the eternal question: 'One lump, or two?'

Undeterred by hats, bustles, and tight high-necked blouses, ladies were enthusiastic tennis players

Boating was a favourite summer pastime. Whether on ornamental lake or Scottish loch, gliding under the Palladian bridge in the park at

Wilton, or tacking into a brisk headwind on Lough Derg, from the male point of view the proximity of water multiplied the chances of rendering chivalrous assistance to ladies whose hoops or bustles made stepping in and out of boats a very real hazard. Ever present was the thrilling possibility of a slip, a splash – foaming petticoats thrashing in the water, a glimpse of a well-turned ankle, a despairing cry . . . What a moment to show one's courage and devotion; to tear off one's coat and dive to the rescue!

Bathing itself was more of an ordeal than a pleasure, performed in strict seclusion in the days of Lord Ernest Hamilton's youth.

> When girls bathed, they had, of course, to discard all their surplus petticoats and things and, in exchange, swathe themselves from head to heel in an impenetrable armour of thick sackcloth and, so protected against any possible betrayal of shape, they bobbed up and down at the end of a short rope . . .
>
> No girl could swim then, nor indeed would swimming have been possible in the heavy protective armour to which they were condemned; but even had it been possible, any such exercise would have been sternly frowned upon by the matrons of the day, as being unladylike and indecorous.[20]

The 4th Lord Langford told the Duke of Portland how, on a summer's day, he bathed in the river with an old peer who had a club foot. Swimming about at the lower end of the pool, he heard frantic shouts from upstream. 'Paddy, me boy! Paddy! For goodness sake catch me corn-plasters, or I shan't be able to walk home.'[21]

By the turn of the century, the excessive modesty which demanded the segregation of the sexes had been overcome. In a letter to his friend H. T. Baker, dated 1 August 1901, Raymond Asquith describes the pleasures of bathing at Clovelly.

> It is the custom of the house to plunge *en echelon* into the Atlantic Ocean as near the centre of it as may be at precisely 5 minutes before 8 every morning. We are rowed out in purple bathing dresses by bronzed descendants of Armada heroes until there is no land in sight but the Island of Lundy and then at a given signal we leap into the blue and bottomless swell and are borne hither and thither like helpless jelly fish in the racing tide.
>
> Having sustained ourselves in the waves so long as our strength holds out, we crawl again into the boats and are ferried back to a great lugger anchored off the harbour mouth where we find our clothes elegantly disposed by careful valets; we cover our bodies; light cigarettes and are taken back to land where we find a herd of black thoroughbred Dartmoor ponies; each man and woman selects a mount and we clamber up a sheer precipice where the occasional ash gives a perilous foothold, and so over a rolling park back to the house, where we are welcomed by a smoking mass of lobsters and great dishes of honey and Devonshire cream.[22]

Despite this easing of social *mores*, bathing retained a certain aura of daring and mystery, beautifully captured in L. P. Hartley's novel *The

Go-Between. Young Leo, deeply conventional and conservative like most prep-school boys, is staying with his precociously sophisticated friend Marcus, youngest son of the Maudsley family. Anxious not to put a foot wrong in this rarefied social milieu, Leo goes with the grown-ups to the river, though he does not intend to swim himself . . .

> I had never been to a grown-up bathing party before. There was nothing surprising in that, for in those days bathing was a pastime of the few and the word denoted an intenser experience than it does now. I was curious about it and almost frightened – this idea of surrendering oneself to an alien and potentially hostile element. Though my knowledge of it was to be only vicarious I felt a tingling on my skin and a faint loosening of my bowels.

At the bathing-platform, an unwelcome surprise awaits them.

> the head and shoulders of a man rose from among the bushes. He had his back to us and did not hear us. He walked slowly up the steps on to the platform between the wheels and pulleys. He walked very slowly, in the exultation of being alone; he moved his arms about and hunched his shoulders, as if to give himself more freedom, though he was wearing nothing that could have cramped him: for a moment I thought that he was naked.
>
> He stood almost motionless for a second or two, just raising up his heels experimentally; and then he threw his hands up, stretched himself into an arc and disappeared. Until I heard the splash I hadn't realized how near the river was.
>
> The grown-ups stared at each other in dismay, and we at them. Dismay turned to indignation. 'What cheek!' said Denys. 'I thought we had the whole place to ourselves.'[23]

Still more bizarre were the preparations for bathing made by the amiable, eccentric Sir Hedworth Williams, as remembered by Sonia Keppel:

> At the foot of his garden was a ruined tower and this he had fitted up for the ladies as a sort of moated grange, equipped with coffers of strangely assorted bathing dresses, and garlands of ivy leaves, and long tresses of bright yellow gun-cotton hair. With these, we were supposed to bedeck ourselves before pursuing him across the public highway into the sea. This might not have been too embarrassing if Hedworth himself had not looked so extraordinary, in a long black tunic down to his ankles and a toga of white Turkish towelling slung from his shoulder. Why no one ever arrested us as lunatics I shall never know.[24]

The Edwardian house party in summer was a livelier affair altogether than its winter counterpart, and the farther from court circles it took place, the more informal the fun.

In Ireland, as far back as the 1860s, the Earl of Desart remembered,

> Life was very carefree and full of delights. In summer cricket and archery, which was then much in vogue . . . Socially, times were then very easy and

Opposite: The Edwardian passion for soul-searching letter-writing often led to trouble. Here a lover's note is whisked out of sight in Sir John Millais's canvas entitled 'Trust Me'

Ping-pong after dinner in 1901

pleasant in Ireland, more so I think than in England; and in my own county [Kilkenny] there were many resident squires, nearly all of them poor, but determined to make life enjoyable and sociable. There was no taint of snobbishness, and no distinction between rich and poor. At a garden-party nobody cared if you came in a donkey-cart or in a coach-and-four. Hospitality was very general and quite unpretentious, and there was an agreeable feeling that one was welcome and might do exactly as one liked as a guest.

Neighbours were constantly in and out of one another's houses, and newcomers to the country were usually given a warm welcome, especially if they were fond of sport in any form . . .

There remained a good deal of the atmosphere of a previous generation which, while it is difficult to describe, was quite different from that of an English house of the same character. I will give an example of this.

There was in the county a delightful house and place called Kilfane, where my elder brother and I were constant guests. Sir John Power, then the Master of the Kilkenny Hounds (his grandfather had been their founder), had large and frequent gatherings of young people. Sir John was a man of peculiar charm, a very typical Irishman, and the most delightful and haphazard of hosts. He had at home four sons, one daughter and an adopted daughter; and when he collected parties of young men, all united in enjoying themselves, it became what I can only describe as an enchanting pandemonium.

When we men arrived to stay, probably in the evening, we were taken to a particular part of the house where all the bachelors' rooms were, with our luggage, and met by a quaint old servant who was like nothing you would ever find in England. His manner of reception was to open all the doors of all the rooms in the bachelors' passage and say, 'Take your choice'. He flung all the luggage into one room, and we all seized what belonged to us and each tried to get possession of the best room.

Then came dinner-time. After we had sat for some time waiting for dinner to be announced, Sir John would come in with a glass in his eye,

Chivalry lives at Lathom House, Lancashire, home of Queen Victoria's stately Lord Chamberlain, who used to tie his plaited beard behind his neck while shooting

walk round the room and say to his wife, 'Lady Power, me dear, have you seen the key of the cellar any where?' The party then searched behind the cushions of the sofas, and under the sofas, and about the room generally. After this game of hunt-the-slipper had been played for a considerable time, the key was discovered in Sir John's pocket, and he disappeared to the cellar.

After an interval we went in to dinner, Sir John at one end of the table and Lady Power at the other. Sir John then said to his wife, all down the table, 'Me dear, I'm sorry to say the cook's not very well.'

This was not encouraging, but things proceeded in a casual way, the truth being that the cook, whenever there was a party in the house, immediately got drunk. The dinner was rather a matter of accident than the pursuance of any regular order. After dancing and the usual sort of thing in the drawing-room, the young men and boys collected and sang and bear-fought till about three o'clock in the morning. How any of our elders slept I don't know, but what I have set down was the ordinary routine of the house when a party was in progress.[25]

However uproarious the fun on other days of the week, the Edwardians still took Sunday seriously. Not with the maniacal fervour of the early Victorians: but even if attendance at church was now more a matter of form than real religious conviction, Sunday was still a day apart.

Church services were a good way to fill a couple of the 24 hours of the weekly moratorium on killing creatures great and small. Foreigners were surprised by the country-wide blanket of inertia that constituted the English day of rest. 'The strict observance of Sunday,' wrote Lady

Randolph Churchill, 'filled me with awe and amazement. I had lived most of my life in Paris, where everything gay and bright was reserved for that day, and could not understand the voluntary, nay, deliberate, gloom and depression in which everyone indulged.'[26]

This passage from *The Conventionalists* by R. H. Benson conveys the languor of a Sunday morning in the country at that date.

> It had been a Sunday precisely like all other Sundays. The males had come down in a long-drawn procession to find the females at breakfast, and a Sunday air had pervaded all things, generated no doubt chiefly by the substitution of trousers for knickerbockers, and the drowsy memory of church bells heard an hour and a half previously. There had followed an hour later another long-drawn procession, through the gardens and down the park, to the church half a mile away – a procession whose head, consisting of Mr Banister, Mary, and Sybil, had appeared in the church three minutes before service began, and whose tail, brought up by Harold himself, had finally caused a reverent turning of heads towards the end of the *Venite*.[27]

The question of how much to put in the collection plate was always a delicate one for guests; but for young Leo, in *The Go-Between*, help came from an unexpected quarter.

> Somewhere on the sunny side of the house . . . the party for church was assembling: a new atmosphere prevailed; voice and movements were restrained, everyone was wearing a decorous air . . . Composing my features into pious lines I strolled about among the gathering guests, but no one paid me much attention, until Mrs Maudsley drew me aside and said, 'Would you like to give that to the collection?' and she slipped a shilling into my hand. I suddenly felt enormously enriched and the thought flashed through me: should I substitute a smaller coin?[28]

A Royal visit to Glorious Goodwood

Rather the same dilemma confronted Frederick Ponsonby when, on a visit to Biarritz in 1908, he found himself seated next to the King in the English church.

> When the clergyman announced that there would be an offertory for some purpose I searched my pockets for some money, but only succeeded in finding a louis, having brought no silver with me, unaware that there would be an offertory. I debated in my mind whether I should put this or nothing in the plate, but it seemed impossible for me to put in nothing while I was in such a conspicuous position.
>
> When the hymn at the end of the service began a beautiful man came round with a plate over which was a red velvet cloth, and went first to the King, who put in a louis: then to me, and I put a louis alongside of the King's. This looked like poker, 'I'll see that louis', but there seemed no alternative.
>
> After church the King was rather vexed and asked if I always put a louis or a sovereign in the bag. I hastily explained that I had nothing else, but he seemed to think I had spoiled his donation. He considered it only right to put in a gold piece, but when I did the same, people thought nothing of his generosity.[29]

In an equally prominent position at church, the sporting Duke of Portland faced an unexpected difficulty.

> For some time it has been my custom to read the First Lesson at the Morning Service on Sunday; and a note of the chapter is sent to me the evening before, written on one of the pink forms which are used here [at Welbeck Abbey] for delivering telephone messages. Many of these forms reach me during the day, and one Sunday I put the wrong paper into my pocket; for, standing at the lectern, I read with horror, *450 partridges*, our bag of the day before, instead of the appointed chapter of Scripture.[30]

For guests at Halton, the opulent country house belonging to Mr Alfred Rothschild, food rather than church was the chief Sunday pre-occupation. According to George Cornwallis-West who, with his wife, the former Jennie Churchill, was a frequent visitor,

> The routine of Sundays at Halton never varied. We saw little of our host in the morning as, despite the fact that they saw each other every day in the week, he was usually closeted with his elder brother, Lord Rothschild, who rode over from Tring. After a huge luncheon, those who were capable of it played tennis, and at about half-past four tiny carriages drawn by dear little ponies, each attended by a diminutive groom in blue livery, were brought round for the use of the ladies, while the rest of us walked up a steep hill to a chalet, from which there was a glorious view. There was another sumptuous tea spread out, and we were shown the pack of black-and-white King Charles's spaniels. After tea, the more sensible members went for a walk to overcome the effects of lunch and prepare for dinner; those less sensible walked down the hill and played bridge until dressing-time.[31]

CHAPTER SEVEN

Exotics, Eccentrics, and PBs

*I*nsular as English society might appear to the outsider, there were certain foreigners who had been taken so warmly to its heart that they acquired the status of mascots.

Foremost among these was the Marquis de Soveral, for some year the Portuguese Minister, who earned the affectionate nickname of the 'Blue Monkey'. With his twinkling black eyes under tremendous eyebrows, dapper though portly figure and luxuriant moustaches up-swept as symmetrically as a buffalo's horns, he was a lively, convivial companion, always good-natured and ready for fun. Wherever the best parties were held, Luiz de Soveral was sure to be there, and innumerable are the Visitors' Books in which his dashing signature careers across the page. He had no sporting ambitions and was happy to entertain the ladies while husbands and lovers were tramping about the muddy woods.

'Well, Soveral, I don't think you are a very keen sportsman,' the Duke of Portland heard King Edward remark when he discovered the Blue Monkey cosily installed by the hall fire at Welbeck while the rest of the men gathered shivering to await the shooting-brake one cold and stormy morning.

'*Pas enragé, Votre Majesté; pas enragé!*' responded the diplomat with his flashing smile.[1] His English was often a direct translation from the French. When questioned about the nature of a recent illness, he startled his hostess by saying airily, 'It was nothing, dear Madame, nothing at all. Only a little gout in the bottom.'[2] It sounds better in French than in English.

Yet a profile of the Marquis de Soveral published in *Vanity Fair* in 1898 shows he was more than just a social butterfly.

MEN OF THE DAY No. 704
Senhor Luiz de Soveral, GCMG

We first hear of him as an Attaché and Secretary of Legation at Vienna; then at Berlin and Madrid. More than twelve years ago he came to London as First Secretary of the Portuguese Legation; and under the auspices of his friend the Chevalier de Souza Correa, the Brazilian Minister, he soon became a popular member of Society. Eight years ago he had the good fortune to settle with Lord Salisbury certain South African differences between England and Portugal; and a year later he was appointed on the spot – a most unusual matter – Envoy Extraordinary and Minister Plenipotentiary to the Court of St James. For two years he was Secretary of State for Foreign Affairs in his own country, during which he arranged a dispute between England and Brazil with respect to the Island of Trinidad, and was made a GCMG; and last year he was reappointed Minister to England.

His individuality is unmistakable, and as he rather jauntily saunters down Bond Street or walks in the Park it is easy to see that the troubles of life sit lightly on him. He is much liked by members of the Royal Family, and he is a grateful person in Society.

He never plays cards, but he occasionally bets a few sovereigns on a race; which he invariably loses. He is a good and a very popular fellow, who never says an ill-natured thing. He always wears white kid gloves, and generally a white flower. He adores a good dinner, yet he is so patriotic that he once nearly called out half the members of the Turf Club because they chaffed him about Portugal being an enemy of England.

He has a great admiration for the ladies.[3]

With the exception of Princess Daisy of Pless, who found Soveral altogether too much of a good thing, the ladies returned the admiration: with his flashing smile and amusing turns of phrase, the Marquis was Society's favourite foreigner. He had none of the hauteur which characterized the conduct of the Austro-Hungarian Ambassador, Count Albert Mensdorff – or Mensdorff-Pouilly-Dietrichstein, to give him his full title – who was the Prince of Wales's cousin twice over, since his grandmother was a sister of the Duchess of Kent (Queen Victoria's mother) and also of Ernest, Duke of Saxe-Coburg and Gotha (father of Prince Albert). Of this double Royal connection, *Vanity Fair* comments dryly that Count Mensdorff 'is naturally pleased about it'.

Mensdorff's pedigree gave him the entreé to English Society, like the rest of the minor German Royalties who claimed blood ties through the marriage of the Royal first cousins Albert and Victoria. When Queen Victoria's eldest daughter, known as Vicky, married the Emperor Frederick of Prussia, family links binding European Royalty became even more intricately knotted. Though the Princess of Wales's relations never received the same warm welcome in England that, for instance, the Emperor Frederick's son did, that had been an unspoken condition of her marriage to the Prince of Wales. Alexandra's breeding was suspect in Queen Victoria's eyes – her grandfather had been a very bad egg indeed – and she made it clear from the outset that her son was marrying Princess Alexandra of Denmark, not her family. Occasional visits in either direction were allowed so long as these were not prolonged, but the expression of Alexandra's strong anti-German sentiments was muffled as diplomatically as possible.

Members of the Russian Imperial family were always exciting and unpredictable guests. With mingled amusement and alarm, Sonia Keppel remembered how, soon after the Russian Revolution had dispossessed these autocrats and scattered them throughout Europe, certain women friends of her mother's

seemed to have taken a vow to find me a 'suitable' husband. Their interpretation of the term seemed to cover a widening field, Lady Lowther's selection falling on the Grand Duke Dmitri Pavlovitch of Russia.

Together with his brother-in-law Prince Yussopoff, in 1916, this glamorous young man had acquired worldwide notoriety through his share in the murder of Rasputin.

In her role of matchmaker, Lady Lowther invited them both to stay in her house party for Ascot.

The Grand Duke was hardly a 'suitable' choice for an English girl of nineteen but, as can be imagined, I was thrilled at the prospect of meeting him. He arrived late on the Wednesday evening, just before dinner, and asked for drinks to be sent up to his room while he dressed. In due course, the rest of the party assembled downstairs and at first, no comment was made on His Imperial Highness' unpunctuality. Then, after an hour's wait, the hostess herself said that dinner would be spoilt and felt that she must go up to find out what was happening.

At intervals during our wait, strange sounds had reached us from the Grand Duke's bedroom above. Apparently, it was his valet's practice always to dress him and, at first, loud laughter and a clinking of glasses had been heard; then scuffling, a few shouts, and then silence. As Lady Lowther

Above left: The Marquis de Soveral, Portuguese Minister at the Court of St James and English Society's favourite diplomat

Above: Count Mensdorff-Pouilly-Dietrichstein, Austro-Hungarian Ambassador and cousin twice over to the Prince of Wales

mounted the stairs, bangings on the door began, accompanied by louder and increasingly angry shouts. After some time, she managed to extract the information that the Grand Duke had locked his door on the inside and had broken the key in the process.

By now Sonia had begun to fear that the Grand Duke's valet must have shared the fate of Rasputin.

With mounting hunger, we listened to the kicks and flow of Slav invective. Then some bright spark said: 'Send for a carpenter, and saw a hole through the door!'

Lady Lowther had taken the house for Ascot week and was not keen to pay heavy damages. When the carpenter arrived, she instructed him to cut out one small panel only, at the bottom.

Through this finally crawled the Heir of All the Russias looking like a bear, on all fours. Hawk-eyed, I examined the valet, who did not look too

State visit by the Shah of Persia. He offered to buy Lady Londonderry, and advised the Prince of Wales to have the Duke of Sutherland executed when he became King

bad. But he gave me a shock again, next morning, when I saw him lying on the doormat outside his master's room, possibly protecting him from renewed onslaughts from the carpenter.[4]

The customs of foreign guests sometimes raised eyebrows at English house parties, though their hosts naturally strove to minimize cultural clashes. When King Chulalonkorn of Siam, attended by many members of his household, paid a visit to Welbeck in August 1897, the Duke of Portland recalled:

> We were rather astonished at the loudness with which His Majesty always spoke. In explanation of this rather tiresome habit, we were told that it is customary in Siam . . . to modulate one's voice according to one's rank: so the King roared like a foghorn. I remember that when H.M. was asked whether he would take port, sherry, claret or madeira, he disconcerted the butler exceedingly by shouting, 'PORT!' at the top of his voice.
>
> When H.M. was shown the drawing room, he lingered behind the rest of the party, in company with my wife, and I heard him say to her in the very opposite of a whisper, 'If I were only English, I should marry for LOVE!' So I thought it best to make a hurried return.[5]

Foreigners had strange fancies. What Lord Londonderry replied to the Shah of Persia's offer to buy Lady Londonderry, history does not record.

Jews were a different matter. The roots of anti-Semitism go deep in England, and the Countess of Warwick's explanation that their introduction into Society was resented because they had brains and understood finance is only part of the story. Despite the centuries during which Jews had made their home in England, they were still regarded as a race apart: grasping, untrustworthy, and too clever by half. How could all their millions be honestly made? Their religious rituals and eating habits were regarded with suspicion by God-fearing Englishmen. The sentiment 'How odd of God to choose the Jews', found an echo in most English hearts. Fear of contamination by an alien race did not originate in Nazi Germany: it has been around for a very long time in every country in which the Jews have settled. It would take more than Queen Victoria's fascination with Disraeli, or the Prince of Wales's admiration for the magnificent Rothschilds to uproot it.

Because the Prince enjoyed the company and needed the advice of such men as Sir Ernest Cassel and the Rothschild brothers, Society was obliged to open its door to them and accept their hospitality in return. It did so reluctantly, and never missed an opportunity to sneer covertly at Jewish ostentation or pretension.

Thus, in *The Shooting Party*:

> 'Is the Israelite not among us?' murmured Sir Randolph, accepting a cup of tea.
>
> He was leaning towards his daughter-in-law Ida, and spoke for her ear alone.

Minnie, some way away from him behind the silver tea-pot and spirit kettle, was particularly fond of Sir Reuben.

'Such a dear man,' she said of him. Indeed, she often addressed him so. 'My dear man,' she would say. 'My dear man, you really shouldn't,' as another costly trinket fell into her lap. He was nothing if not generous with his millions.

'Hush,' said Ida reprovingly. 'He fell into a bog and is having a mustard bath.'

'You don't say. A bog? There aren't any bogs.'

Minnie had heard him.

'He got his feet wet,' she said gently. 'Crossing a ditch. I persuaded him to let me send Hopkins along to him with a mustard bath. You know they can be so comforting.'

'Ah, well of course if a fellow will come out shooting inadequately shod.'

'He was not inadequately shod,' said Ida firmly. 'He was shod the same as everyone else. I particularly noticed.'[6]

In *The Edwardians*, the Dowager Duchess makes less effort to hide her prejudice when she tells her grandson.

'King or no King, I don't like those Jews: I saw a lot of their horrid names to-day, when I was looking through the Visitors' Book. She ought to have put the book away before I came, if she didn't want me to find out. They're no fit company for her or for you. I daresay they've been putting ideas in your head – perhaps they want you to go into business with them? A name like yours would be the making of them. Don't you listen.'[7]

But the Prince liked them, and Society had to grin and bear it. Attitudes changed slowly, but change they did. Lord Rosebery's marriage to Hannah, the plump, plain, but enormously rich only daughter of Mayer de Rothschild, owner of Mentmore Towers, occasioned much ill-natured comment. He was said to be marrying her for her money, but a letter written at the time of his betrothal shows he appreciated his bride for her sweet nature as well as her worldly goods.

> One line to say that I am really engaged and very happy in my engagement [he wrote to his friend Mrs Duncan early in 1878]. The awful deed was done at 4.25 pm on Jan. 3. May I never go through such another ordeal.
> You do not know my future wife. She is very simple, very unspoilt, very clever, very warm-hearted, and very shy. This description is for your private eye. I never knew such a beautiful character.[8]

Lord Rosebery was not the first well-bred Englishman to marry a Rothschild daughter. Hannah's cousins Annie and Constance had already married into the Hardwicke and Battersea families, undermining English prejudice which had received a considerable jolt two years earlier when, in 1876, Queen Victoria created her dear Prime Minister Benjamin Disraeli Earl of Beaconsfield.

In 1885, urged on by Gladstone, she agreed to bestow a barony on Nathaniel Mayer Rothschild, thereby provoking another spate of snide comment among English diehards.

> Jews all over the world were thrilled at what they regarded as a triumph over prejudice, a step towards racial equality. Yet when onlookers saw the portly frame of Lord Rothschild emerging from his brougham at New Court, social equality was not the first phrase that sprang to mind. 'King of the Jews' seemed more apt a description. Indeed, a story went the rounds that a Polish Jewish immigrant, who was spending the Day of Atonement at an East End synagogue, suddenly heard someone whisper: 'The Lord has come!' He prostrated himself before the Messiah: then saw the famous top hat of Lord Rothschild.[9]

Nathaniel Mayer Rothschild was the Prince of Wales's first and probably his closest Jewish friend. They had met in 1861 during the Prince's short spell at Oxford University, on the few occasions when he slipped the leash and went out with the University Drag, hunted by Charles Carrington and paid for by Nathaniel Rothschild.

One friendship led to another. Nathaniel introduced the Prince to his brothers Alfred and Leo; his father Lionel and uncles Mayer and Anthony. The family was widespread in Europe, with cousins in France and Austria. Soon the Prince was also acquainted with other rich Jews: the Beits, the Sassoons, Cassels, and Hirsches.

Compared to many of his set, the Prince of Wales was not rich and he had expensive tastes. Racehorses, cigars, presents, gambling, travel: the demands on his purse were never-ending. His wife was extravagant with her dress-bills and he had a growing family to support. In the circumstances it made sense to cultivate the acquaintance of men who knew how to make money as well as spend it. Rumours that the Rothschilds paid the Prince's debts are probably unfounded. More likely he sought their advice on matters financial and they in turn were careful to see that his investments showed a profit.

As much as their company, the Prince enjoyed the lavish hospitality of his Jewish friends. At the housewarming party given by Baron Ferdinand de Rothschild at Waddesdon Manor, near Aylesbury, the guests arrived in pouring rain, which had beaten to the ground the geraniums that filled the flowerbeds, scattering their petals and almost tearing their roots from the soil. At five the next morning, an early-waking guest went to the window to see if the storm had passed, and saw an army of gardeners silently at work, taking out the damaged plants and replacing them with fresh ones. When the house party strolled out to see the gardens after breakfast, the flowerbeds bloomed as if the storm had never touched them.

Halfway between a French château and an Oriental palace, Waddesdon Manor – the dream translated into solid Bath stone by Baron Ferdinand – is about as unlike the traditional English manor house as any building could be. Clean lines and classic symmetry were anathema to the Victorian eye. Ferdinand's architect, Gabriel-Hippolyte Destailleur, who was required to incorporate into his plans the twin towers of the Château de Maintenon, the dormer windows of Anet, the great staircase of Blois, and the chimneys of Chambord, did well to produce no monstrous hybrid eye-sore but a huge folly of faintly ridiculous charm – a monument to all that was extravagant in Victorian taste.

Halton House, near Wendover, built by Ferdinand's cousin Alfred, was less successful. 'An exaggerated nightmare of gorgeousness and senseless and ill-applied magnificence', was one verdict quoted by Virginia Cowles in her history of the Rothschild family.[10] Eustace Balfour was more specific.

> I have seldom seen anything more terribly vulgar. Outside it is a combination of a French château and a gambling house. Inside it is badly planned, gaudily decorated . . . O, but the hideousness of everything, the showiness! the sense of lavish wealth thrust up your nose! the coarse mouldings, the heavy gildings always in the wrong place, the colour of the silk hangings! Eye hath not seen nor pen can write the ghastly coarseness of the sight.[11]

Waddesdon, on the other hand, excited wonder rather than horror. The site had been chosen on a whim by Ferdinand when out hunting with the South Oxfordshire Hounds in the early 1870s. He bought the land from the Duke of Marlborough, levelled off the top of the Chiltern outcrop on which he wished to place his new home, and constructed a railway 14 miles long to bring building materials to the site. The surrounding hillside was landscaped and planted with oaks, beeches, and conifers to produce an instant park. He imported antique French furniture, carpets, and tapestries to furnish the 70-odd rooms, and dotted the

gardens with ponds, fountains, statues, and classical allegorical groups in shining white marble. Seven years after work began, Waddesdon was ready to amaze the fashionable world.

To illustrate the quality of Rothschild hospitality, Mr Asquith used to tell the following story of a visit to Waddesdon. He was woken on his first morning by a footman, followed by an underling with a trolley, and asked:

Waddesdon Manor, built by Baron Ferdinand de Rothschild on a Chiltern outcrop and surrounded by an instant park of mature trees. Architectural inspiration was derived from a variety of French chateaux, including Blois, Anet, and Maintenon

'Tea, coffee, or a peach off the wall, sir?'
'Tea, please.'
'China tea, Indian tea, or Ceylon tea, sir?'
'China, if you please.'
'Lemon, milk, or cream, sir?'
'Milk, please.'
'Jersey, Hereford, or Shorthorn, sir?'

The Prince of Wales was a frequent visitor to Waddesdon. A letter written by Lady Battersea in 1884 lists some of its delights.

The Christy Minstrels and a Hungarian Band performed alternately and gave great satisfaction, particularly the latter. But the house itself with all its wonders, pictures, objets d'art, and magnificent couches and satin cushions and palms and photos of crowned heads with autograph signatures, was a never-ending source of pleasure. Lady Jane said it was *seraphic*.[12]

Out of doors, there were more marvels.

We used to go and feed the ostriches with bread [wrote Lady Warwick]. He had aviaries, too, filled with lovely birds. Naturally he wished to adorn the hill on which the Manor stood, but he did so in such a fashion as to enable him to enjoy its full beauty during his life-time – to do this he transplanted full grown forest trees. As a frequent visitor I saw these trees take root though some were of enormous size when taken from their original home.[13]

In 1890, Waddesdon received a still rarer accolade when Queen Victoria asked Baron Ferdinand if she might pay him a visit. She was entirely captivated after her drive through the grounds in a Bath chair pulled by a pony, and wrote: 'The host was as delightful as the place was beautiful.'[14]

Naturally enough, the legendary Rothschild generosity was often exploited. Alfred, most eligible of bachelors, was an enthusiastic patron of the arts and used to pay world-famous artistes royal fees to entertain a handful of his friends. He suffered from dyspepsia and ate only the plainest food, though his guests had the best of everything.

> He used to ride every morning in the park, followed by his brougham [Lady Warwick remembered]. Park-keepers soon learnt how generous the millionaire was; they used to put stones on the road by which he would enter, then, when he came in sight, they would hasten to remove them – a courtesy which he invariably rewarded. He was shrewd enough to know just how the stones got there, but this childish device amused him, so he pretended ignorance.[15]

Unlike the Duke of Westminster, Rothschild did not resent being 'done', though he nearly suffered a seizure when Lillie Langtry, who

The Princess of Wales breakfasting at Sunningdale Park in 1889, with Princess Victoria and the Hon. Juliet Stonor. Maria, Marchioness of Ailesbury (standing), still wears her famous ringlets

had been guest of honour at one of his 'adoration dinners', responded all too literally to his ritual question, 'What shall I give you, beautiful lady?'

Unerringly her acquisitive eye alighted on a priceless diamond-and-enamel Louis XVI snuff box that was lying on a nearby table among other treasures, and she picked it up, saying casually, 'Oh, this will do'. 'He had a weak heart,' she recalled, 'and for a moment I thought I had stopped it. When he got his breath he promised me something much prettier, and out came one of the well-known gift-boxes.'[16]

Another of the Prince's Jewish friends, the financier Sir Ernest Cassel, bore such a marked resemblance to him that the scurrilous old story that Albert Prince Consort's father had been his mother's Jewish footman was reactivated. Sir Ernest played up the likeness by adopting the same style of dress and, when the Prince injured his shoulder, Sir Ernest also began to shake hands with his elbow held close to the body: just as some ladies devotedly copied the Princess of Wales's stiff-kneed limp. It was all part of keeping in the swim.

Others preferred to indulge their eccentricity. Caroline, Duchess of Montrose, was a striking figure at the races, wearing a Homburg hat above features lavishly adorned with paint, and hair of a brilliant metallic gold that did not even pretend to be real. She owned a number of good horses and raced under the *nom de course* of 'Mr Manton'. At the age of 70 she surprised Society by marrying Mr Henry Milner, then aged 24.

Lady Charles Beresford was equally heavy-handed with cosmetics, and Maria, Marchioness of Ailesbury, wore long corkscrew ringlets on either side of her lined face up to an advanced age. Lady Florence Dixie was known as a rough diamond and hard as nails. She used to alarm her friends by strolling in the park with a none-too-tame jaguar in attendance; while the Dowager Duchess of Abercorn preferred to spend the evening of her days at Coates House, on the Petworth estate, fishing in an ornamental pond for perch, which her footman then carefully unhooked and returned to the water.

In an earlier generation Lord John Scott, brother of the Duke of Buccleuch, was a notable eccentric who was so fond of a scrap that on his way home from hunting he would offer a sovereign to any young man who agreed to a bout of fisticuffs. It must have been a curious spectacle: the nobleman and the ploughboy slogging it out bare-knuckled in the gathering dusk, while Lord John's second horseman held the reins and the coats, and kept the ring by the roadside.

Some hosts even allowed their private whims to override simple courtesy towards their guests. The crusty old Earl of Dudley had an irrational dislike of black or dark colours, and refused to let any member of his family wear them. Unaware of this foible, Lady Randolph Churchill went to a ball at Dudley House

> in what I thought a particularly attractive costume – dark blue and crimson roses. To my discomfiture my host came up to me and nearly reduced me to tears by asking why I came to his ball in such a 'monstrous dress'.
>
> At Witley Court in Worcestershire [she adds], this old tyrant insisted

Far left: The Jewish banker, Sir Ernest Cassel, accentuated his resemblance to the Prince of Wales by adopting the same mannerisms

Left: The Maharajah Duleep Singh, deposed ruler of the Punjab, became a Christian and Society favourite until his shabby treatment by the India Office caused an unbridgeable rift

on his shooting-party guests wearing shoes and morning coats for breakfast instead of the hobnailed boots and weatherbeaten tweeds they would have preferred.[17]

Even after the First World War, when hosts had in general become more accommodating in the matter of dress, Lord Ashcombe insisted that female guests wore gloves in the house all day and forbade anyone to smoke in the drawing-room or play cards on Sunday; while Lady Ashcombe surprised young Sonia Keppel by referring to her throughout tea in the third person singular. 'Will the young lady have a scone and some home-made strawberry jam?' Luckily, a friend had warned Sonia about the gloves.

> Just before dinner, a housemaid brought me a pair of elbow-length, white kid gloves. 'His Lordship's compliments, miss, and will you please wear them.' My progress downstairs coincided with the other female members of the party, all similarly buttoning on new white kid gloves. Thus arrayed, we were all formally armed-in to dinner.[18]

Another Society favourite, at once exotic and eccentric, was the Maharajah Duleep Singh, who rented the Elveden estate near Thetford from Lord Iveagh. Son of the great Ranjit Singh, the one-eyed 'Lion of the Punjab', Duleep Singh had been deposed in childhood. For 30 years he lived in Suffolk, where he and his sons Albert and Victor, locally known as 'The Black Princes', were popular and convivial hosts.

In *The Big Shots*, J. G. Ruffer tells how Duleep Singh clashed with Queen Victoria on the unlikely subject of underwear.

Opposite: A Royal snowball fight during King Carlos of Portugal's visit to Chatsworth, December 1904. The Illustrated London News *notes that though the King started the fun, etiquette demanded that Dom Carlos's own person should be unassailed*

One day the Queen remonstrated with him because she had been told that he refused to wear woollen underclothing during the winter; and that in spite of his English guardian's repeated entreaties, and the presentations made to him of the dangerous English winter, he continued to refuse to do so.

'Ma'am,' he replied, 'I cannot wear flannel next to my skin. It makes me long to scratch, and you would not like to see me scratching myself in your presence.'

The Queen hurriedly dropped the subject.[19]

His gallant fellow Sikh Sir Partab Singh of Idar charmed English hosts with his beautiful manners. Even when he injured his ankle in a polo fall, he appeared in the evening at Sandringham in tight military boots, though the Prince noticed that he was in considerable pain. After dinner both he and the Princess of Wales begged Sir Partab to sit down, but nothing would induce him to do so in their presence. Clearly it was time to pull rank.

> they turned to Lord Roberts, and asked him to persuade Sir Partab to be seated. Lord Roberts did so; and at once Sir Partab put his hands palm to palm before his face, in salute, and popped down into a chair. He explained that it was impossible for him to disobey for one second the orders of the *Bahadur*.[20]

Another small band of exotics who added colour to the social scene were the women whose looks had earned them the rather misleading title of 'Professional Beauties', or 'PBs'.

These were not, as the cynical modern reader might assume, prostitutes, actresses, or fashion mannequins. On the contrary, they were respectable ladies, often of high rank. Lady Helen Vincent, Lady Randolph Churchill, and Georgina Countess of Dudley were all PBs, and the distinguishing factor which set them aside from ordinary amateur beauties was that they allowed photographic portraits of themselves to be displayed in shop windows.

Copies of these photographs were bought by admirers who could never hope to meet their idol in the flesh, rather as today's teenagers collect posters of favourite pop singers. And just as modern pop stars are divided into those who claim it is their duty to the public – that is, believe it may further their career – to make their images readily available, and others who shun publicity for fear of sating the public appetite, so some PBs revelled in being mobbed wherever they went, while others professed to find the whole business a little vulgar.

A hostess who could promise an appearance by one or more PBs knew the success of her party was assured. They were therefore inundated with invitations to every kind of dinner, ball, and house party, where little more was required of them than that they should simply *be there* and look lovely.

Most celebrated of the Professional Beauties was Lillie Langtry, whose meteoric rise from being the drably dressed wife of a nobody to the most talked-of and admired woman in London, if not England, was truly remarkable.

At this distance, the secret of Lillie Langtry's success is hard to divine.

Below left: Georgina Elizabeth, Countess of Dudley, whose looks were so much admired that old ladies climbed on park benches to watch her drive past

Below right:
Would you like to sin
With Elinor Glyn
On a tiger-skin?

Or would you prefer
To err with her
On some other fur?

Lillie Langtry, the 'Jersey Lily' who took London by storm

Sex appeal? Charisma? Magnetism? She was not witty or even particularly vivacious, but whatever her magic she used it with unswerving dedication, rapidly relegating rival PBs to the second division.

Like every legendary beauty from Helen of Troy to Lady Diana Cooper, she had the right looks for her time. A modern eye can gaze unmoved at the straight lines of that stern profile; those calculating eyes and the thick white column of neck. Handsome, certainly, but not to our taste. But after years of seeing women with nipped-in waists and sudden unlikely bulges, men felt a thrill of discovery at the vision of Lillie Langtry's statuesque uncorseted body, plain black dress and gold-glinting hair drawn into a simple knot at the nape of the neck. No 'rats' or false fringes of hair. No pads, combs, or laces. This was new. This was what women ought to look like. Overnight Mrs Langtry became the rage. Artists besought her to sit for them. Hostesses showered her with invitations. The haemophiliac Prince Leopold pinned a portrait of her to the wall of his sickroom, whence it was removed by a disapproving Queen Victoria. The heavy-lidded eyes of the Prince of Wales rested on her thoughtfully, and before long his brougham was seen outside her front door. Sulkily her husband withdrew into the shadows: Mrs Langtry had arrived.

She had known what it was to be poor, and many of the stories told about her show an unattractively grasping nature. Certainly she treated poor Frank Langtry with contempt, and claimed she had only married him for his yacht. At a ball which Baron Ferdinand de Rothschild gave for Crown Prince Rudolph of Austria, he offered a dozen of his lady guests new dresses from Doucet in Paris, a princely gesture since this fashionable couturier charged as much as £300 for a single gown. Yet for Lillie Langtry this was not enough. She ordered a petticoat to go under her gown, and was rather taken aback when she received a bill for it, with a note to say that Baron Ferdinand had not authorized the ordering of petticoats.

During the evening, she received another set-down. It was a warm night, and while partnering Crown Prince Rudolph in the cotillion, she recalled in her memoirs

> he danced with great zest, the natural consequence was that he got very hot, which caused a friend of mine whose soubriquet was 'Mrs Sloper' to whisper: 'Take care of your dress; there are marks on it. Make him put on his gloves.' This I proceeded to do at the first opportunity, calling attention to the finger marks around the waist in support of my request. And what do you think the young man's delicate reply was? *'C'est vous qui suez, Madame.'*[21]

Like many swift-rising stars, Lillie's soon faded, and though the Prince of Wales and other admirers loyally supported her efforts to make money on the stage, she had no real talent. She found it hard to come to terms with the inevitable loss of her youth and beauty; but her daughter married into the aristocracy, becoming Lady Malcolm of Poltalloch, and her grand-daughter Mary, whose face was a softer version of Lillie's own, became Lady Bartlett.

The following lines of doggerel give a clue to the half-mocking, half-worshipping attitude of the late-Victorian male to the ladies of his circle:

First Lady Dudley did my sense enthral,
Whiter than chiselled marble standing there,
The Juno of our earth, divinely tall,
And most divinely fair.

And next with all her wealth of hair unroll'd
Was Lady Mandeville, bright-eyed and witty;
And Miss Yznaga, whose dark cheek recall'd
Lord Byron's Spanish ditty.

The Lady Castlereagh held court near by –
A very Venus, goddess fair of love;
And Lady Florence Chaplin nestled nigh,
Gentle as Venus' dove.

As gipsy dark, with black eyes like sloes,
A foil for Violet Lindsay, sweetly fair,
Stood Mrs Murietta; a red rose
Was blushing in her hair.

And warmly beautiful, like sun at noon,
Glowed with love's flames our dear Princess Louise,
Attended by the beautiful Sassoon,
The charming Viennese.

Then Lady Randolph Churchill, whose sweet tones
Make her the Saint Cecilia of the day;
And next those fay-like girls, the Livingstones,
Girofla-Giroflé!

And then my eyes were moved to gaze upon
The phantom-like, celestial form and face
Of the ethereal Lady Clarendon,
The loveliest of her race.

The beauteous sister of a Countess fair;
Is she, the next that my whole soul absorbs.
A model she for Phidias, I declare,
The classic Lady Forbes.[22]

CHAPTER EIGHT

North of the Border

Apart from one brief visit by George IV in 1822, Scotland had seen no reigning British monarch since the days of Charles I when in 1842 Queen Victoria decided to visit the northern part of her realm.

It was a courageous decision by the young Queen for Scotland was, in modern terms, a security risk. Historically the Scots had always been eager to afford aid and comfort to England's enemies and welcomed any opportunity to twist the lion's tail. After the disastrous defeat of the Young Pretender, Charles Edward Stuart, in 1746, long Scottish memories kept green the recollection of how Highlanders were massacred by the hated redcoats, and clans stripped of their distinguishing marks. A century later they still toasted the 'King over the Water' and cursed the name of 'Butcher Cumberland' – Queen Victoria's great-great-uncle –

Creature comforts among the high tops: a Royal picnic at Carn Lochan. (Right to left) Queen Victoria, Prince Albert, Princess Alice, Prince Louis of Hesse, Princess Victoria, John Brown (kneeling) and J. Grant (with bottle)

also known as Sweet William by the English and Stinking Billy by the Scots.

Queen Victoria was determined to do what she could to close this dark chapter in Anglo-Scottish relations, but she could hardly have anticipated how far her Scots subjects would go to meet her. She had a rapturous welcome as she travelled to Edinburgh, Perth, Taymouth, and Stirling, and the wild grandeur of the scenery struck a chord in her ardent, romantic nature.

She came, she saw, she fell in love with Scotland and its people. Before she sailed away on *Trident*, a large steam boat belonging to the General Steam Navigation Company, she was already making plans to return.

During those two centuries of Royal neglect, with no jealous eye to check their growing power, Scottish noblemen had become virtually petty kings, keeping semi-regal state. They maintained bodyguards which amounted to small personal armies, and owned vast tracts of land on which, to all intents and purposes, everything animate and inanimate belonged to them.

After the revival of the Marquessate of Breadalbane in 1885, some wag wrote – half in mockery, half in envy –

> From Cairndour to Taymuir the land is all the Marquess's,
> The mossy howes,
> The heathery knowes,
> And ilka bonny park is his.
>
> The bearded goats
> The toozie stots,
> And a' the braxy carcases;
> Ilk crofter's rent,
> Ilk tinker's tent,
> And ilka collie's bark is his.
>
> The muircock's craw,
> The piper's blaw,
> And ghillie's hard day's wark is his;
> From Cairndour to Taymuir, the world is all the Marquess's![1]

So magnificent a subject was able to offer his sovereign lady hospitality on a grand scale. Scottish nobility flocked to his castle to welcome her. The house party gathered at Taymouth Castle, home of the 6th Earl of Breadalbane, included the Dukes and Duchesses of Buccleuch, Abercorn, and Roxburghe; the Duchess of Sutherland and her daughter Lady Elizabeth Leveson-Gower, Lord Lauderdale, Lord Lorne, son of the Duke of Argyll, Sir Anthony Maitland, Mr and Mrs William Russell, a whole family of Pringles, and Lady Breadalbane's two brothers, the Messrs Baillie.

When the Royal party arrived after a two-hour drive through the hills from Dunkeld, Lord Breadalbane's guard of Highlanders was drawn up at the castle gate to greet them.

Taymouth Castle, home of the Earl of Breadalbane, gave Queen Victoria her first heady taste of Highland hospitality

In her diary, the Queen recorded the scene:

Taymouth lies in a valley surrounded by very high, wooded hills; it is most beautiful. The house is a kind of castle, built of granite. The *coup d'œil* is indescribable. There were a number of Lord Breadalbane's Highlanders, all in the Campbell tartan, drawn up in front of the house, with Lord Breadalbane himself in a Highland dress at their head, a few of Sir Neil Menzies' men (in the Menzies red and white tartan), a number of pipers playing, and a company of the 92nd Highlanders, also in kilts. The firing of the guns, the cheering of the great crowd, the picturesqueness of the dresses, the beauty of the surrounding country, with its rich background of wooded hills, altogether formed one of the finest scenes imaginable. It seemed as if a great chieftain in olden feudal times was receiving his sovereign. It was princely and romantic. Lord and Lady Breadalbane took us upstairs, the halls and stairs being lined with Highlanders.[2]

That evening, after the Queen had dined, there was a display of fireworks in the illuminated grounds, followed by reels danced 'to perfection, to the sound of the pipes, by torchlight, in front of the house. It had a wild and very gay effect'.

Next day Albert was taken shooting by Lord Breadalbane while the Queen and her hostess walked up the hill in pelting rain to admire the view across the loch. Victoria was stoical about the weather, too enthralled by the noble sweep of hills to worry if her feet were wet or dry. From her constant references to the beauty of the mountains, it is clear

*Recommended for its
healthy situation and
rebuilt to accommodate the
Royal family, Balmoral
Castle became Queen
Victoria's favourite home*

their appeal for her amounted to fascination, while for Albert they evoked happy memories of youthful holidays in the Alps. Both would find England 'sadly flat' when their tour was over.

Their visit to Taymouth Castle concluded with the whole party, except the delicate Lady Breadalbane and Duchess of Sutherland, embarking in boats to be rowed 16 miles up Loch Tay to Auchmore. It was a lovely way to leave.

> We saw the splendid scenery to such great advantage on both sides. Ben Lawers, with small waterfalls descending its sides, amid other high mountains wooded here and there; with Kenmore in the distance; the view, looking back, as the loch winds, was very beautiful. The boatmen sang two Gaelic boat-songs, very wild and singular; the language so guttural and yet so soft. Captain McDougall, who steered, and who is the head of the McDougalls, showed us the real 'brooch of Lorn', which was taken by his ancestor from Robert Bruce in a battle. The situation of Auchmore is exquisite; the trees growing so beautifully down from the top of the mountains, quite into the water, and the mountains all round, make it an enchanting spot. We landed and lunched in the cottage.[3]

Everything pleased her: the wild scenery, the handsome, active people with their soft speech and natural courtesy, the wildlife, the grim grandeur of Scottish castles.

From that first tour in 1842 sprang Queen Victoria's desire for a Highland home of her own, where she and Prince Albert and their growing brood could withdraw from the complications of court and politics, and live a simple, healthy life surrounded by noble hills and loyal Highland servants.

Six years later, the dream had become reality. The charming small castle of Balmoral on Deeside, chosen partly on the recommendation of the Queen's physician for its healthy situation, cast an immediate and lasting spell over the Royal couple. The simple sturdy old building had to go – it was so cramped that when the gentlemen played billiards, the ladies had to move their seats every few minutes to get out of the way of the cues – and Victoria and Albert set a trend many of her rich subjects were soon to follow by building a substantial modern house on the site, complete with all the turrets, towers, crenellations, and ornamentations dear to the Victorian heart.

No one could call Balmoral comfortable, and the furnishings were enough to make sensitive souls feel quite ill. There were tartan carpets, curtains and upholstery; severed stuffed stags' heads staring glassy-eyed and accusing from the walls; the usual clutter of small tables loaded with silver-framed photographs; amazing sky-blue wallpaper patterned with gold fleurs-de-lys – but for the Queen, throughout the happy decade up to the death of Prince Albert, it was 'perfection'.

House parties at Balmoral during those years were for the most part family affairs, augmented by equerries, ladies-in-waiting, and the occasional reluctant statesman. As the Royal children grew up, suitable young men and girls were sometimes invited to join the party with their parents.

Princess Victoria – Vicky – accepted Prince Frederick William of Prussia's posy of white heather and his proposal of marriage there in 1855; and 15 years later Princess Louise took a walk from the Glassalt Shiel to the Dhu Loch in company with Lord Lorne, with the same satisfactory result.

Deer-stalking occupied the time and energy of the men of the Royal party, and word of the excitement to be found in this hitherto little-known sport quickly spread among rich southerners. Since red deer breed too rapidly for the poor feeding in the Highlands to support them, a yearly cull is essential to control deer numbers. Stags are shot in late summer and autumn, before the rut, or mating season; hinds in mid-winter. Such wild and wary animals are difficult to approach near enough to shoot, and the skill needed to stalk them on the steep, barren hill-tops gives the sport a peculiar fascination. Soon an ever-growing stream of rich English sportsmen flowed northward annually, and traditional land-owners such as the Duke of Sutherland and the Earls of Seafield and Breadalbane found to their astonishment that millionaire tenants were eager to rent their outlying deer-forests for outrageous sums. Five thousand pounds for ten weeks' sport was not unusual.

In some cases, these would-be lairds bought their forests outright. It was the ultimate status symbol. No matter how barren or remote the situation, Victorian energy, engineering skill, and money were ready to challenge and overcome the formidable logistical difficulties of building or remodelling large houses in the middle of nowhere – a task which generally had to begin with the construction of roads and bridges to bring materials to the site.

Glens that had heard little save the roar of rutting stags and keening cry of eagles since the Highland Clearances of the 1780s, when the crofting population had been driven out to make way for sheep, now echoed once again with human activity. The Victorians built for comfort and durability, though even the grandest Scottish houses retained some curiously primitive arrangements. At Inveraray Castle, seat of the Dukes of Argyll, a strange procession used to take place from the house to the bridge over the Aray every morning after breakfast. Over each of the twenty or so male guests, 'a footman carried an umbrella. They marched to a spacious privy under the bridge, where they sat facing each other in a row. When the last man had finished, the platoon marched back two by two to the house, each with his footman and umbrella.'[4]

Huge quantities of dressed stone, timber, slate, and hundreds of tons of cement were painstakingly transported by rail, road, or in some cases, water, generally by local contractors. The surge of business gave a powerful boost to the Highland economy. Not only the building trade, but the cabinet-makers, upholsterers, hauliers, farriers, ironmongers, and provision merchants prospered, though these last found it necessary to supplement their stocks of basic foodstuffs with all manner of delicacies

Responsible stalkers shoot stags of inferior physique and leave the best to breed. Here the right-hand beast has a 'switch' top – an unforked antler which makes him a lethal fighter – and the left-hand stag is past his prime

for the sophisticated southern palate. The tradition lingers on: Scottish grocers are some of the best in the world.

Outside Kinnaird House, 1869. Dogs were used to pull down a wounded beast

Once the building was finished, the lodge furnished, and stalkers and ghillies handsomely arrayed in tweed knickerbocker suits of the new laird's personal choice, it was time to show off all this northern splendour to the admiring gaze of friends. Soon it was common to see a fashionable sporting man with his rifles and fishing rods paying £5 for his ticket on the night-sleeper train from London to Inverness. There he would change to a smaller train which would, in due course, deposit him at some bleak and lonely halt, where he would soon find himself, in the words of Augustus Grimble, 'in mortal combat with a very tough chop in a Highland inn'.[5] The last lap of his long journey would be in the dog-cart sent by his host to convey him to the lodge.

Deer-stalking has a fascination all its own. Not only is it a sport but a science and craft; not only an exciting hunt, but a necessary operation to maintain a balance in a precariously poised ecology. Deer-stalking differs from other field sports in the demands it makes on the hunter. A man or woman must be physically fit even to climb within sight of a stag, and mentally tough to surmount the many setbacks he or she is bound to encounter. It is no use arriving exhausted at the summit, for that is only the *hors d'œuvre*. The real business will begin only when a shootable beast has been identified and an approach-route worked out.

In that barren wilderness of peat, sedge, and heather, stretching to limitless horizons, the red-brown dots scattered among the stones on some steep face look very small and far away. Time and again an almost imperceptible shift in the wind, or the unexpected movement of hare, sheep, or grouse, or even the bark of a wary hind foils the stalker, and he sees his quarry gallop effortlessly over the skyline to which he himself has climbed with so much labour. A swirl of mist may block out visibility just as he raises the rifle, or a stag which has lain quietly cudding for an hour with just the tips of his antlers showing, may spring up and trot smartly away, high-stepping over the tussocks, before the stalker can move his numbed hands.

So many things can – and do – go wrong that when the stalk is successful the triumph feels well-earned. The stag is a beautiful animal. He is also a worthy, wary, subtle opponent, and outwitting him is all the fun of the game. The shot itself is no more than the declaration of 'Checkmate' at the end of a hard-fought match.

My father used to compare the stag to a crusty old gentleman sitting in a nightclub surrounded by lovely girls, digesting his dinner and keeping a wary eye on young whippersnappers at other tables who might try to lure away one of his harem. Unknown to him, hired assassins are lurking behind a screen.

Bang!

The old gentleman staggers up, takes a couple of steps and falls stone dead. The ladies scatter with their young lovers. Unlike the hunted fox, the tortured salmon, or the game bird forced to fly into a hail of lead, the stag has an easy passage to the next world.

Jennie Churchill did not see deer-stalking in quite this light, but the roots of her distaste seem to lie less in the death of the stag than in the fact that it was caused by one of her own sex, and badly executed, at that.

> Personally [she wrote], although I see no harm in a woman shooting game, I cannot say I admire it as an accomplishment . . . Not long ago, while in Scotland, I saw a young and charming woman, who was surely not of a bloodthirsty nature, kill two stags in one morning. The first she shot through the heart. With the aid of a powerful pair of field-glasses, I watched her stalk the second. First she crawled on all-fours up a long burn; emerging hot and panting, not to say wet and dirty, she then continued her scramble up a steep hill, taking advantage of any cover afforded by the ground, or remaining in a petrified attitude if by chance a hind happened to look up.
>
> The stag meanwhile, quite oblivious of the danger lurking at hand, was apparently enjoying himself. Surrounded by his hinds, he trusted to their vigilance, and lay in the bracken in the brilliant sunshine. I could just see his fine antlered head when suddenly, realising that all was not well, he bounded up, making a magnificent picture as he stood gazing round, his head thrown back as if in defiance. *Crash! Bang!* and this glorious animal became a maimed and tortured thing. Shot through both forelegs, he attempted to gallop down the hill, his poor broken limbs tumbling about him, while the affrighted hinds stood riveted to the spot, looking at their lord and master with horror, not unmixed with curiosity. I shall never forget the sight, or that of the dogs set on him, and the final scene, over which I draw a veil.[6]

A horrid sight: though the massive shock of the bullet would have temporarily anaesthetized the wounded stag until the dogs bounded up to pull him down. Wounding a stag is the stalker's nightmare, and it is to minimize this risk that every amateur 'rifle' – no matter how good a shot – should be accompanied to the hill by a professional stalker whose authority over him is absolute, and whose business it is to see that he not only shoots the right stag, but shoots it dead.

The nineteenth-century threshold of tolerance of cruelty to children, animals, and birds being even higher than our own, some of the sporting feats recorded by visitors to the glens make a modern gorge rise. The large party, including a number of ladies, who drove up Glen Tilt to watch the big-game hunter Sir Samuel Baker knife a stag to death could hardly have been accused of squeamishness.

Organized deer-drives, too, were messy, brutal affairs which wounded more deer than they killed, but on few occasions was the operation a more total flop than when the socially aspiring banker Sigmund Neumann, who had rented the deer forest of Invercauld from the Farquharsons, invited the Prince of Wales to a deer-drive in 1898.

> Everything went wrong [recalled Frederick Ponsonby]. In the first place the deer refused to be driven in the proper direction; whether this was sheer bad luck or owing to the lack of skill on the part of the keepers it is difficult to say. Deer when they are conscious of being driven invariably go straight back through the beaters and therefore it has to be done in a subtle manner. Whatever the cause was, the drive that lasted two hours proved a failure and no one got a shot.
>
> The Prince of Wales, who knew the difficulties, took it with great equanimity and made light of it, but when the luncheon proved a fiasco, it was quite a different matter. Neumann, full of apologies for the failure of the drive, led us off to luncheon. He had made all the arrangements himself so that there should be no mistake. We walked down a path in single file and he assured us that it was not far. After half an hour's walk we came to a wood and Neumann explained he had chosen this sheltered spot in case it was a windy day. It seemed an ideal place but there were no signs of anything to eat. He told us to wait a moment while he looked about and, like a hound who is trying to pick up the scent, he circled round and round but with no success.
>
> The Prince of Wales, who by that time was getting very hungry, began to make very scathing remarks about rich men undertaking things they knew nothing about and ended by shouting suggestions to the wretched Neumann, who was still scouring the countryside at a trot.[7]

A passing shepherd at last shed light on the mystery, though it brought little comfort to Neumann to be told that his servants had taken the luncheon to a place five miles away which, though written similarly, was pronounced quite differently. Begging Ponsonby to explain matters to the Prince and persuade him to walk to the road, Neumann set off at the best pace he could muster to fetch some form of transport.

> H.R.H. on hearing the explanation called Neumann every synonym for an idiot, but urged by hunger he agreed to walk to the road, which took us

Opposite: View through the drawing-room window. 'Summer in Cumberland', 1925, by the Borders artist James Durden

*The end of a day's stalking
in Glen Tilt on the Atholl
estates in the 1880s*

about half an hour. It was then past two and there, on a heap of stones, we sat silently waiting for a conveyance. Conversation was at first tried, but eventually lapsed into gloomy silence. It was past three when a wagonette arrived.[8]

When one considers the kind of luncheon to which the Prince was accustomed, it is easy to understand his chagrin. For a typical Royal shooting meal, sent out to the rifles from Balmoral during a deer-drive in the Abergeldie woods, the menu consisted of:

> Homard Naturel, Sauce Remoulade
> Ragoût de Mouton Provençal
> Poulet et Langue à l'Anglaise
> Salade Vosigienne
> Epinards au Beurre
> Pommes de Terre Maître d'Hôtel
> Tarte de Framboises et Groseilles
> Compote de Pêches
> Pouding au Riz
> Apple Dumpling.[9]

While the men were away to the hill, most of the ladies of the party devoted their time to sketching, walking, fishing, and gossip. It was not until evening that both sexes foregathered for dinner and an analysis of the day's sport. This could be a testing experience for, as General Henry Hope

Crealock, author and illustrator of the splendidly produced *Deer-Stalking in the Highlands of Scotland*, expressed it:

> The entrance into the dining room of a stalking house is a critical moment . . . Mortification and vexation of spirit await the unlucky wight who has missed a good chance or, blundering his shot, has wounded and lost his beast . . . Chaff is no name for what he may expect, and woe betide him if he tries to stammer lame excuses . . .
>
> As the stalker of the day walks into the dining room all eyes are turned on him, and he is saluted with a general query from all: 'Well, what have you done?' But the question need not be asked: you can generally tell by the way he comes into the room what has taken place on the hill.
>
> If he has blood, triumph is in his eye, his gait is brisk and joyous, and he is full of chaff; while if he has failed, he has not a word to say for himself, looking very meek and 'umble . . . The bachelor seems to me to have much the best time of it when he misses; for he has not to undergo a curtain lecture and chaff besides from the wife of his heart, and beyond his own mortification there is nothing to follow.
>
> But the poor married man has, I suspect, a rough time of it . . . for I notice the wife is as jealous of her husband's reputation and as keen for

'Take him now, sir.' Though most modern rifles are fitted with telescopic sights, little else has changed in a hundred years

blood as her lord. How often has one watched the lady's manner on entering the drawing-room! If her husband has missed, she comes in very quietly and is civil to everyone; but if he has killed a good stag, she enters the room with her nose *en l'air*, and an expression on her face of 'Thank God I am not as other women are – my man don't miss.' Then follows the smoking-room ordeal, when you have to stalk your beasts all over again and give all the details.[10]

Of all types of sporting country house party, the deer-stalking one bears the closest resemblance now to its counterpart a century ago. Compare old photographs with those taken last year: the tweeds were baggier in Edwardian days, but they are basically the same in material and cut. More chins wore beards in those days, and the gentleman stalker was not ashamed to ride the first ascent, but riding was then as natural a way for a man to travel as on his own feet.

Far more striking than the differences are the similarities between then and now: the essential boots, the telescopes slung across the chest, the trusty thumbstick and pulling-ropes with which to drag the dead stag down to the pony-path. Today's heavy, hairy garrons, or deer-ponies, with their rounded saddles strongly breeched and hung about with neatly coiled straps by which the stag will be secured, are bred and trained in just the same way as their ancestors; their headcollars, nosebags, and ancient rusty bits were probably made when Queen Victoria was on the throne.

Even the expressions of the nineteenth-century stalking party setting out from the lodge bear a marked resemblance to those captured by today's camera. The gentlemen rifles look competent and keen, yet with that touch of anxiety which will put an edge on their performance. Are they fit for the hill? Will they 'blow up' before reaching the high tops? Will they – awful thought – have to ask the stalker to slow down? Will they bring off a good shot at 150 yards, or miss ignominiously? If so, can they blame it on the rifle?

All these questions will be answered in the next few hours; meantime, nerves are strung tight.

The stalkers and ghillies have seen it all. They stand in attitudes of negligent hill-craft, sure of their own strength and skill, yet their thoughts are busy too. Will the mist come down and ruin the stalk? Will the gentleman suffer an attack of paralysing 'stag fever' at the *moment critique*, and be incapable of squeezing the trigger? Have the big bunch of stags glimpsed yesterday evening moved over the march during the night? Does the gentleman carry a dram with him?

The ponies look placidly resigned. Their role is to wait at the top of a marked path until a wisp of smoke high on the hillside signals that a stag has been shot. Then they will be led to the nearest negotiable spot so that the carcase can be loaded, carefully balanced and securely lashed to the deer-saddle.

Training a deer-pony to carry a dead stag which can weigh up to 20 stone, which smells of blood and the rank taint of the rut, and is equipped with long, sharp, branching antlers, is a painstaking business. Few ponies can be considered steady until they are 8 or 9 years old, and many live to a

great age. Even the most reliable is ritually blindfolded in the pony-boy's coat, sleeves wrapped round to knot under the hairy chin, while the dead stag is hoisted and adjusted on the saddle. Then the girths are hauled so tight that it seems the pony will be lifted off his feet; the breeching and balance are checked; and the garron wheels to lumber home with his unwieldy burden, his vast rump swaying as, with surprising nimbleness, he picks his way down the rough path.

Though telescopic sights have largely replaced open ones, and many stalkers communicate by walkie-talkie, there are still ponies as well as Argocats to bring home the stags on Highland deer-forests. The picturesque yet workmanlike procession of men and ponies, on which so many lens-shutters click, is in all essentials (except deer-hounds) the same as that Landseer which painted 100 years ago.

Nor do the elements of after-dinner entertainment in Scottish stalking parties differ much from those our great-grandparents knew. A little homespun music, some silly games, prolonged study of the Game Book in some deep armchair from which a discreet snore may now and then be heard . . . Nothing too taxing for men who have spent eight or nine hours scrambling up hills and sliding down them, crawling knee-deep in freezing burns, soaked with sweat one minute and rain the next; men who have made quarter-mile sprints in squelching boots, and inched on their bellies over jagged rocks. It was, and is, the task of the party's livelier ladies to bully and tease them into playing games – Racing

Highland finery: the
Prince of Wales dancing a
reel at a Ball at Braemar

Demon, perhaps, or Clumps, General Post, Are You There, Moriarty? or
that perennial favourite, The Game. In a huge, haunted Gothic lodge,
with the wind soughing among the turrets and the unearthly roar of stags
in the policies, what could be more deliciously spine-chilling than a game
of Murder, involving much creeping about in the dark and sudden eerie
shrieks?

So, as the clock's hands steal towards midnight, the sporting heroes
stumble upstairs, wondering if they will ever bend their knees again; and
the die-hards gather in the billiard-room with a decanter of Lagavulin
malt whisky to steady their aim until, just as the game grows exciting, the
peremptory shut-down of the electricity generator plunges the lodge into
blackness, and brings the evening to a close.

Stalking parties have a timeless quality, partly because modern
technology has changed so little of the age-old sporting ritual, partly
because the extreme remoteness of many Highland deer-forests means
that once guests have arrived, they tend to stay put. This promotes a
feeling of continuity: a team spirit in which relationships become established – if only for a few days – and each guest assumes his or her proper
place in that team. Private jokes and buzz-words evolve. One guest

adopts the role of Clown, another of Sage. There will be a Principal Beauty; a Tomboy; some Belles Jeunes Filles en Fleur, and perhaps an Impossible Woman. Several grades of Sporting Man will emerge – Fisherman, Catcherman, Best Shot, Lousy Shot and so forth. Inevitably, most parties will include their Crashing Bore.

At times this agreeable remoteness leads to drama. Someone falls ill or breaks a leg: the nearest telephone is 10 miles away down the strath. Here is the chance for heroic feats of rescue work and derring-do; for men to scramble up impossible slopes with stretchers, for panting messengers to hurry back and forth, for women to show off their nursing skill and vie with one another in being Too Too Wonderful. It is all – in retrospect at least – the greatest fun.

In the 1970s a guest at Loch Choire, a splendidly isolated deer-forest rented from the Countess of Sutherland, slipped on rocks at the lip of a waterfall while grouse-shooting, and went over it, gun and all. As he fell, the 12-bore discharged itself, but since the terrain was rough and the line of guns well spaced out, the accident went unseen. When the party gathered for lunch they realized a man was missing, but thought he must be searching for a lost bird.

When finally a hunt was made and the accident discovered, the unlucky guest had been in the water the best part of an hour and was in a bad way. The operation to bring him back to the lodge without further damage taxed all the party's ingenuity. A boat was sent 4 miles down the loch to fetch a bed, and this was ferried to the head of the loch and carried to the waterfall. Five hours after the accident the party was back at the lodge; but another five would elapse before the ambulance, summoned by radio to transport the casualty over 12 miles of unmade track, eventually deposited him safely in hospital.

More recently still, when taking a Sunday walk on the very day we arrived at Glenkinglass, another inaccessible lodge in Argyllshire, I got left behind and sat down to rest in the sun. Gradually I became aware of – and puzzled by – a faint cry. It sounded like *Help! Help!*

Impossible, I thought, and at once rationalized it into the bleating of a sheep. Then it occurred to me that the boys who had walked on ahead might be shouting into a gully to make it echo. That night I asked if they had; but they looked surprised and denied it.

Two days later, another guest came down to breakfast saying she had been woken by a voice shouting for help, and when the stalking party assembled outside there could be no more doubt. Someone *was* shouting; and now, high on the opposite face, field-glasses revealed a blob of fluorescent orange. Stalking was abandoned. There was a general rush up the hill, where we found a Dutchman with a broken leg, who had fallen into a steep-sided gully *five days earlier* and been imprisoned there, shouting, ever since. The heavy rain of the previous night had turned his dry gully into a rushing torrent, which bowled him down to within earshot of the lodge; but when he managed painfully to crawl from his prison, it was to see the lights below him suddenly extinguished, as the generator switched off for the night.

One look at his leg convinced even the keenest amateur quacks in the party that this was out of their league. We summoned an RAF helicopter and watched entranced as it hovered over the hillside while men slid down on ropes and strapped the casualty to a stretcher, then winched him into the belly of the chopper. All ended well, but he was lucky. Glenkinglass was the only house within a 7-mile radius of where he fell.

Dramas apart, the heady experience of being a laird, however temporarily, affects men strangely. Just as the mildest man with a tiller in his grasp imagines himself Bligh of the *Bounty*, lairdship brings out the best in some hosts and the worst in others.

In the second volume of his autobiography, *Georgian Afternoon*, L. E. Jones tells the story of his own fall from grace as the guest of Mr Edward Wagg, a senior partner of the City firm of Helbert Wagg and Company, and Laird of Glenlochay.

> In most English houses the routine, however well starched, is softened or bent to suit the visitors, there is an implicit conferring of a 'freedom' in the welcoming handshakes; the hostess will even wait, after dinner is upon the table, for a tardy guest. But at . . . Glenlochay it was the guests who had to shed their free and easy ways; it was the host, the little holy man, silver-haired and benevolent, to whose habits all must conform.
>
> It was not for him, on the stroke of eight o'clock, to count heads, or to make sure that the principal lady guest was present, before going in to dinner. If she was not down, that was her affair. The Laird rose and led the way into the dining-room, ahead of his guests. Once there, he carved the joints or the birds with a craftsman's attention; so that the principal lady might well hope to slip unnoticed into the chair at his side and so to escape the loss of 'a life'. But if she did so she had forgotten J.K. For there was a tradition at Glenlochay, imparted by the seasoned to the novice guests, that to each newcomer so many 'lives' were allowed; when these had been lost, it was the end of you. You were not asked again. To be late for a meal cost a life; to knock out your pipe on the metalwork of the wagonnette cost another. You very properly lost one if you omitted to tell the Laird that it had taken more than one shot to kill your stag, or forgot to confess your misses. The notches against you were made and counted in J.K.'s head. But nobody ever pretended to discover just how many 'lives' were allowed, or whether the allowance was the same for all.
>
> I lost my last life, after seven years of punctuality and of truthfulness about the day's stalking, by falling ill. It was true that I fell ill with a certain lack of consideration. A specialist from Edinburgh had to be sent for and given a meal; I was carried out of the Lodge on a stretcher and put into an ambulance; there was a good deal of fuss and agitation. All the same, when two years later I had completely recovered and was stalking again in other forests, it was a shock to discover there was to be no forgiveness for me. I was never invited again.[11]

A cautionary tale. It could happen to anyone.

CHAPTER NINE

Below Stairs

ehind the green baize door lay the power-house of every large
country house: the servants' hall. Without labour-saving
machines, but with a very deeply rooted conviction that any
attempt to make the servants' work easier carried a grave risk of
undermining their morals and, in consequence, the whole social structure,
employers were careful to keep their staff busy. The routine of cleaning
and maintaining these enormous houses and waiting on their masters
demanded an army of domestics as well as outdoor servants. Judged by
modern standards, they worked long and hard, but there were compensa-
tions. Domestic service was not then considered demeaning work for the
free-born Englishman or woman: on the contrary, there was a good deal
of prestige, even glamour, attached to being part of a noble household
where the standard of living for the humblest scullerymaid was higher
than she could expect in her own home.

Jobs at the local 'big house' were eagerly sought. Thus in *The
Edwardians*:

> It was . . . seldom that any complete stranger obtained a situation at
> Chevron. The system of nepotism reigned . . . Thus Mrs Wickenden [the
> housekeeper] and Wickenden the head carpenter were brother and sister;
> their father and grandfather had been head-carpenters there in their day;
> several of the housemaids were Mrs Wickenden's nieces, and the third
> footman was Vigeon's nephew. Whole families, from generation to genera-
> tion, naturally found employment on the estate. Any outsider was regarded
> with suspicion and disdain. By this means a network was created, and a
> constant supply of young aspirants assured. Their wages might range from
> twelve to twenty-four pounds a year. To do them justice, it must be said
> that the service they one and all gave to Chevron was whole-hearted and
> even passionate. They considered the great house as in some degree their
> own; their pride was bound up in it, and their life was complete within the
> square of its walls.[1]

The staff of a great country house was divided into two teams (as it
were regular regiments), the males headed by the house steward, and the
females under the command of the housekeeper. A third, so to speak
irregular, regiment was composed of outdoor servants: the stable staff,

the gardeners, porter's lodge attendants, window-cleaners, boilermen, coalman and watchman, together with the staff of the laundry who, though female, enjoyed a degree of autonomy. In all three regiments an almost military discipline prevailed, governed by a strict hierarchy. A population census taken in 1891 revealed that 16 per cent of the English worked in domestic service – a figure that seems less surprising when you consider that the Duke of Westminster, for instance, employed a staff of over 300 at Eaton Hall alone.

The officer class of servants was known as the 'Upper Ten' and the other ranks as the 'Lower Five', though these figures bore no relation to the number of servants in the house. The steward, leader of the Upper Ten, was a figure of considerable power, responsible for engaging and dismissing all male staff except for his master's personal valet; for paying wages and bills, ordering household supplies, organizing travel arrangements, and keeping accounts.

Next in rank was the groom of the chambers, who rang the bell for prayers, and whose duty it was to see that all was in order in the house, upstairs and down, with particular attention to fires, writing-desks, lamps and candles – always a potential hazard – and the security of doors and windows.

The butler was generally responsible for the wine, the silver, the proper conduct of meals; for checking the condition of fires before the gentry entered the reception rooms, sorting the day's mail, receiving visitors and taking up their cards in the morning (a duty handed over to the footmen in the afternoon) and, in some households, ironing the newspapers.

Another powerful figure among the upper servants was the master's personal valet, who was expected to be on call early and late. He roused his employer in the morning, brought shaving water, put out and cared for his clothes; packed, unpacked; bought tickets, arranged transport, and waited up to whatever hour his master decided to go to bed.

Cooks and chefs also belonged to the higher echelon of servants and jealously guarded their privileged status. As the vogue for lavish entertaining grew, it became fashionable to employ French chefs who were often considerable artists, and to take a perverse pride in their outbursts of Gallic temperament.

In the female hierarchy, the housekeeper ruled the roost, kept the housekeeping accounts and the keys to the storerooms, and engaged female staff. She was usually an imposing, black-clad figure at whose belt jingled a multitude of keys, very conscious of her dignity and careful to allow no familiarity from underlings. The only female servant with the independence to challenge the housekeeper's authority was the lady of the house's personal maid, counterpart to the master's valet, whose duties did not fall directly within the housekeeper's sphere of influence. All other female servants, from the head housemaid to the most junior scullery-maid, went in fear of the housekeeper's displeasure; and like all petty tyrants she exulted in her power.

Below the head housemaid came five more grades of housemaid,

Servants at Petworth, Sussex, collected by Mrs Percy Wyndham. (far left) the under-butler; (middle) Mrs Smith, the housekeeper; (left) Phillips, Lord Leconfield's coachman

who worked in pairs: sewing-women, kitchenmaids of various degrees, several scullerymaids in their early teens, stillroom maids who made jams, scones, and other tea-time delicacies, and a dairymaid who was responsible for milk, cream, butter and egg supplies.

There were, besides, other female servants whose place in the household was less clearly defined. The governess, who often belonged to the gentry by birth but was, through misfortune or accident, obliged to earn her own living, walked an uncomfortable tightrope between family and servants and was often a sad, lonely figure. The lady of the house's secretary had an equally invidious position – one moment a confidante, almost a friend; the next an underling to be ordered around or sharply criticized.

A traditional hostility existed between nursery and kitchen. Day and night nurseries were at the top of the house and kitchens at the bottom, so food habitually arrived cold and unpalatable on the nursery table. Then Nannie would rise in her wrath and despatch a succession of trembling nursery-maids down the back stairs to the kitchen with complaints, earning the bitter enmity of Cook and the first kitchenmaid, whose duty it was to prepare nursery meals. It must be said, though, that Nannie's complaints were generally justified. The diet of offal, greasy mutton, overcooked vegetables and stodgy or slimy puddings which were considered suitable food for children was uniformly disgusting. Victorian and Edwardian nursery lore decreed that anything delicious must be bad for young digestions, so even in the richest households the children and their hapless attendants lived on penitential fare.

Attendants brought with visiting children were regarded with acute suspicion by the home team. In the persona of the housekeeper's son in his novel *Tono-Bungay*, H. G. Wells describes the closing of ranks

Children saw their parents
only at set times and were
largely reared by nannies.
A mother pays her
morning visit to the
nursery

among the Bladesover staff when the Honourable Beatrice Normandy
came to stay.

She was eight, and she came with a nurse called Nannie; and to begin with I
did not like her at all.

Nobody liked this irruption into the downstairs rooms; the two 'gave
trouble' – a dire offence; Nannie's sense of duty to her charge led to requests
and demands that took my mother's breath away. Eggs at unusual times,
the reboiling of milk, the rejection of an excellent milk pudding – not
negotiated respectfully, but dictated as of right. Nannie was a dark,
long-featured, taciturn woman in a gray dress; she had a furtive inflexibility
of manner that finally dismayed and crushed and overcame. She conveyed
she was 'under orders' – like a Greek tragedy. She was that strange product
of the old time, a devoted, trusted servant; she had, as it were, banked all
her pride and will with the greater, more powerful people who employed
her, in return for a lifelong security of servitude . . . She was sexless, her
personal pride was all transferred, she mothered another woman's child
with a hard, joyless devotion that was at last entirely compatible with a
stoical separation. She treated us all as things that counted for nothing save
to fetch and carry for her charge.[2]

Other visiting servants received a warmer welcome. Though country house parties made a lot of extra work for the resident staff, they brought a whiff of glamour from the outside world to servants' halls tired of their own company, besides providing opportunities for fascinating gossip about their masters and flirtation among themselves. Since hostesses were inclined to invite the same friends to their houses year after year, the servants became almost as well acquainted as their employers, and below-stairs mimicked most faithfully the social rituals of above-stairs.

Down in the steward's room the butler offered his arm gravely to the Duchess of Hull's maid, and conducted her to the place at his right hand. Lord Roehampton's valet did the same by Mrs Wickenden the housekeeper. Mrs Wickenden, of course, was not married, and her title was bestowed only by courtesy. The order of precedence was very rigidly observed, for the visiting maids and valets enjoyed the same hierarchy as their masters and mistresses; where ranks coincided, the date of creation had to be taken into account, and for this purpose a copy of Debrett was always kept in the housekeeper's room – last year's Debrett, appropriated by Mrs Wickenden as soon as the new issue had been placed in Her Grace's boudoir. The maids and valets enjoyed not only the same precedence as their employers, but also their names. Thus, although the Duchess of Hull's maid had stayed many times at Chevron, and was indeed quite a crony of Mrs Wickenden's, invited to private sessions in the housekeeper's room, where the two elderly gossips sat stirring their cups of tea, she was never known as anything but Miss Hull, and none of her colleagues in the steward's room would ever have owned to a knowledge of what her true name might be.[3]

In some large households it was the custom to call first footmen by a particular Christian name, and the second and third footmen by others, no matter what their real names might be. Upper servants were addressed by their surnames except on the occasions when they stayed away from home, at which times they adopted their masters' names. 'I say, Stanhope, did you clean Rosebery's boots?' one manservant was heard to call out to another, to the amusement of Lord Leicester's listening granddaughter.

Running a large household, particularly when there were guests, was an intricate and demanding business, requiring good teamwork. Servants who were difficult seldom lasted long.

I am worried by my new maid turning out dreadfully huffy with the Duke's household, and unmanageable when I tell her to show my gowns to other people [confided Lady Frederick Cavendish to her diary while on a visit to Chatsworth]. She is going. It perplexes me sadly how all I say and do, though it is not without prayer, seems to fail utterly with one maid after another. This is the 4th I have had that has behaved ill in her rapports with some fellow-servant or other, and they have not a notion that they can be in the least to blame, though by their own showing (certainly in this one's case) it all grows out of the pettiest jealousy and pride. There is a code of morals among them . . . the supreme and pre-eminent commandment of this code being, 'Thou shalt never let thyself be put upon; and thou shalt attribute the meanest motive to the conduct of thy fellows.'

Still at Chatsworth a month later, she notes: 'To my inexpressible relief and comfort, my odious little maid went off, and gentle, pleasant-looking, quiet little Mrs Parry came, who will probably turn out to be a Felon, but is meanwhile very soothing.' Alas, barely two months elapse before this gloomy prophecy is fulfilled. 'To my bewilderment and dismay last night, my poor maid Parry, who is married, announced in a tremulous voice that, when she had been with me only a few days, she suddenly and unexpectedly discovered that she was several months gone with a luckless baby! My head span.'[4]

Despite all her prayers, Lady Frederick lacked the knack of handling servants. After her own conversion to Socialism, the Countess of Warwick could make a clear-eyed assessment of what was wrong with the master-servant relationship upon which large country houses depended so heavily. Even when masters were charitably disposed (as she was herself), their charity was suspect for there were strings attached.

> The landowning class expected a certain fealty, a certain acceptance of the view of those who gave the 'dole'. Blankets, soup, coal, rabbit and the rest were all paid for, though not in cash – because the recipients were the poorest of the poor – but in subservience, in the surrender of all personality, and in a certain measure of humility from which there could be no escape.
> Snobbery ran riot, from the lodge-keeper who opened the gates with a profound obeisance, to the little children who were instructed to pull their forelocks or make a curtsey. We paid in cash and took in kind . . .
> Democracy had not arisen, and could not arise while the great country

houses were a power in the land. Even on the rare occasions when a great place was let for the shooting or hunting season, the people who took it would follow the same rules of life and the same comical etiquette was maintained below-stairs . . . The 'Stately Homes of England' have had their selfish day.[5]

When there was a house party, that selfish day began early for the servants who ran the machine. First awake would be the scullerymaids, called by the night watchman on his final round at 5.30 a.m. Shivering in the bleak dawn light that filtered into their attic bedrooms, they would splash their faces with cold water in token cleanliness, and dress in their morning uniform of ankle-length, striped print dresses with leg-of-mutton sleeves, thick black stockings, white aprons, and frilled white cotton caps.

Their first task was to clean and light the huge kitchen range on which most of the cooking was done; and for this they replaced their white aprons with rough sacking ones before setting to work with brushes and blacking, ash-bucket, and thin dry sticks of kindling. The range was the heart of kitchen operations and it was imperative to have it burning well before Cook and the kitchenmaids arrived to prepare breakfast first for the staff, then for the gentry.

The hours between half-past six when the senior kitchen staff descended the stairs and nine o'clock when the gong announced breakfast saw continuous activity in the kitchen and servants' hall. Early-morning tea-trays had to be set for the ladies' personal maids to carry to their

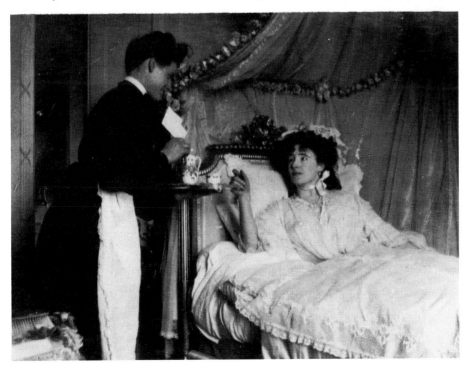

From her bed, Elinor Glyn gives morning orders for the staff

High-ceilinged, stone-floored kitchens were equipped with massive utensils and functional simplicity. There were few labour-saving gadgets and Cook's word was law

mistresses; great iron kettles must be filled and put to heat on the range; and the table in the servants' hall had to be laid with plain white crockery.

Then the copper must be filled and lit for the valets' jugs of shaving-water; more brass jugs of hot water for the ladies' ablutions; bread and butter was cut and placed in alternate triangles of white and brown on every breakfast-tray. The junior housemaids would already have cleaned the steel grates in the morning-room, library and drawing-room, burnishing the bars (still hot from the previous night's fire) with a special burnisher made of rows of fine chain sewn on to a leather backing. Scorch marks on the bars were abraded with emery paper, and the firedogs and fenders polished.

At Chatsworth, writes the present Duchess of Devonshire,

It took two hours to do this. They swept the carpets and used tea-leaves or wet paper to absorb the dust. The upper housemaids followed with the dusting. Everything had to be ready by 8 a.m. and the blinds were pulled as

soon as the rooms were cleaned to prevent the light from reaching the
books and paintings . . .

For the upper housemaids, besides all the ordinary work, there was
'maiding' to do. They looked after the lady guests in the bedrooms allocated
to them for cleaning, unpacked for them when they arrived, called them in
the morning, pressed their clothes, ran the bath, squeezed the toothpaste on
the brush, turned the stockings to slip the feet into and laid an evening dress
and clean underclothes on the bed before dinner.

Hot water was carried to the bedrooms in brass cans, and placed in the
china bowl on the washstand with a clean and folded linen towel under the
handle. This was done four times a day before meals and the slops taken
away afterwards in white china slop pails. The coal fires in the bedrooms
were lit about four p.m. so that it was reasonably warm when it was time to
dress for dinner. The last round of the bedrooms was made at ten p.m. with
hot-water bottles, the fires were made up and the final can of hot water put
on the wash-stand.[6]

In the grandest houses, where the heavy work of carrying water and
coal would have been beyond the housemaids' strength, men were
employed – strong, silent giants whom the young Lady Diana Manners,
daughter of the Duke of Rutland, regarded with some awe.

The watermen are difficult to believe in today. They seemed to me to
belong to another clay. They were the biggest people I had ever seen, much
bigger than any of the men of the family, who were remarkable for their
height. They had stubbly beards and a general Bill Sikes appearance. They
wore brown clothes, no collars, and thick green baize aprons from chin to
knee. On their shoulders they carried a wooden yoke from which hung two
gigantic cans of water. They moved on a perpetual round. Above the
ground floor there was not a drop of hot water and not one bath, so their
job was to keep all jugs, cans, and kettles full in the bedrooms, and morning
or evening to bring the hot water for the hip-baths. We were always a little
frightened of the watermen. They seemed of another element and never
spoke but one word, 'Water-man' to account for themselves.

If anyone had the nerve to lie abed until eleven o'clock, which can
seldom have happened, there were many strange callers at the door. First
the housemaid, scouring the steel grate and encouraging the fire of the night
before, which always burned until morning, and refilling the kettle on the
hob until it sang again. Next the unearthly water-giants. Then a muffled
knock given by a knee, for the coal-man's hands were too dirty and too full.
He was a sinister man, much like his brothers of the water, but blacker far
and generally more mineral. He growled the single word, 'Coal-man' and
filled one's bin with pieces the size of ice-blocks.[7]

It was generally when a guest fell ill that these invisible toilers were
briefly glimpsed. Though the Victorians and Edwardians treated death
with a casualness that we find unfeeling, they were mortally afraid of
infection and illness.

Sufferers from any malady which was supposed to be in any degree
catching were isolated in a remote part of the house, which was fenced-off
with vinegar-soaked sheets. Beyond these sheets no one ever penetrated

except doctors, nurses, and housemaids. I always used to wonder [wrote Lord Ernest Hamilton], even in my very youthful days, why it was that doctors, nurses, and housemaids never caught things which were supposed to be fatal to the high-born.[8]

So many children of those large nineteenth-century families were struck down before reaching maturity that germs – those silent, invisible carriers of disease – were most heartily dreaded. It was with some trepidation that young Leo in *The Go-Between* by L. P. Hartley discovered his friend Marcus still in bed after breakfast one sunny morning.

'It was decent of you to trickle along,' said Marcus languidly from the bed, 'but don't come in. I have a headache and some spots and Mama thinks it may be measles. She didn't say so, but I know.'
'Hard cheese, old man,' I said. 'But what about the jolly old quarantine?'
'Well, cases do develop when it's over. But the doctor's coming and he'll know. What fun for you if you get it . . .' Marcus said, 'You'd better not stay here breathing in my ruddy germs.'
'Oh, God, perhaps you're right . . . Shall I slink across the room and get my prayer-buggins?'
Last term it had been fashionable to call a book a 'buggins'.
'Yes, but hold your breath.'
I filled my lungs, dashed to the chest of drawers, snatched up the prayer-book and, scarlet in the face regained the door.
'Good egg, I didn't think you could,' said Marcus, while I gasped. 'And have you got any old button or such-like for the collection?'
Again the under-water dash to the chest of drawers but this time I had to come up for air. As I gulped it down I had a distinct feeling of several germs, the size of gnats, going down my throat.[9]

Servants belonging to the Lower Five grades scrambled through as much as possible of their work of cleaning, sweeping, dusting, and polishing before the family party and guests came down to breakfast at nine, for once the gentry were abroad in the ground-floor rooms, housemaids and their cleaning-boxes had to vanish. Early-rising guests were not popular since any maid surprised cleaning was supposed to bob a curtsey and leave the room, creeping back to finish whatever she had been doing only when she could be sure the room was once more empty. Equally tiresome were guests who kept popping back to their bedrooms, interrupting the busy housemaids at work in pairs making beds, emptying slops, replacing used towels with clean ones and re-laying the bedroom fire. Two well-trained maids could 'do' a bedroom in ten minutes, but so tight was their work schedule that the smallest delay made it difficult for them to complete their tasks before it was time to join the rest of the staff for lunch in the servants' hall.

While the housemaids and kitchenmaids were toiling invisibly, the footmen were splendidly on view. They were chosen for their looks. A handsome face and a good pair of shoulders to set off a gold-laced livery were important qualifications for the post, and it was said that 'calves

Laundry-maids enjoyed a degree of autonomy and could flirt with garden and stable staff on their way to and from the drying-grounds

came before character' when engaging a footman.

Their day would also have begun early, since they were responsible for cleaning boots, trimming lamps, and carrying coals into the living-rooms. They laid the tables for breakfast and tea, while the more elaborate luncheon and dinner settings were supervised by the under-butler, or head footman. Generally guests and family helped themselves to breakfast and tea, but the footmen waited on them at luncheon and again at dinner, when they were splendidly turned out in full-dress livery with knee-breeches, silk stockings, and powdered hair.

At Welbeck and Longleat, writes Adeline Hartcup in her fascinating study *Below Stairs in the Great Country Houses*,

> there were special footmen's powder rooms, fitted with long mirrors and wash-basins along one side. The footmen took off their jackets, hung them up, and covered their shoulders with towels. Then they ducked their heads in water, rubbed soap in their hair to make a lather, and combed it stiffly through. Powder puffs came into action as they took turns to dust each other's hair with either violet powder or (in some cases) ordinary flour. This dried to a firm paste and it was important that it should not be shaken off and seen on a livery jacket. It was quite an ordeal. Some footmen found that they caught cold from waiting with damp heads in draughty passages or at

Meals in the servants' hall were as formal as those in the dining-room. Visiting servants were often known by their employer's name

open doors. They often had to stand for a whole evening, stock still and statuesque though longing to scratch their itchy scalps.[10]

The Upper Ten servants ate only their meat course with the lower orders in the servants' hall. Then they swept out in a stately procession to finish their meal in the more rarefied atmosphere of the steward's or housekeeper's room, leaving the Lower Five to gossip and giggle and put their elbows on the scrubbed deal table for a few precious minutes of unsupervised relaxation.

Soon, though, dirty plates and vegetable dishes would be piling up in the scullery as the footmen brought them through from the dining-room, and the little scullerymaids would sigh, gulp down their last mouthfuls of beer or tea, wipe their mouths with the backs of their hands, and scuttle back to begin on the mountain of washing-up.

Silver and glass from all four meals would be washed by the footmen in the under-butler's pantry, where huge wooden sinks were installed to minimize the risk of breakages.

During the afternoon the footmen were kept busy running errands or delivering messages. They took turns for 'carriage duty', which involved standing on the platform at the back of the coach, ready to jump down and open gates, pay tolls, hold the horses' heads or lower the step for passengers to descend. Carriages were chilly, draughty vehicles, and footmen were expected to be ready with rugs, warmed bricks, or umbrellas as the need arose. When the carriage drew up before a house, one footman would run to the horses' heads, while the other helped the passengers out of the carriage.

A footman would accompany a lady and her maid on shopping expeditions, ready to carry parcels and hail cabs. Meanwhile his colleagues left at home would answer the door to afternoon callers, look after the downstairs fires, and carry tea in and out of the drawing-room. One would draw curtains and light lamps; another attend the gentlemen in the smoking-room and check that the silver candlesticks were ready on the tray to light the ladies up to bed.

Their day was a long one and did not end until the last reveller had mounted the stairs, when the footmen on duty had the final chore of raking out the fires ready for the maids to clean next morning, and extinguishing candles and lamps.

Such a life left little opportunity for recreation and entertainment, and free time was strictly limited. The housekeeper was entitled to a modest social life, and might arrange her day's work to include an hour's gossip with the mistress's personal maid or some other special crony in the comfortable privacy of her sitting-room, but for the lower servants when one job ended another began.

H. G. Wells was himself a housekeeper's son and knew what such children suffered.

> I hated tea-time in the house-keeper's room more than anything else at Bladesover. And more particularly I hated it when Mrs Mackridge and Mrs Booch and Mrs Latude-Fernay were staying in the house. They were, all three of them, pensioned-off servants. Old friends of Lady Drew's had rewarded them posthumously for a prolonged devotion to their minor comforts, and Mrs Booch was also trustee for a favourite Skye terrier. Every year Lady Drew gave them an invitation – a reward and encouragement of virtue with especial reference to my mother and Miss Fison, the maid. They sat about in black and shiny and flouncey clothing adorned with gimp and beads, eating great quantities of cake, drinking much tea in a stately manner and reverberating remarks.
>
> I remember these women as immense. No doubt they were of negotiable size, but I was only a very little chap and they assumed nightmare proportions in my mind. They loomed, they bulged, they

In the afternoon, footmen ran errands or took turns for carriage duty, opening gates, paying tolls, or ensuring the passengers' comfort with rugs, hot-water bottles and umbrellas. A phaeton outside Cawdor Castle

impended. Mrs Mackridge was large and dark; there was a marvel about her head, inasmuch as she was bald. She wore a dignified cap, and in front of that upon her brow her hair was *painted* . . .

Then there was Miss Fison, the maid who served both Lady Drew and Miss Somerville, and at the end of the table opposite my mother, sat Rabbits the butler. Rabbits, for a butler, was an unassuming man, and at tea he was not as you know butlers, but in a morning coat and a black tie with blue spots. Still, he was large, with side whiskers, even if his clean-shaven mouth was weak and little. I sat among these people on a high, hard, early Georgian chair, trying to exist, like a feeble seedling amidst great rocks, and my mother sat with an eye upon me, resolute to suppress the slightest manifestation of vitality.[11]

Keeping the lower orders in their place was a special preoccupation of the upper servants. Only once a year were these barriers lowered to permit a degree of familiarity. This was on the occasion of the servants' Christmas ball, Christmas party, or tenants' supper – tradition varied from one big house to another. The 6th Duke of Portland, always noted for his generosity towards his servants, used to give a Twelfth Night Ball for 1,200 of his tenants, servants, and local tradesmen and their families in the huge underground ballroom and three vast reception rooms which had been constructed by his eccentric cousin, the 5th Duke, who had a badger-like passion for burrowing tunnels and hollowing out subterranean chambers. Fifty waiters were imported to wait on the servants, and a whole orchestra was brought from London to entertain them.

The dark-haired Duchess, who had before her marriage been the Scottish beauty Winifred Dallas-Yorke, radiant in full ball dress and

Outdoor workers at a large country house included gardeners, grooms, a coachman, shepherds, and farmhands

jewels, would open the dancing with the steward, while the Duke partnered his housekeeper, resplendent in blue satin. Titled guests who had celebrated the Christmas festivities at Welbeck Abbey would cause wild flutterings in the hearts of housemaids as they bowed and asked for the pleasure of a dance.

Memories of those enchanted hours would warm and comfort through many long months of polishing grates and scouring greasy pans in the year ahead. Wine, beer, and lemonade flowed lavishly throughout the hall, and with exemplary tact the Duke and Duchess made a habit of leaving Welbeck early next morning, leaving their staff to recover from their hangovers in peace.

In the huge armoury at Hatfield House, Lady Salisbury distributed presents to her servants, farm-workers, cottagers and their families under an immense Christmas tree decorated with candles and glittering baubles. The Salisburys entertained frequently: a children's party in January was followed by a ball for friends and neighbours; then a tenants' ball and another for the servants. At the tenantry dinner a special service of china which included 276 meat dishes, 48 pie dishes, three dozen butter boats and 500 plates was brought from the store-room and disposed on long trestle tables for the farmers and their wives to eat their fill.

In the early years of the nineteenth century, Mr Coke of Norfolk – later the 1st Earl of Leicester – kept open house at his annual sheep-shearing gatherings, known as the Holkham Clippings. These lasted several days, and were the forerunners of the modern agricultural show, putting on display the county's finest livestock and crops, and demonstrating new agricultural methods and tools.

> At the 1802 sheep-shearing [writes Adeline Hartcup] two hundred guests 'dined on plate' and the dinner was considered even better than the one at Woburn because of Holkham's nearness to the sea 'which gives plenty of fish'. In 1804, Coke invited all the agriculturalists and breeders at the Woburn sheep-shearing to come the following week to Holkham, when not only the house, but every inn and farmhouse in the neighbourhood was filled with visitors.
>
> Each year more people turned up at the clippings. There were two hundred in 1810, and three times as many eight years later. In 1819 the Duke of Sussex, George III's seventh son, who seldom missed the occasion, was among the five hundred or more guests dining in the state apartments at an early meal which was followed by a late supper for house guests. The Duke was there again in 1820 and in 1821, a year of great agricultural distress, when even Coke had to take care of his pennies and the forty-third and last sheep-shearing took place.
>
> Never had so many people turned up. There were about eighty staying in the house, and the first day's activities began when the house party came out to join the huge crowd waiting outside – tenants and local farmers, Norfolk friends with their own house parties, visitors from other counties and scientists from even farther afield. On each of the four days between five and seven hundred people rode out to inspect the various farms, crops, herds and farm processes, and then came back to Holkham at three o'clock for dinner.[12]

Class barriers were briefly lowered on the night of the Servant's Ball, when a Duchess would lead off with her steward while the Duke begged his housekeeper for the honour of a dance

These were house parties on a grand scale, where local farmers were made just as welcome as visiting noblemen. The annual 'Audit Dinner' which followed the examination of their accounts was another lavish beano for Coke of Norfolk's lucky tenants, who sat down 40- or 50-strong to feast on roast meat, Norfolk dumplings, and mince pies, and to drink their landlord's health and prosperity in bowls of steaming punch.

Such parties, dinners and balls did much to keep relations sweet between masters and servants, but the high days and holidays were few and far between, and the servants would not have been human had they not at times resented the yawning gulf between themselves and their employers.

Yet in one respect servants had the upper hand. For all their apparent power, in any practical sense the gentry were helpless – and proud of it. Waited on hand and foot from cradle to grave, none of them had the slightest idea how anything worked, nor did they want to know. It was not considered quite the thing for any gentleman or lady to display proficiency in a practical field. This ignorance extended into every detail of ordinary domestic life and was ruthlessly exploited by servants.

Members of the *beau monde* [explained Lord Ernest Hamilton] had, of course, to pay very dearly for the ignorance and inefficiency in which they took such pride. Those who served them in various capacities and who smirked and bowed before them in such unctuous servility, took every advantage behind their backs of a situation which seemed specially designed by Providence for the improvement of their own bank balances and which they themselves, of course, lost no opportunity of encouraging. Even in the matter of sport, amusement, or daily routine, the fine ladies and gentlemen could do nothing for themselves. Servitors took their railway tickets for them, laced their boots, paid their cab-fares, affixed their salmon-flies – did everything for them, in fact, except blow their noses. Can it be wondered at that, under such conditions, the belief gradually took root that disaster would follow if anyone but a servitor put his hand to the simplest practical operation? It was an article of belief, in my primrose days, that a house would at once blow up if anyone but the footman lighted the gas.[13]

As Hilaire Belloc put it:

> Lord Finchley tried to mend the electric light
> Himself. It struck him dead, and serve him right.
> It is the business of the wealthy man
> To give employment to the artisan.[14]

Exploitation was a two-way traffic, but in the matter of country house parties, masters leaned very heavily on their servants, whose skills and sheer hard work were the nuts and bolts upon which the whole elaborate edifice depended. When the First World War plucked away those vital nuts and bolts, the country house party began its slow decline.

A DISTINCTION

" Do you dance—or *jazz*? "

CHAPTER TEN

The Long Week-End

Among the flower of British youth who died in the mud of Flanders during the First World War, were many sons of the aristocracy who would have inherited great houses had they lived; and when the war was over at last in 1918, the girls who would have married them and reared the next generation of landowners had to look elsewhere for mates, or else remain single – the choice preferred by a surprising number.

This wholesale destruction of promising young men struck at the roots of the traditional closed society which had ruled England for so long; neither it nor the country house party was ever the same again.

The survivors did their best. When the ravages of shell-shock, mustard gas, and trench-foot had been patched up, and shattered limbs and tattered nerves as far as possible repaired, the depleted ranks of the *jeunesse dorée* began to gather again for shooting parties and cricketing week-ends (the once socially suspect word 'week-end' had now replaced the cumbersome 'Saturday to Monday' in all but the starchiest vocabularies); for hunting and golfing and tennis and coming-of-age balls; but those who had known the old order found the changes in both guests and entertainment hard to approve.

Eligible young men were scarce and greatly in demand. After four years of bitter warfare these men were very different creatures from the well-mannered schoolboys who had answered the bugle's call. Cynicism had replaced the starry-eyed idealism with which they had gone to war. They had been through hell: now they wanted to squeeze every last drop of pleasure from what remained of their youth. They were heroes. They had survived the war to end all wars, which had killed so many of their friends. They were in no mood to observe a lot of pettyfogging social rules about answering invitations and writing bread-and-butter letters.

Invitations continued to shower on them, no matter how recklessly they broke those stuffy old rules. They could pick and choose their amusements, flit from flower to flower, chuck a party here and turn up without being asked there, with none of their fathers' fear of social ostracism. Hostesses gritted their teeth and accepted these new casual manners, no matter how little they liked them. If they did not invite the right sort of young man to their house parties, how would their daughters

Opposite: As American fashions in drinking and dancing swept across the Atlantic, the rigid structure of Society began to crumble

Officers wounded in the First World War practise racing on crutches beneath the windows of Longleat, where they were sent to convalesce

find husbands? Better let the young people enjoy themselves in their hectic modern way than risk one's darling daughter being left on the shelf or – still worse – marrying someone who was Not Quite Our Class, Dear.

All sorts of barriers and taboos were disappearing as the style of entertaining changed. Gone was the reassuringly leisurely – if sometimes tedious – ritual of the Edwardian house party. Instead of a carefully worded letter of invitation sent weeks in advance, a popular young man might now expect to receive a garbled message telephoned to the porter at his club: 'Lady A would like Mr B to make up the party at Castle X this week-end and bring a friend; but if he is already engaged will he look in the card-room and see if any of her lot are there and would come instead.'

Music had undergone so profound a change that the old guard could hardly bring themselves to call the sounds they heard 'music'. Instead of the melodious strains of Strauss waltzes, the loud primitive rhythms of jazz echoed in country house ballrooms, and a whole host of new dances with ugly – even indelicate – names: Breakaway, Black Bottom, Conga, and Charleston swept in from America with the remorseless rapidity of Atlantic fronts.

Even the amiable Duke of Portland disapproved.

At the few balls I have attended since the War, I found couples of all ages, young, middle-aged, and definitely old, solemnly performing what seemed to be flat-footed, negro antics, to the discordant uproar – I will not call it music – of a braying brass band. The only advantage I could see, and that was a very doubtful one, was that middle-aged and elderly couples, who had long ceased to dance, could once again take the floor. This may have been good for their health, but it certainly was not so for the dignity or beauty of their appearance. Heated youth is not a particularly beautiful spectacle; but how much worse is heated and frisky old age![1]

Yet the changes in men and music were small compared to the extraordinary transformation that had taken place in young women. The modern miss was barely recognizable. Her shingled hair clung like a sleek cap to her small, neat head. Her boyish figure was so utterly devoid of pectoral protruberances that in Edwardian eyes she *had* no figure. Her slender silken legs were shamelessly on display instead, and her pretty fresh face was painted as gaily – and with as little attempt at concealment – as that of an actress.

Modern! shuddered the old guard, averting their eyes; but the young men thought her perfectly ripping.

> And then she's slim [marvelled A. P. Herbert],
> So swift and slim,
> Electric wires in every limb!
> And she can ride and she can swim,
> And she can dance till stars grow dim,
> And, waking fresh as violets,
> Play eighteen holes or seven sets,
> Or paint, or cook,
> Or write a book,
> Or fence, or vote,
> Or sail a boat,
> Will run a mile or run a man
> (And run the office if she can),
> Defend a burglar, drive a 'plane,
> And in the evening dance again.[2]

Members of the Herbert family pose informally for this conversation piece by Sir John Lavery in the Double Cube Room at Wilton House, home of the Earls of Pembroke. Overmantel and wall panelling were designed to take portraits by Van Dyck

No crinoline hoop to catch her foot as she climbed a stile, no uncut tresses to escape from their confining pins – how the Double Duchess's generation must have envied their granddaughters' uncorseted freedom! Over the next two decades the modern girl evolved into two distinct types: the tomboy prototype Joan Hunter Dunn, furnished and burnished by Aldershot sun, who would take on any man at any game and probably beat him; and the tiny, brittle, birdlike, ultra-smart women beloved of the current Prince of Wales.

In her novel *Love in a Cold Climate*, Nancy Mitford's young narrator, Fanny, encounters the second variety of fashionable woman at the first grown-up house party she attends.

> Veronica was small and thin and sparkling. Her bright gold hair lay on her head like a cap, perfectly smooth with a few flat curls above her forehead. She had a high bony nose, rather protruding pale blue eyes, and not much chin. She looked decadent, I thought . . . but all the same it was no good denying that she was very, very pretty and that her clothes, her jewels, her make-up and her whole appearance were the perfection of smartness. She was evidently considered to be a great wit, and as soon as the party began to warm up after a chilly start it revolved entirely round her. She bandied repartee with the various Rorys and Rolys, the other women of her own age merely giggling away at the jokes but taking no active part in them, as though they realised it would be useless to try to steal any of her limelight, while the even older people who surrounded the Montdores at the two ends of the table kept up a steady flow of grave talk, occasionally throwing an indulgent glance at 'Veronica'.
>
> Now that I had become brave I asked one of my neighbours to tell me her name, but he was so much surprised at my not knowing it that he quite forgot to answer my question.
>
> 'Veronica?' he said, stupefied. 'But surely you know Veronica?'
>
> It was as though I had never heard of Vesuvius. Afterwards I

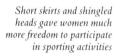

Short skirts and shingled heads gave women much more freedom to participate in sporting activities

discovered that her name was Mrs Chaddesley Corbett and it seemed strange to me that Lady Montdore, whom I had so often been told was a snob, should have only a Mrs, not even an Hon. Mrs, to stay, and treat her almost with deference. This shows how innocent, socially, I must have been in those days, since every schoolboy (every Etonian, that is) knew all about Mrs Chaddesley Corbett. She was to the other smart women of her day as the star is to the chorus, and had invented a type of looks as well as a way of talking, walking, and behaving which was slavishly copied by the fashionable set in England for at least ten years.[3]

Innocent Fanny may have been, but she had enough social acumen to sense the faintly *déclassé* aura emanating from Mrs Chaddesley Corbett and her clique. Patriotism in the First World War had been ill-rewarded. Those true-blue aristocrats who had responded to their country's call as patricians should, sending their sons, servants, and hunters to the war without flinching (and certainly without trying to wangle exemption for any of them), now found themselves deprived of all that had made their lives worth living. With no son left to inherit the family home, no servants to maintain it, taxes rising, income falling, stables empty, big rooms eerily silent, what was the point of struggling to keep the old place up to former standards? Better far to sell up to one of those rich City men who had made a packet in the war and now thought a few thousand acres and a big house would buy respectability.

So the ancient family that had been rooted to its land for three, four, five hundred years quietly faded away like a tree from which too many branches have been lopped; and in its place came the City men who had made their pile in ways that were probably best not enquired into too closely, and wanted to spend it on turning their sons into country gentlemen.

All healthy societies follow this pattern of renewal. No tears need be shed for the ancient family which has simply had its day. Similar replacement took place after the Wars of the Roses and at the Dissolution of the Monasteries. It happened again at the Restoration and after the Act of Union. Self-made men on the winning side were rewarded with estates taken from the losers; the only difference in the case of the First World War was one of scale. Never before had so many old families gone to the wall at once.

The new society which took their place was less hidebound in every way, and admitted to its ranks all sorts of people whom Theresa, Marchioness of Londonderry (for instance) would never have allowed to cross her doorstep. Actors, film stars, artists, authors, racehorse trainers, and men who worked all week in offices now enjoyed week-end parties at great country houses which, if not as grand as in former days, were a good deal more lively. (Though even in the glossiest of these gatherings, a sensitive nose like young Fanny's quivered at the faint yet unmistakable scent of *parvenu*.) The new rich had made their money from brewing or ship-building, army contracts or tobacco. Those who still depended on land for their dwindling revenues regarded them with a mixture of envy and contempt.

EWART'S
"BRILLIANT" GEYSER

halves the housework—it supplies instant and constant hot water night or day—no fire to stoke—as useful in the kitchen as in the bathroom.

Write for the free booklet " Ewart's Geysers in the Home." It shows how every hot water problem can be dealt with instantly and economically.

EWART & SON LTD., 346 Euston Road,
London, N.W.1.   (*Est.* 1834.)   'Phone : Museum 2570.

HOT WATER INSTANTLY NIGHT OR DAY

More or less malicious stories circulated regarding the social gaffes of these newcomers, the origins of their fortunes, and their desire to lose the label of Johnnie-come-lately. The first Lord Doverdale, for instance, a paper manufacturer by the name of Partington, bought Westwood Park near Droitwich from the Pakington family, together with most of its furniture and pictures. He was supposed by the uncharitable to have altered the labels on several portraits of Pakington forebears, substituting 'rt' for the 'k'.

Another Edward, Prince of Wales, had begun to make pleasure the main purpose of his life. Like his grandfather and namesake, he was not particularly choosy about the company he kept, regarding the population as either Royal or non-Royal, with no precise distinctions among the second category.

The Prince was not an imposing figure. Slightly built and slope-shouldered, he wore his ultra-fashionable clothes without distinction. He spoke with a rather common, faintly Transatlantic accent, deliberately adopted, and was an enthusiastic importer of American fashions and crazes. Nevertheless, he had a certain magnetism. Sir Alan Lascelles, who served him as assistant private secretary, wrote after their meeting in November, 1920: 'To St James' Palace, where I made my bow to H.R.H. He won me completely – he is the most attractive man I've ever met.'[4]

This enthusiasm was short-lived. No man is a hero to his valet and a private secretary, too, has a good chance to study his master's feet of clay. Sir Alan soon revised his opinion. By the time of the Abdication, he was firmly convinced that anyone as shallow, selfish and irresponsible as the Prince of Wales would make a disastrous King of England.

Meantime, all the Prince asked of his associates was that they should not bore him – and the fast, fashionable people who formed his circle did their best to keep boredom at bay.

They danced, they smoked, they drank astonishing mixtures of alcohol in the new-fangled cocktails that had arrived from America in the wake of the jazz craze and revolutionized the tedious hour before dinner. They held 'theme' parties in odd locations – swimming pools or skating rinks – they dressed up as babies, or medieval knights, or Renaissance Florentines; they drove on wild treasure-hunts along leafy country lanes or through the streets of London; in Lady Diana Cooper's words they were 'very irritating to others and utterly delightful and satisfying' to themselves.

The fun was fast and furious. Old photographs show the guests and hosts at house parties in strange clothes, continually posing and posturing as if to say, 'Look at us! Look how we're enjoying ourselves!' but the more frantically they pursued pleasure the more, in its habitual perverse way, pleasure eluded them.

Cocktail parties were by no means to everyone's taste.

> This party is rather a bore [complained A. P. Herbert],
> I shall go to such parties no more.
> Will somebody kind
> My overcoat find
> And quietly show me the door?
> I'm weary of standing about,
> Making silly remarks in a shout;
> The sandwiches taste
> Of photograph-paste,
> And now the white wine has run out![5]

Despite such strictures, hostesses welcomed the cocktail party fashion. It was an easy way to entertain large numbers of guests now that servants were becoming scarce. Few who had left domestic service during the war had felt inclined to return to it: besides, the enormous labour of keeping big houses clean and warm was gradually being lightened by ingenious new machines. The invention of the vacuum cleaner was a major breakthrough which made it possible to dispense with the services of at least a brace of housemaids; the steam iron speeded laundry work, and the miraculous power of electricity banished at a stroke the work of lamp-filling, wick-trimming, grate-scouring, range-blacking, and kindred chores; it also reduced the work of carrying coal and provided the inestimable blessing of hot water on tap.

Proprietary brands of polishes and cleaners of everything from silver to harness replaced the old home-made concoctions and found a ready market. In the garden, motorized lawnmowers superseded the horse-drawn variety, and the substitution of cars (noisy, unreliable, and smelly though they were) for carriage-horses made large reductions in the stable staff possible. Few owners gave up their horses without a pang. Even before the First World War there had been painful scenes when the new form of transport met the old in narrow streets.

Driving his sister Daphne behind a pair of mettlesome greys in Dornford Yates's novel *The Berry Scene*, Boy Pleydell spots a car in the distance:

Posing and posturing in clothing the old guard would have considered scandalous: a Guinness house party at Luggala

> Before Law and Order had seen it, I turned to the left. It was no good asking for trouble. But when I had fetched a compass, to enter the square at St Giles, there was another car fuming some fifteen paces away.
>
> Happily the square was not crowded, for the greys, with one consent, proposed to mount the pavement, if not to enter some shop.
>
> I spoke over my shoulder to William.
>
> 'Ask the chauffeur to stop his engine. Be very polite.'

*Girls learned quickly how
to repair motor-cars as well
as paint their faces*

With the tail of my eye I saw my order obeyed, but the chauffeur only laughed and let in his clutch.

There was only one thing to be done.

As the car moved forward towards us, I stood up, lashed Law and Order and let them go. Oblivious to all but the pain, the greys leaped forward, flung past the moving car and down the length of the square.

To this day I do not know how we entered Bellman Lane, but I managed to pull them up before we had reached its end.

William came running, white-faced.

'All's well,' I said, 'but stand to their heads a minute.'

While he was there, I gave the reins to Daphne and went to their heads myself. I did my best to repair the wrong I had done them, soothing them and making much of the handsome pair.

Then I turned to the groom, who clearly had news to tell.

'Yes, William. What do you know?'

'It was just beginning, sir. Joe Chinnock had got the chauffeur, and Mr Bertram was there.'

'Then we'll hear all about it later. They're all right now, I think; so we'll get along.'

But I felt better already. Joe Chinnock came out of our village, and plied a blacksmith's trade.[6]

On that occasion, at least, the wicked motorists reap what they have sown. The chauffeur ends up in the horse-trough and his master in court; but the Pleydells realize they cannot turn back the clock. A week later they own a car themselves, and taste the joys of motoring 60 miles to lunch with friends.

As far as the country house party was concerned, this new mobility

proved a mixed blessing. It gave guests rather too much independence and undermined the authority of their host. Motor cars encouraged people to flit here and there in search of pleasure instead of settling down to enjoy whatever entertainment had been planned for them. It destroyed a house party's group spirit. It was all very well to let guests treat your house as their own; less agreeable to see them treat it as an hotel.

Except in the more inaccessible parts of the country it was now rare for a house party to last more than three nights, and conducting a romance or even furthering an acquaintance was difficult on so tight a schedule. It did not help if the charming girl – or man – you took a shine to on the first evening disappeared to visit other friends next morning, leaving you to start from scratch with someone else.

That indefatigable social butterfly Henry – known as 'Chips' – Channon, American by birth but by 1935 a Member of Parliament and integral part of the English fashionable scene, began the year enthusiastically with a visit to Elveden, now back in the hands of the Guinness family, into which Chips had married.

> *8 January 1935* . . . of all the Iveagh houses, I like Elveden best. I love its calm, its luxurious Edwardian atmosphere. For a fortnight now I have slept in the Kings' bed, which both Edward VII and George V have used. And this morning, in the wee sma' hours, I had a humiliating accident – I somehow smashed the royal Chamber pot. It seems to be a habit of mine, and one much to be discouraged. At Mentmore once, staying with the Roseberys, I broke Napoleon's pot in similar circumstances, a very grand affair covered with 'N's and Bees.[7]

The social pace was hot. The Channons were invited everywhere and by July even such an addicted partygoer as Chips was beginning to flag.

> What a bore week-ends are [he complained to his diary]. Forty-eight hours social crucifixion. Ours this summer have been curious. 13 June, the Dufferins, in a hideous villa, with cocktails, gramophones, pekes and bridge. 20 June, Sutton Courtenay, roses, the river, and the youth of England splashing in the Thames, and Norah, the sublime Norah. Russian ballet, food in the courtyard, Chopin, colour, gardening, a riot, but a healthy riot of the senses, and a deep thirst for life. 27 June, Villa Trianon, Versailles, super sophistication. Toile-de-Jouy, French princesses, Sèvres, gardens lit by Wendel, flowers, one feels, by Cartier. 4 July, Tredegar; glorious house, but the feel and even smell of decay, of aristocracy in extremis, the sinister and the trivial, crucibles and crocodiles.[8]

Two years later his incipient disenchantment had turned into active dislike of country house parties. '*2 July 1937* Cliveden. I really wonder why we came here. I hate weekends, and so often feel désœuvré and bored in other people's houses, and there is nothing so out of date as a 1900 house, which Cliveden is, with its famous views and vistas.[9]

Even nocturnal passage-creeping, though still a recognized part of country house party life, had become much less exciting. People no longer pretended to be shocked, which removed the delicious *frisson*

Opposite: Lady Diana Manners, youngest daughter of the Duke of Rutland, married the politician and diplomat Duff Cooper, and won international renown when she starred in the stage production of 'The Miracle'

Right: Sir Henry ('Chips') Channon: American-born MP, diarist, and indefatigable partygoer

Far right: A younger Lady Londonderry, daughter of Viscount Chaplin, as Queen Joanna of Scotland in the 'Pageant of England', 1935

of tiptoeing along dark corridors in search of the beloved's room; and the risk of running into an early-rising maid on one's return trip was much reduced. There were times, though, when this general attitude of *laissez-faire* produced problems of its own.

Returning from an early morning stroll with the lion of the house party, the fascinating Duc de Sauveterre, Nancy Mitford's young narrator in *Love in a Cold Climate* finds Hampton Place in uproar:

> The front door opened on a scene of great confusion, most of the house party, some in tweeds and some in dressing-gowns, were assembled in the hall, as were various outdoor and indoor servants, while a village police-men, who in the excitement of the moment had brought his bicycle in with him, was conferring with Lord Montdore. High above our heads, leaning over the balustrade in front of Niobe, Lady Montdore, in a mauve satin wrap, was shouting at her husband:
>
> 'Tell him we must have Scotland Yard down at once, Montdore. If he won't send for them I shall ring up the Home Secretary myself . . .'
>
> It seemed that there had been a burglary during the night and that nearly everybody in the house, except Lord and Lady Montdore, had been roundly robbed of jewels, loose cash, furs, and anything portable of the kind that happened to be lying about. What made it particularly annoying for the victims was that they had all been woken up by somebody prowling in their rooms, but had all immediately concluded that it must be Sauveterre, pursuing his well-known hobby, so that the husbands had merely turned over with a grunt, saying, 'Sorry, old chap, it's only me, I should try next door,' while the wives had lain quite still in a happy trance of desire, murmuring such words of encouragement as they knew in French.[10]

If you ask any upper class young adult of the late thirties why their generation paid so little heed to the visibly mounting menace of German National Socialism, you are likely to get one of two answers: 'We couldn't believe Germany would fight again'; or, 'We were too busy enjoying ourselves to bother about what was happening in Germany.'

Both answers are true as far as they go. It *did* seem incredible that the ruined and bankrupt country humiliated by the Treaty of Versailles should rise from its ashes with revenge in mind; and it *was* a full-time business for the dedicated socialite to keep abreast of the English social scene. The small world of the Edwardians had now expanded to the point where there were groups within groups, and it was hardly possible to know what was happening in all of them.

But an equally valid though less creditable reason was that among England's upper crust, Hitler had plenty of admirers. He was, they said at country house parties up and down the land, not a bad chap at all. Look at the way he had put Germany back on its feet – built roads, stamped out unemployment, made things hum. As for reports of his followers' ill-treatment of Jews, what of it? Hadn't those filthy Hebrews been asking

Presentation to the Sovereign was an important landmark in a girl's entry to Society. Here a debutante makes her curtsey to King Edward VIII

The Duke and Duchess of Windsor's unconcealed admiration for Hitler gave a boost to Nazi morale

for it for years, with their tiresome talent for making money and their stubborn refusal to integrate with the rest of the population? They were so sharp they shouldn't be surprised if they cut themselves. It wasn't decent to be so rich: a little rough handling wouldn't do them any harm. And so on and so forth.

Despite the efforts of King Edward VII, despite respect and admiration for individual Jews such as Disraeli or the Rothschilds, Cassels and Sassoons, the old fear and suspicion of the alien race was deep-rooted among the English upper classes. In fiction, as in life, Jews made convenient scapegoats – ready-made villains for granite-jawed clubland heroes such as Richard Hannay, Bulldog Drummond, and Jonathan Mansel to pit their wits against.

Hitler's hugely successful public relations exercise in staging the 1936 Olympic Games in Berlin completed the wool-pulling over English eyes which were only too pleased to be so blinkered. Distinguished English visitors eagerly accepted invitations to the Games and revelled in the lavish hospitality of the Nazi hierarchy. Lord and Lady Kemsley arrived in Kiel in their private yacht; Chips and Lady Honor Channon flew to Templehof to be met by their personal ADC, Baron von Geyr, and a Government car driven by a brown-shirted stormtrooper, both of which were put at their disposal for the whole of their visit. Lord Jellicoe and Kenneth Lindsay, MP, represented the Houses of Lords and Commons respectively; and Sir Austen and Lady Chamberlain accompanied the

Kemsleys (though as he refused to set foot on German soil he saw nothing of the Games).

A more objective – indeed, critical – eye watching the Nazis at play belonged to Sir Robert Vansittart, a diplomat of wide experience who was brother-in-law to the British Ambassador, Sir Eric Phipps, one of the few who perceived the menace of Nazism and constantly reiterated these fears to Whitehall, where they went unheeded. In a letter of 24 April 1936, Phipps wrote: 'The fact is that the Germans want to do that almost impossible thing (even with old English ladies and Bishops), viz., to deceive *everybody all the time.*'[11]

Despite Nazi hospitality and propaganda, despite Hitler's personal efforts to charm him and his wife, Sir Robert Vansittart remained hostile to everything National Socialism stood for. Chips Channon was more easily wooed, though now and again his diary sounds a warning note.

After an evening garden party given by Goering in the grounds of the huge new Air Ministry, where the *corps de ballet* from the Berlin Opera danced on the lawn, and the guests were entertained with merry-go-rounds, shooting-galleries, wine and beer booths and charming actresses in Tyrolean costume, he wrote: 'It was fantastic. Peasants dancing and *schuhplattling*, vast women carrying pretzels and beer, a ship, a beerhouse, crowds of gay, laughing people, animals . . . "There has never been

Sir Robert Vansittart at the Anglo-German talks of 1931. His warnings about Hitler and Nazi intentions were ignored by Whitehall until too late. With Prime Minister Ramsey MacDonald (left) and the German Foreign Minister (right)

anything quite like this since the days of Louis Quatorze", someone remarked. "Not since Nero", I retorted.'[12]

He was right. Not Rome alone, but the whole civilized world was about to erupt in flames while the English fiddled, and told one another the Nazis weren't half as black as they were painted. The veteran statesman David Lloyd George visited Hitler in Berchtesgaden in September 1936, and wrote so enthusiastic an account of the interview that he was said not only to have whitewashed Hitler, but blacked his boots as well.

Soon Sir Robert Vansittart was removed to the post of chief diplomatic adviser to the Foreign Secretary, where he could do little to obstruct the growth of Anglo-German friendship. Sir Oswald Mosley's British Fascist Party continued to attract new members, and Neville Chamberlain reiterated his promise of 'Peace in our time'.

King George V had died in January 1936. After an uneasy reign lasting less than a year, the abdication of his successor, King Edward VIII, to marry the twice-divorced American Wallis Simpson shook English Society to its foundations. With considerable mental anguish, social high-flyers such as Chips Channon and Lady Diana Cooper faced the fact that they had put their money on the wrong Royal horse. The future lay with the dull, decent, dutiful, domestic Duke of York and his vivacious little Duchess, neither of whom had ever wanted to be smart or witty any more than they had coveted the Crown.

As the Duke of Windsor sailed away to lifelong exile, a good many of his ideals went with him, among them that of friendship with Nazi Germany. Slowly British public opinion awoke to the fact that Hitler had been allowed to go not only far enough but a great deal too far. Men like Harold Nicolson and Duff Cooper, who had opposed Nazism ever since Hitler seized power in Germany, now found their fears shared by friends who had hitherto laughed at them. Germany's military might had grown unchecked despite all Sir Eric Phipps's warnings. For years these had been gathering dust in Whitehall files. Suddenly – too late – they were hideously relevant. By 1939 Austria had been annexed, Czechoslovakia swallowed. Now Hitler's troops threatened to overrun Poland.

With deep reluctance, English heads were withdrawn from the sand in which they had been buried, and blinkered eyes uncovered to see how perilously the balance of power in Europe was out of kilter. The long week-end was over. If England was to survive, she would have to fight for her life.

CHAPTER ELEVEN

Letting in the Jungle

To form some idea of the straits to which the owners of large country houses were reduced during the Second World War, one only has to look at the number that were offered to the National Trust at that time.

In 1942, the Trust was 47 years old and had a membership of 6,000. It owned 75,000 acres and about a half-dozen historic houses, and was administered by a skeleton staff, four male and four female. James Lees-Milne, who had been invalided out of the Army in 1941, rejoined the National Trust's Headquarters Staff, then based at West Wycombe Park, as its Historic Buildings Secretary. It was his job to assess the interest and importance of the houses offered to the Trust by owners who could no longer afford to maintain them.

This demanded patience and tact as well as a clear idea of what was and what was not acceptable. It is not an easy decision to hand over to strangers the home that has been your family's pride for centuries, and frequently the owners most eager to be quit of their hereditary burden jibbed when it came to discussing details of the endowment they must make before the National Trust agreed to preserve the house. Giving your home away is bad enough. Paying to give it away was more than some could stomach. Yet what alternative had they? Such owners were usually old, struggling to manage without the servants they had depended on all their lives, in despair as they realized the impossible cost of maintaining ancient roofs and fabric. Often the decision to offer the house to the National Trust had been precipitated by the death in action of one or more sons; nerves were raw, and negotiations had to be handled with great delicacy.

These problems were compounded when the proposed gift proved unacceptable or the endowment inadequate. In February 1943, James Lees-Milne had

> a horrible day with Colonel Pemberton at Pyrland Hall near Taunton. He is a fiendish old imbecile with a grotesque white moustache. When I first saw him he was pirouetting on his toes in the road. He has an inordinate opinion of himself and his own judgement. He is absolutely convinced that Pyrland is the finest house in Somerset and he is doing the Trust a great service in bequeathing it . . .

James Lees-Milne was appointed in 1941 Historic Buildings Secretary to the National Trust. Through his efforts much of England's heritage of country houses was saved from ruin

I was drawn into several acrimonious arguments with the old man, whom I cordially disliked, for he insisted in contradicting whatever I said. He gave me an exiguous lunch of bread and cheese, both hard as wood, a baked potato in its own skin, dry as sawdust, and watery apple with Bird's custard. Ugh!'[1]

The hospitality he received at Stourhead, home of Sir Henry Hoare, was an improvement on Colonel Pemberton's, though the house's owners verged on the picaresque.

Sir Henry is an astonishing nineteenth-century John Bull, hobbling on two sticks. He was wearing a pepper and salt suit and a frayed grey billycock over his purple face . . .

En route for Stourhead I sat in the back of the car beside him and behind an old chauffeur of immense, overlapping fatness who had an asthmatic wheeze, like a blacksmith's bellows. Sir Henry talked about his bad knee, and told me he had lost a knee-cap. I found myself shouting, for he is rather deaf, 'Do you find it much of a handicap having no knee-cap?' After the third repetition I decided that my remark was inept.

Lady Hoare is an absolute treasure, and unique. She is tall, ugly and eighty-two; dressed in a long black skirt, belled from a wasp waist and trailing over her ankles. She has a thick net blouse over a rigidly-upholstered bosom, complete with stiff, whaleboned high collar round the throat. Over this a black and white check jacket, evidently reinforced with stays, for it ends in tight points over her thighs. The sleeves are exaggeratedly mutton-chop. She has a protruding square coif of frizzly grey hair in the style of the late nineties, black eyebrows and the thickest spectacle lenses

I have ever seen. She is nearly blind in one eye. She is humorous and enchanting . . .

The Hoares took me round the house, which is packed to the brim with good things, and some ghastly things like cheap bamboo cake stands and thin silver vases filled with peacocks' feathers . . .

For dinner we had soup, whiting, pheasant, apple pie, dessert, a white Rhine wine and port. Lady Hoare has no housemaid, and only a cook and butler. But she said with satisfaction, 'The Duchess of Somerset at Maiden Bradley has to do all her own cooking.'

We ate in the little dining-room at a long table, Sir Henry with his back to a colonnaded screen, Lady Hoare with hers to the window. He spoke very little, and that little addressed to himself. She kept up a lively, not entirely coherent prattle. She said to me, 'Don't you find the food better in this war than in the last?' I replied that I was rather young during the last war, but I certainly remembered the rancid margarine we were given at preparatory school when I was eight. 'Oh!' she said. 'You were lucky. We were reduced to eating rats.' I was a little surprised, until Sir Henry looked up and said, 'No, no, Alda. You keep getting your wars wrong. That was when you were in Paris during the Commune.'[2]

Country house parties were impossible in such circumstances. Even people who retained one or two servants rejected by the Armed Forces on the grounds of age or incapacity were under too much strain to enjoy themselves. The entries in James Lees-Milne's diary which describe a week-end spent with Lord and Lady Kennet at Fritton capture the weary edginess of wartime.

Friday, 7 August We dined off rabbit, claret, nectarines and raspberries. I am already getting a few spots from all this fruit . . .

Saturday, 8 August I stroll about with K [Kathleen, widow of Captain R. F. Scott of the Antarctic, who had later married the 1st Lord Kennet] in the morning after being given breakfast in bed. I find myself strangely tired and long to be left alone with the book I have picked up here, Geikie Cobb's on the Ductless Glands, instead of embarking on intense conversations with K so early in the day. I give up, for one must pull one's weight a bit in other people's houses when one has been such a fool as to visit them . . .

Sunday, 9 August The others sail spasmodically on the lake in their beastly boats, but the water bores me and I don't go near it. When we all meet up the fun is not furious and the conversation not sparkling. I feel discontented and unwell. Indeed, I wonder why on earth I ever came.[3]

Food rationing and national exhaustion made even the simplest form of entertaining difficult after the war ended, and the Labour Government which swept to power in 1946 brought a host of new worries to the owners of large country houses. Not only were rates and taxes rising steeply. There was also a growing section of the public that had begun to take a proprietary interest in England's historic houses and demand their preservation – at the owner's expense. In a modern version of Morton's Fork, these unfortunates found themselves unable to keep their houses up, and forbidden to pull them down.

The stately homes of England [sang Noel Coward's four lordlings]
We proudly represent,
We only keep them up
For Americans to rent;
Now the pipe that supplies the bathroom's burst
And the lavatory makes you fear the worst,
(It was used by Charles the First
Quite informally; and later by George the Fourth
On a journey north.)
The state apartments keep their
Historical renown.
It's wiser not to sleep there,
In case they tumble down;
But if they should happen to catch on fire –
Which with any luck they might –
We'll fight
For the stately homes of England![4]

How many owners must have been sorely tempted to strike the match that would have made a bonfire of some vast Victorian pile, impossible to clean or heat, a bottomless pit of expense that no one would buy, an ever-reproachful reminder of days that had gone for good?

Though many stately homes were intrinsically beautiful – Longleat, for instance, or Hever Castle in Kent, or Burghley House in Lincolnshire (to name only a sample) – a great many others were not only huge but hideous, built or enlarged when Victorian architecture was at its ugliest.

England's largest country house: Wentworth Woodhouse, Yorkshire, seat of the Earls Fitzwilliam

Even the monstrosities of Eaton Hall and Welbeck Abbey paled into insignificance beside Wentworth, seat of the Earls Fitzwilliam, the largest country house in England, uncomfortable, unwieldy, and with 300 bedrooms.

Despite the temptations, few owners went so far as to destroy their properties. Instead, with remarkable resilience, they sought ways of making silk purses from these huge, intractable sows' ears. The ugliest houses were generally sold for a song to local authorities who turned them into schools, nursing homes, or lunatic asylums. Others had wings lopped off to restore them to more manageable proportions, which were often their original ones. Some became hotels, country clubs, or conference centres; still more resourceful owners opened their homes to the public, reasoning that if the taxpayer wanted such houses preserved, he must pay for them himself. Where the architectural interest was not enough of a draw to fill the coach-parks, adventurous spirits found new ways to drum up custom: a motor museum at Beaulieu, home of Lord Montagu; lions at Longleat, seat of the Marquess of Bath; giraffes, sea-lions, gorillas, and zebras to supplement the long-standing attraction of rare deer at the Duke of Bedford's home, Woburn Abbey. Today there is hardly a great country house in England that does not boast a garden centre selling plants, shrubs, rustic seats, and dried-flower arrangements in the huge walled kitchen garden where once twenty or more gardeners toiled to supply family needs alone.

Certain noble owners developed an unexpected talent for publicity and competed keenly to draw the biggest crowds of lolly-licking sightseers; but such natural showmen were rare. More often it was only his deep love of his family home and reluctance to be the one to part with it that compelled an owner to open his doors to the public.

The 10th Duke of Beaufort, Master of the Horse to Queen Elizabeth II and known as 'Master' to all who hunted with him, found an original solution to the problem of making public use of his land without ruining its character. His generosity in inviting the British Horse Society to stage a three-day event annually in his park, for the purpose of training and selecting a British equestrian team, has made Badminton famous throughout the sporting world. The first horse trials were held there in 1949, and the event now attracts a quarter of a million visitors every year, as well as an enormous amount of trade. The steady success of British three-day event teams in international competitions owes much to the Duke of Beaufort and his successor, who continues the tradition of keeping open house for the competitors and their grooms throughout the competition, as well as entertaining a large and frequently Royal house party in Badminton itself. Part of the beauty of the scheme is that for the rest of the year the Duke has the house and grounds to himself, unlike those owners of stately homes who have opted for safari parks or museums, which inevitably place certain constraints upon their own freedom.

Quite apart from the constant need to supervise the public who are making free with his house and grounds in the inimitable way of the British – dropping litter, feeding animals despite all prohibitions, pushing open doors marked 'Private' and plucking cuttings from choice shrubs – the owner of a stately home is liable to find himself caged in his own house. The wing set apart for family use is probably no bigger than an ordinary house and very much less convenient, having been designed as part of a whole, not complete in itself. There is unlikely to be room to accommodate even a dozen guests: on the other hand, it is difficult to entertain a rollicking house party in state apartments while the paying public is walking through them.

In the years immediately after the Second World War, house party guests had to be prepared for anything. A degree of eccentricity was considered smart. Evelyn Waugh was not easily surprised, but life in Lord Walston's household struck him as sufficiently bizarre to deserve comment.

> I went to such an extraordinary house on Wednesday [he wrote in 1948]. A side of life I never saw before – very rich, Cambridge, Jewish, socialist, highbrow, scientific, farming. There were Picassos on sliding panels & when you pushed them back plate glass & a stable with a stallion looking at one. No servants. Lovely Carolean silver unpolished. Gourmets' wines and cigars. The house a series of wood bungalows, more bathrooms than bedrooms. The hostess at six saying, 'I say shall we have dinner tonight as Evelyn's here. Usually we have only Shredded Wheat. I'll see what there is.' Goes to tiny kitchenette and comes back. 'Well, there's grouse, partridges, ham, a leg of mutton and half a cold goose' (literally). 'What does anyone want?' Then a children's nannie dining with us called 'Twinkle' dressed with tremendous starched frills and celluloid collars, etc. and everyone talking to her about lesbianism and masturbation. House telephone so that generally people don't bother to meet but just telephone from room to room.[5]

During the lean fifties and early sixties, the only times the great houses came to life were for coming-of-age parties or coming-out balls. A system of *quid pro quo* now operated. If you accepted an invitation to another girl's ball, you were honour bound to ask her to yours. If your parents preferred to launch you with a series of cocktail parties, you might still accept a friend's ball, but to accept her cocktail party as well put you under an uncomfortable obligation which you might be able to discharge by asking her to join your party at Ascot (a useful riposte if her parents were divorced and thus ineligible for the Royal Enclosure).

Despite this rather bureaucratic insistence on evenhandedness, people were generous about lending their houses for balls, and when there was one in the offing neighbours rallied round most gallantly with offers to accommodate six, eight, or even ten young people who might be total strangers both to their hosts and to one another. Gone were the close-knit family ties, the restrictions of birth and breeding that had kept the Edwardian house party world within such comfortable limits. Two world wars, two influxes of new money and standards, plus a much looser interpretation of the terms 'lady' and 'gentleman' had thrown open the social scene to anyone with the money and will to compete there.

A pride of lions at Longleat House, Wiltshire, home of the Marquess of Bath. In partnership with Jimmy Chipperfield, of the circus family, he established one of England's first safari parks

These house parties were only a pale shadow of their Edwardian predecessors. Very young men have not the confidence or sophistication to be rewarding guests, and 'debs' delights' were either well-mannered, safe, dull boys fresh from public school, or fascinating raffish young men with the warning label FI – Financially Insecure – or NSIT – Not Safe In Taxis – scribbled against their names in the invitation lists passed from one hostess's hand to the next. In the same way, girls who had been educated at single-sex boarding schools, then briefly 'polished' in Paris, Florence, or Geneva, were inclined to blush when confronted by males, and preferred to giggle with old school-friends instead of trying to extend their acquaintance.

Yet, however haphazardly, young people got to know one another well over those spring and summer months when every night there were three or four London balls to choose from and every week-end a house party in a different part of the country. These followed, as far as possible, the old pattern of hospitality whose rules had been laid down by the Marlborough House Set – the main difference being the extreme youth of the guests. One seldom met a man over 25 years (by which age he would have finished with National Service and university and might have begun to think about marriage as well as his career). For the sad fact was that after the Second World War scions of even the noblest houses could no longer look forward to a life of uninterrupted leisure. Work had become a necessary part of a gentleman's life. Fledgling stockbrokers, merchant bankers, and publishers would stumble bleary-eyed into their offices after dancing all night with girls who were – most unfairly – free to sleep until noon if they pleased. There was a brisk trade in hangover cures and a fair

Sad scene of dereliction at Mavisbank, Midlothian, designed by William Adam. By 1976 it had become a graveyard for wrecked cars

number of nervous breakdowns among young men who burned the candle at both ends too enthusiastically.

It was difficult for hostesses to rope in a quorum of young men for daytime festivities, and further complications arose when social life impinged upon office hours. Many were the 'grandmother's funerals' arranged during Ascot week; and young men gallantly risked their jobs in order to escort debs to the Fourth of June, Henley, Wimbledon or Glorious Goodwood.

Their week-ends, at least, were their own and they made the most of them. Breathless young men would sprint along the platform at Paddington just in time to leap aboard the west-bound 4.45 which would get them to Kemble, Evesham, or Hereford in time to change before dinner. Dashing little red MGs would zigzag through the rush-hour traffic heading north, south, east, or west of London, at the start of a 100 mile journey to the country house where they were due to change, dine, and dance the night away.

In those pre-disco days, country bands were reluctant to break the Sabbath, particularly north of the border, so coming-out balls or hunt balls were held on Friday night. By the time 'breakfast' was served at 3 a.m., young men who had done a full day's work at the office were asleep on their feet, and it was not unknown for them to nod off at the wheel when driving their partner home through the misty dawn.

'Shall I give you my Shakespeare monologue?' one deb used to ask if she noticed her escort yawn. 'Five minutes or ten. Guaranteed to keep you awake.' If even this remedy failed there was nothing for it but to pull into a lay-by and let him sleep it off, knowing there would be curious stares at breakfast; the inevitable question from one's hostess, half jocular, half censorious: 'What time did *you* two get in?' 'Oh, sometime after six, I suppose.'

There was a certain kudos in being the last back. Anyone obliged to accept her hostess's offer of a lift home felt a miserable failure.

More entertainment would fill Saturday: point-to-point meetings in spring; tennis or swimming parties or picnics in summer. There would probably be a small informal dance on Saturday night, carpets rolled back and gramophone stacked with crooners. The couples swaying with closed eyes about the dimly-lit floor in the small hours of Sunday morning were more often in the throes of exhaustion than passion, and though some mothers reckoned that only a third of the year's debs would end their first season virgin, sleeping around was – by modern standards – surprisingly rare. Before the pill, pregnancy was a very real fear and, since most debs' delights were hardly the stuff of which dreams are made, not worth risking. Occasionally word would filter through the tea parties and cocktail parties that a girl had had to postpone her dance because of 'emergency appendicitis', and heads would nod wisely. Everyone knew what *that* meant.

From the vantage point of the eighties, when young partygoers arrive with a precautionary sleeping-bag rolled up in the back seat of the car, and expect to be slung out after breakfast next morning, I feel immensely grateful to those generous hosts and hostesses of the late fifties, who entertained callow strangers so unstintingly. It must have cost

Vegetation encroaches at Grange Park, Hants, designed by William Wilkins

them untold time and effort, as well as money. Sometimes they hired staff for the occasion. When they didn't the strain was inclined to show.

'Put your shoes outside your door if they need cleaning. The gardener's boy will see to them.' But if you heard shoes being dropped outside your door early next morning and were tactless enough to open it, you would probably come face to face with your host, and the fiction of the 'gardener's boy' would be blown. Better to pretend, with your hosts, that a large, willing, but strangely invisible staff was padding silently from room to room, stoking boilers, pulling curtains, turning down beds and lighting fires, as well as cooking and washing-up, while the house party sunned itself on the terrace or read the Sunday newspapers.

I remember the time when six of us were parked for the week-end of a friend's ball in a lovely old moated house in Herefordshire. We travelled down by train and were met at the station by a neat soldierly figure in chauffeur's uniform. He drove us the dozen miles to the house and carried in our cases.

His wife, the housekeeper, showed us to our rooms. She apologized on behalf of Colonel and Mrs H—. They would have liked to be there to greet us, but had to go to a meeting. Please would we start dinner without them, since the dance began at 10.30?

The chauffeur changed into a black coat and waited on us at table as we ate a delicious dinner. He plied us all with wine and the boys with port and brandy until the party became very merry.

There was still no sign of Colonel and Mrs H— when we left the table, well after eleven, so the housekeeper said we had better start for the dance, and our host and hostess would follow in the other car.

The chauffeur drove us another 15 miles to the floodlit castle where we found the ball in full swing. I am ashamed to say I never gave our absent hosts another thought until the chauffeur was driving us home, half-asleep, through the pearly dawn, when someone remarked what a a pity it was that Colonel and Mrs H— had missed the whole party.

The chauffeur gave him a sideways glance. 'Oh dear, didn't they find you, sir? They were there, all right. They got there only a few minutes after we did.' He shrugged. 'I suppose in all that crowd . . .'

It seemed reasonable enough. I didn't smell a rat then, or even next morning, when we woke just in time to eat a delicious cold lunch and scramble into our whites for tennis and a tea party at another house. Hardly had we returned from that, than we had to bathe and change for drinks and dancing with still more neighbours . . .

So it went on. Colonel and Mrs H— had gone to church when we woke, but the chauffeur drove us to another party and picnic lunch on the river; then suddenly it was seven o'clock and we must hurry to catch the train back to London.

We all wrote extravagant bread-and-butter letters, saying how much we had enjoyed it all, and how sorry we were never to have seen our kind hosts. Of course, if they *had* been there, we might not have laughed so loudly or eaten and drunk with such abandon. Or were they? That chauffeur's smile . . . I still wonder.

If the twenties had seen the dawn of the Age of the Common Man, by the late 1960s it had reached its high noon. Though money was again available for private entertaining, it tended to accumulate in different hands from before the war. Egalitarianism became the fashion and marks of distinction and privilege were carefully erased even by those who had once been proud of them. Peers dropped their titles like hot bricks.

Regional accents replaced the clipped 'Oxford English' formerly heard over the air-waves, and Etonians cultivated the nasal intonation of Brum for protective colouring.

Denim, once the uniform of the labouring French peasant, now clothed the noblest English legs, and rollneck sweaters were preferred to collars and ties.

Manners took a sharp turn for the worse. Meaningless yet agreeable gestures of chivalry towards women shrivelled in the scorn of militant feminism. Men remained sprawled in their chairs as women entered the room, walked on the inside of pavements, and stopped opening car doors for them. Invitations went unanswered or were curtly refused by telephone. Boorish behaviour became the norm and there seemed little hope of reversing the trend.

All this was deeply discouraging for party-givers. Even with the support of numerous servants, entertaining people in your home is hard work and always has been. When guests express neither pleasure nor gratitude and leave your house looking like Passchendaele, serious doubts arise as to whether the game is worth the candle.

There was now, besides, an ever-present fear of bad publicity. The

Gatcombe Park, Gloucestershire, bought by H.M. the Queen from R. A. Butler as a home for Princess Anne and Captain Mark Phillips. The annual Horse Trials they hold there attract top-class Eventers

spirit of envy was strong in Fleet Street, and editors considered fashionable hostesses fair game. Nor could party-givers depend on the loyalty of
their guests to keep their mouths buttoned. It was distressing and
distasteful for a hostess to read a highly-coloured account of her party
couched in terms calculated to foment class hatred in the gossip columns
of the gutter press: doubly so when she knew the information must have
been supplied by one of her guests. But now so many members of the
upper classes earned their living in journalism and photography, what
could she expect?

Gatecrashing – originally a twenties phenomenon – became so
prevalent that party-givers found it necessary to hire bouncers and
security guards for the purpose of ejecting uninvited guests. I remember a
dance at Cliveden which a number of young bloods from Oxford decided
to gatecrash. Using Commando techniques, they slipped through the
security net and infiltrated the grounds, then found a convenient garden
shed in which to change into their hired evening rig of starched white
shirt, white tie, and tails. Alas for them, they had been misinformed: the
invitations had specified Black Tie. Dressed like the waiters, they stuck
out like sore thumbs, were quickly spotted and unceremoniously hustled
out.

The result of these social tribulations was that private entertaining
went underground – and there, for the moment, it remains. Instead of
courting publicity, wise and resourceful hostesses now take steps to
muzzle the press, cultivating the acquaintance of newspaper proprietors
and persuading them to call off their newshounds. There has also been a
radical pruning of guest-lists to eliminate blabbers. Every detail of a
showbiz party is nowadays made available to an avid public, but a
week-end party attended by cabinet ministers, Royalty and captains of
industry is likely to go unreported – by special request. Eminent people
have perfected the art of enjoying themselves out of range of the telephoto
lenses. When the Prince of Wales enjoys a day's hunting while staying
with friends, he joins the Field unobtrusively as they jog to the first
covert. It is better than attracting attention at the meet. There is, besides, a
tacit understanding that if public figures are harried beyond a certain
point, they might decide to lay down the burden of public life. There is,
after all, a precedent within living memory, and it is no part of any
newspaper proprietor's strategy to kill the goose that lays the golden eggs.

Chroniclers of the future are unlikely to find whole bookshelves lined
with memoirs of country house parties in the late twentieth century.
Diary-keeping is out of fashion, and memoirs intended for publication
tend to concentrate on more serious matters. Yet the urge to entertain is as
strong as ever: however invisibly, the fun goes on.

Much has changed, yet much remains. Where once it required
courage to opt out of church-going on Sunday, it now takes a brave man
to insist on going. House party routine is more flexible than it was, but
still the hostess calls the tune. Like any healthy institution, it has adapted
to the times. While the stately homes of England remain, country house
parties will continue to flourish.

Notes

Introduction
1 Anon., Christchurch MS.

Chapter One *The Small World*
1 V. Sackville-West, *The Edwardians* (Hogarth Press, 1930).
2 Lady Frederick Cavendish, *Diaries*, Vol. II (London, 1912).
3 Isabel Colegate, *The Shooting Party* (Hamish Hamilton, 1980).
4 Sackville-West, *The Edwardians*.
5 Frances Warwick, *Afterthoughts* (London, 1920).
6 Ibid.
7 Ibid.
8 Mrs Alexander, in *Hymns Ancient and Modern*.
9 Lord Ernest Hamilton, *Old Days and New* (Hodder, 1923).

Chapter Two *The Widow and the Rake*
2 The Duke of Portland, *Men, Women, and Things* (Faber, 1937).
1 Lady Frederick Cavendish, *Diaries*, Vol. I (John Murray, 1912).
3 Frederick Ponsonby, *Recollections of Three Reigns* (Eyre & Spottiswoode, 1952).
4 James Lees-Milne, *Ancestral Voices* (Chatto & Windus, 1975).
5 Portland, *Men, Women, and Things*.
6 Ponsonby, *Recollections*.
7 Frances Warwick, *Afterthoughts* (London, 1920).
8 Ponsonby, *Recollections*.
9 *Queen Victoria's Highland Journals*, edited by David Duff (Webb & Bower, 1980).
10 Ibid.
11 Ponsonby, *Recollections*.
12 Ibid.
13 Ibid.
14 Cavendish, *Diaries*, Vol. I.
15 Ibid.
16 James Lees-Milne, *Another Self* (Hamish Hamilton, 1970).
17 Isabel Colegate, *The Shooting Party* (Hamish Hamilton, 1980).
18 Lord Ernest Hamilton, *Old Days and New* (Hodder, 1923).
19 Ibid.
20 Elinor Glyn, *Romantic Adventure* (Nicolson & Watson, 1936).
21 Warwick, *Afterthoughts*.
22 Portland, *Men, Women, and Things*.
23 Ponsonby, *Recollections*.
24 Ibid.
25 Ibid.

Chapter Three *Four Hostesses*

1 Lady Frederick Cavendish, *Diaries*, Vol. II (John Murray, 1912).
2 Frances Warwick, *Afterthoughts* (London, 1920).
3 Lady Eleanor Stanley's letter quoted by Anita Leslie in *Edwardians in Love* (Hutchinson, 1972).
4 The Duchess of Devonshire, *The House* (Macmillan, 1978).
5 The Duke of Portland, *Men, Women, and Things* (Faber, 1937).
6 Warwick, *Afterthoughts*.
7 J. G. Ruffer, *The Big Shots* (Debrett, 1977).
8 Christopher Hibbert, *The English: A Social History, 1066–1945* (Guild Publishing, 1987).
9 Elinor Glyn, *Romantic Adventure* (Nicolson & Watson, 1936).
10 Ibid.
11 Ibid.
12 Ibid.
13 Ibid.
14 Ibid.
15 Ibid.
16 Lord Ernest Hamilton, *Old Days and New* (Hodder, 1923).
17 Hibbert, *The English*.
18 Ruffer, *The Big Shots*.
19 Lady Randolph Churchill, *Reminiscences* (Butterworth, 1908).

Chapter Four *Sporting House Parties*

1 Frances Warwick, *Afterthoughts* (London, 1920).
2 The Duke of Portland, *Men, Women, and Things* (Faber, 1937).
3 Lady Randolph Churchill, *Reminisicences* (London, 1908).
4 Ibid.
5 Roger Mortimer, *The History of the Derby Stakes* (Cassell, 1962).
6 Ibid.
7 Ibid.
8 Ibid.
9 Ibid.
10 Warwick, *Afterthoughts*.
11 Frederick Ponsonby, *Recollections of Three Reigns* (Eyre & Spottiswoode, 1952).
12 Transcript of court case, 1891, in *The Times*, quoted by Virginia Cowles, in *Edward VII and his Circle* (Hamish Hamilton, 1956).
13 Portland, *Men, Women, and Things*.
14 Transcript of court case, *The Times*.
15 Lord Ernest Hamilton, *The Halcyon Era* (Hodder, 1925).
16 Lady Frederick Cavendish, *Diaries*, Vol. I (John Murray, 1912).
17 Churchill, *Reminiscences*.
18 Ibid.
19 Ibid.
20 John Welcome, *The Sporting Empress* (Michael Joseph, 1975).
21 *Margot Asquith: Autobiography* (Butterworth, 1920).
22 R. S. Surtees, *Mr Sponge's Sporting Tour* (Bradbury & Evans, 1853).
23 Hamilton, *Halcyon Era*.

Chapter Five *Fine Feathers*

1 A. P. Herbert, *Tantivy Towers* (Ernest Benn, 1930).
2 Lord Ernest Hamilton, *Old Days and New* (Hodder, 1923).
3 Christopher Hibbert, *King Edward VII* (London, 1976).
4 Ibid.
5 Lord Ernest Hamilton, *The Halcyon Era* (Hodder, 1925).
6 Ibid.

7 V. Sackville-West, *The Edwardians* (Hogarth Press, 1930).
8 Lady Randolph Churchill, *Reminiscences* (London, 1908).
9 Isabel Colegate, *The Shooting Party*. (Hamish Hamilton, 1980).
10 Lady Frederick Cavendish, *Diaries*, Vol. I (London, 1912).
11 Ibid.
12 Frederick Ponsonby, *Recollections of Three Reigns* (Eyre & Spottiswoode, 1952).
13 Hamilton, *Old Days and New*.
14 Frances Warwick, *Afterthoughts* (London, 1920).
15 Elinor Glyn, *Romantic Adventure* (Nicolson & Watson, 1936).
16 Hamilton, *Old Days and New*.
17 H. J. Bruce, *Silken Dalliance* (Constable, 1948).
18 The Duchess of Devonshire, *The House* (Macmillan, 1978).
19 Hamilton, *Old Days and New*.
20 The Duke of Portland, *Men, Women, and Things* (Faber, 1937).
21 Sackville-West, *The Edwardians*.
22 Ibid.
23 Ibid.
24 Ibid.
25 Portland, *Men, Women, and Things*.
26 R. S. Surtees, *Mr Sponge's Sporting Tour* (Bradbury & Evans, 1853).
27 Devonshire, *The House*.
28 Warwick, *Afterthoughts*.
29 Hamilton, *Old Days and New*.
30 Christopher Hibbert, *The English: A Social History, 1066–1945* (Guild Publishing, 1987).
31 Devonshire, *The House*.
32 Fanny Cradock, *The Lormes of Castle Rising* (W. H. Allen, 1980).
33 Hamilton, *Halcyon Era*.
34 Colegate, *The Shooting Party*.
35 Hamilton, *Halcyon Era*.
36 Hibbert, *The English*.
37 Ibid.
38 George Cornwallis-West, *Edwardian Hey-days* (Putnam, 1930)
39 Elinor Glyn, *Romantic Adventure*.
40 Warwick, *Afterthoughts*.
41 Sackville-West, *The Edwardians*.

Chapter Six *The Marriage Mart*

1 Elinor Glyn, *Romantic Adventure* (Nicolson & Watson, 1936).
2 Ibid.
3 The Duke of Portland, *Men, Women, and Things* (Faber, 1937).
4 Ibid.
5 Lady Randolph Churchill, *Reminiscences* (Butterworth, 1908).
6 Frederick Ponsonby, *Recollections of Three Reigns* (Eyre & Spottiswoode, 1952).
7 Lord Ernest Hamilton, *Old Days and New* (Hodder, 1923).
8 Lady Frederick Cavendish, *Diaries*, Vol. II (John Murray, 1912).
9 Sonia Keppel, *Edwardian Daughter* (Hamish Hamilton, 1950).
10 Frances Warwick, *Afterthoughts* (London, 1920).
11 Cavendish, *Diaries*, Vol. II.
12 Ibid.
13 Letter by H.D.G. Leveson-Gower quoted by Christopher Simon Sykes, in *Country House Camera* (Weidenfeld, 1980).
14 Lord Ernest Hamilton, *The Halcyon Era* (Hodder, 1925).
15 John Welcome, *The Sporting Empress* (Michael Joseph, 1975).
16 Ponsonby, *Recollections*.
17 Churchill, *Reminiscences*.
18 Warwick, *Afterthoughts*.

19 James Lees-Milne, *Another Self* (Hamish Hamilton, 1970).
20 Hamilton, *Old Days and New*.
21 Portland, *Men, Women, and Things*.
22 Sykes, *Country House Camera*.
23 L. P. Hartley, *The Go-Between* (Hamish Hamilton, 1953).
24 Keppel, *Edwardian Daughter*.
25 The Earl of Desart, *A Page from the Past* (Cape, 1936).
26 Churchill, *Reminiscences*.
27 R. H. Benson, *The Conventionalists* (Hutchinson, 1909).
28 Hartley, *The Go-Between*.
29 Ponsonby, *Recollections*.
30 Portland, *Men, Women, and Things*.
31 George Cornwallis-West, *Edwardian Hey-days* (Putnam, 1930).

Chapter Seven *Exotics, Eccentrics, and PBs*

1 The Duke of Portland, *Men, Women, and Things* (Faber, 1937).
2 Ibid.
3 From *Vanity Fair* series, 'Men of the Day' (1898).
4 Sonia Keppel, *Edwardian Daughter* (Hamish Hamilton, 1950).
5 Portland, *Men, Women, and Things*.
6 Isabel Colegate, *The Shooting Party* (Hamish Hamilton, 1980).
7 V. Sackville-West, *The Edwardians* (Hogarth Press, 1930).
8 Virginia Cowles, *The Rothschilds: A Family of Fortune* (Hamish Hamilton, 1973).
9 Ibid.
10 Ibid.
11 Ibid.
12 Ibid.
13 Frances Warwick, *Life's Ebb and Flow* (London, 1902).
14 Cowles, *The Rothschilds*.
15 Warwick, *Life's Ebb and Flow*.
16 Cowles, *The Rothschilds*.
17 Lady Randolph Churchill, *Reminiscences* (Butterworth, 1908).
18 Keppel, *Edwardian Daughter*.
19 J. G. Ruffer, *The Big Shots* (Debrett, 1977).
20 Portland, *Men, Women, and Things*.
21 Cowles, *The Rothschilds*.
22 Churchill, *Reminiscences*.

Chapter Eight *North of the Border*

1 Source unknown to the author.
2 *Queen Victoria's Highland Journals*, edited by David Duff (Webb & Bower, 1980).
3 Ibid.
4 James Lees-Milne, *Ancestral Voices* (Chatto & Windus, 1975).
5 Duff Hart-Davis, *Monarchs of the Glen* (Cape, 1978)
6 Lady Randolph Churchill, *Reminiscences* (Butterworth, 1908).
7 Frederick Ponsonby, *Recollections of Three Reigns* (Eyre & Spottiswoode, 1952).
8 Ibid.
9 Hart-Davis, *Monarchs of the Glen*.
10 Henry Hope Crealock, *Deer-Stalking in the Highlands of Scotland* (Longman, 1892).
11 L. E. Jones, *Georgian Afternoon* (Rupert Hart-Davis, 1958).

Chapter Nine *Below Stairs*

1 V. Sackville-West, *The Edwardians* (Hogarth Press, 1930).
2 H. G. Wells, *Tono-Bungay* (Macmillan, 1912).
3 Sackville-West, *The Edwardians*.
4 Lady Frederick Cavendish, *Diaries*, Vol. I (John Murray, 1912).

5 Frances Warwick, *Afterthoughts* (London, 1920).
6 The Duchess of Devonshire, *The House* (Macmillan, 1978).
7 Diana Cooper, *The Rainbow Comes and Goes* (Rupert Hart-Davis, 1958).
8 Lord Ernest Hamilton, *Old Days and New* (Hodder, 1923).
9 L. P. Hartley, *The Go-Between* (Hamish Hamilton, 1953).
10 Adeline Hartcup, *Below Stairs in the Great Country Houses* (Sidgwick & Jackson, 1980).
11 Wells, *Tono-Bungay*.
12 Hartcup, *Below Stairs*.
13 Hamilton, *Old Days and New*.
14 Hilaire Belloc, *Cautionary Verses* (London, 1910).

Chapter Ten *The Long Week-End*

1 The Duke of Portland, *Men, Women, and Things* (Faber, 1937).
2 A. P. Herbert, *Ballads for Broadbrows* (Ernest Benn, 1930).
3 Nancy Mitford, *Love in a Cold Climate* (Hamish Hamilton, 1949).
4 Sir Alan Lascelles, *End of an Era* (Hamish Hamilton, 1986).
5 Herbert, *Ballads*.
6 Dornford Yates, *The Berry Scene* (Ward Lock, 1947).
7 Sir Henry Channon, *Diaries*, edited by Robert Rhodes James (Weidenfeld, 1975).
8 Ibid.
9 Ibid.
10 Mitford, *Love in a Cold Climate*.
11 Duff Hart-Davis, *Hitler's Games* (Century, 1986).
12 Channon, *Diaries*.

Chapter Eleven *Letting in the Jungle*

1 James Lees-Milne, *Ancestral Voices* (Chatto & Windus, 1975).
2 Ibid.
3 Ibid.
4 Noel Coward, 'The Stately Homes of England', from *Cavalcade*.
5 *Letters of Evelyn Waugh*, edited by Mark Amory (Weidenfeld, 1980).

Select Bibliography

Asquith, Margot, *Autobiography* (Butterworth, 1920).

Benson, R. H., *The Conventionalists* (Hutchinson, 1909).

Bruce, H. J., *Silken Dalliance* (Constable, 1948).

Cavendish, Lady Frederick, *Diaries*, Vols I and II (John Murray, 1912).

Channon, Sir Henry, *Diaries*, edited by Robert Rhodes James (Weidenfeld, 1967).

Churchill, Lady Randolph, *Reminiscences* (Butterworth, 1908).

Colegate, Isabel, *The Shooting Party* (Hamish Hamilton, 1980).

Cornwallis-West, George, *Edwardian Hey-Days* (Putnam, 1930).

Cradock, Fanny, *The Lormes of Castle Rising* (W. H. Allen, 1980).

Desart, The Earl of, *A Page from the Past* (Cape, 1936).

Devonshire, The Duchess of, *The House* (Macmillan, 1978).

Girouard, Mark, *Life in the English Country House* (Yale University Press, 1978).

Glyn, Elinor, *Romantic Adventure* (Nicolson & Watson, 1936).

Hamilton, Lord Ernest, *The Halcyon Era* (Hodder, 1925).

——, *Old Days and New* (Hodder, 1923).

Hartley, L. P., *The Go-Between* (Hamish Hamilton, 1953).

Hibbert, Christopher, *King Edward VII* (London, 1976).

——, *The English: A Social History, 1066–1945* (Guild Publishing, 1987).

Jones, L. E., *Georgian Afternoon* (Rupert Hart-Davis, 1958).

Keppel, Sonia, *Edwardian Daughter* (Hamish Hamilton, 1950).

Lascelles, Sir Alan, *End of an Era* (Hamish Hamilton, 1986).

Lees-Milne, James, *Another Self* (Hamish Hamilton, 1970).

——, *Ancestral Voices* (Chatto & Windus, 1975).

Mitford, Nancy, *Love in a Cold Climate* (Hamish Hamilton, 1949).

Mortimer, Roger, *The History of the Derby Stakes* (Cassell, 1962).

Ponsonby, Sir Frederick, *Recollections of Three Reigns* (Eyre & Spottiswoode, 1952).

Portland, The Duke of, *Men, Women and Things* (Faber, 1937).

Ruffer, J. G., *The Big Shots* (Debrett, 1977).

Sackville-West, V., *The Edwardians* (Hogarth Press, 1930).

Surtees, R. S., *Mr Sponge's Sporting Tour* (Bradbury & Evans, 1853).

Warwick, Frances, *Life's Ebb and Flow* (London, 1902).

——, *Afterthoughts*, (London, 1920).

Waugh, Evelyn, *Letters of Evelyn Waugh*, edited by Mark Amory (Weidenfeld, 1980).

Welcome, John, *The Sporting Empress* (Michael Joseph, 1975).

Index

Acknowledgements

The publishers are grateful for permission to reproduce extracts as follows:
A. P. Watt on behalf of R. M. L. Humphreys and D. C. Humphreys: *The Berry Scene* by Dornford Yates. Constable & Company Ltd: *Silken Dalliance* by H. J. Bruce. David Duff: *Queen Victoria's Highland Journals* published by Webb & Bower Ltd. The estate of the late Duke of Portland: *Men, Women and Things*. Debrett's Peerage Ltd: *The Big Shots* by J. G. Ruffer. Century Hutchinson Ltd and Harper & Row Inc.: *Hitler's Games* by Duff Hart-Davis. John Johnson Ltd: *The Sporting Empress* by John Welcome. Sidgwick & Jackson Ltd: *Below Stairs in the Great Country Houses* by Adeline Hartcup. Copyright © Crawley Features, 1973, reproduced by permission of Curtis Brown Ltd.: *The Rothschilds: A Family of Fortune* by Virginia Cowles. From *The Edwardians* by Vita Sackville-West copyright 1930 by Vita Sackville-West, in the United States copyright 1930 by Doubleday, Doran Company Inc., renewed © 1958 by Vita Sackville-West, reproduced by permission of Curtis Brown Ltd, London. Methuen, London: 'The Lyrics of Noel Coward' in *The Stately Homes of England* by Noel Coward. Century Hutchinson Ltd: *Edwardians in Love* by Anita Leslie. Scribner Publishing Co. Inc. and Chatto & Windus and

the Hogarth Press: *Ancestral Voices* by James Lees Milne. Constable & Co. Ltd: *Silken Dalliance* by H. J. Bruce. George Weidenfeld & Nicolson Ltd: *The Letters of Evelyn Waugh*, ed. Mark Amory. Grafton Books: *Georgian Afternoon*, by L. E. Jones. Macmillan Publishers Ltd and Holt, Rinehart & Winston Inc: *The House* by the Duchess of Devonshire. Macmillan Publishers Ltd: *Tono-Bungay* by H. G. Wells; *Recollections of Three Reigns*, by Frederick Ponsonby. Grafton Books: *The English* by Christopher Hibbert. W. H. Allen: *The Lormes of Castle Rising* by Fanny Craddock. Jonathan Cape Ltd: *A Page from the Past* by Sybil Lubbock and the Earl of Desart. George Weidenfeld & Nicolson Ltd: *Diaries of Sir Henry Channon*, ed. Robert Rhodes James. The publishers have made every attempt to trace the copyright holders of quoted extracts and apologize for any errors or omissions.

Illustrations

Reproduced by gracious permission of Her Majesty the Queen: 12, 26, 37, 79, 137 (right), 138, 144; The Architectural Press Ltd: 210, 211; B. T. Batsford Ltd Archives: 132 (Courtesy of Lord Skelmersdale), 162 (Courtesy of the Duke of Atholl), 181 (Courtesy of the Earl of Cawdor); Courtesy of Lady Anne Bentinck: 19 (left); British Tourist Authority: 209; Camera Press: 31; Courtesy of Christie's Ltd: 33, 55 (right); Clwyd Record Office: 182; A. C. Cooper Ltd: 149 (right), 175; Courtauld Institute of Art: 137 (right); *The Daily Telegraph*: 204; Dublin Civic Museum: 130; Essex Record Office: 62; The Hulton Picture Library: 63, 66, 68, 75, 76 (left and right), 90, 91, 92, 93, 95, 98 (right), 118 (left and right), 123, 148 (left), 150, 153, 158, 159, 190, 198 (right); Mansell Collection: 28, 39 (left), 48 (left), 50 (left), 55 (left), 116 (right), 196, 206; Mary Evans Picture Library: 2, 6, 14, 22 (left and right), 34, 43, 48 (right), 54, 56, 58, 59, 60, 71, 72, 78, 82, 87, 98, 101, 103, 109, 110, 122, 124 (right), 125, 131, 133, 143, 155, 156, 163, 165, 166, 172, 174 (left and right), 180, 184, 185, 192, 195; The National Monuments Record: 176; The National Portrait Gallery, London: 19 (right), 50 (right), 51, 80 (left and right), 88, 15 (left and right), 116 (left), 124 (left), 137 (left), 147 (right), 198 (left); Popperfoto: 199, 200, 201; Private Collection: 70, 126, 137 (right); *Punch*: 17, 39 (right); Rex Features: 213; The Royal Academy of Arts: 189; Sotheby's Ltd: 140; Weidenfeld and Nicolson Archives: 15, 84, 120, 127, 147 (left), 171 (3 pictures), 179, 188, 194; York City Art Gallery: 148 (right).